Recommended Bed & Breakfasts™
Southwest

HELP US KEEP THIS GUIDE
UP TO DATE

Every effort has been made by the author and editors to make this guide as accurate and useful as possible. However, many things can change after a guide is published—establishments close, phone numbers change, facilities come under new management, etc.

We would love to hear from you concerning your experiences with this guide and how you feel it could be improved and kept up to date. While we may not be able to respond to all comments and suggestions, we'll take them to heart, and we'll also make certain to share them with the author. Please send your comments and suggestions to the following address:

The Globe Pequot Press
Reader Response/Editorial Department
P.O. Box 480
Guilford, CT 06437
Or you may e-mail us at:
editorial@globe-pequot.com

Thanks for your input, and happy travels!

Recommended
BED&
BREAKFASTS™

Southwest

June
Naylor

Guilford, Connecticut

Cover illustration: Michael Crampton
Cover and text design: Nancy Freeborn/Freeborn Design
Map design: *osprey*design
Illustrations: by Mauro Magellan

Library of Congress Cataloging-in-Publication Data
Naylor, June.
 Recommended bed & breakfasts. Southwest/June Naylor.—1st. ed.
  p. cm.—(Recommended bed & breakfasts series)
 Includes index.
 ISBN 0-7627-0759-3
  1. Bed and breakfast accommodations—Southwestern States—Guidebooks. I. Title II. Series

TX907.3.S69 N39 2001
647.94—dc21   2001023693

Manufactured in the United States of America
First Edition/First Printing

In memory of my grandparents,
Chili and June,
John and Pauline

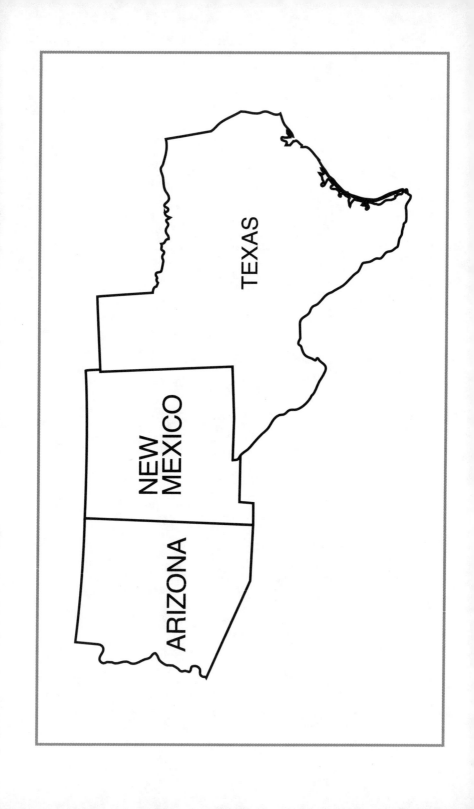

Contents

Introduction

Whether traveling out of necessity or desire, bed-and-breakfast travelers hold a special appreciation for lodgings that are loaded with personality. Chain motels and hotels are the cat's meow for some people, but if you're reading this, you're probably somebody who wants charm, surroundings with heritage or loads of design, decor that involved plenty of thought or effort. Lucky you—that's exactly what you'll find at B&Bs that fill these pages.

In traveling the Southwestern states, which in this case include Texas, New Mexico, and Arizona, you'll discover tremendous diversity in B&Bs. Because settlers became particularly busy in Texas about 150 years ago, Victorian homes make up the bulk of B&B lodgings in the Lone Star State. This legion of beautifully restored, antique-filled places is augmented, however, by a number of interesting B&B alternatives, such as ranches, lodges, and renovated old hotels.

In New Mexico choices range from Victorian homes to adobe houses and more, while Arizona's offerings include mountain retreats, contemporary homes, and elegant desert retreats.

In Texas there's a heavy concentration of bed-and-breakfast lodgings in the towns of Fredericksburg, Galveston, Jefferson, and San Antonio. In New Mexico you'll find B&Bs thickly clustered in Santa Fe and Taos, while Arizona's B&B population in most dense in Sedona. This book couldn't possibly include all the worthy B&Bs in these states, but you're likely to enjoy the choices that are offered here.

The common denominator, of course, is the inclusion of breakfast with your room rate. The description of breakfast can vary wildly from place to place, so be sure to inquire. Note also that in almost every case, these bed and breakfasts were chosen for a sense of style and comfort, which often includes a private bathroom for each bedroom. Whereas travelers in Europe are accustomed to finding shared baths at B&Bs, most bed-and-breakfast patrons on this side of the pond desire their own privy. (More on this follows.)

There are several things to keep in mind as you peruse the places in this book, of course. Decor might have been changed the week after the place was visited for the purposes of writing this guide, and in some cases, the B&B or inn might have been sold. The new owner might continue to run it as a B&B, but that's not always the case. Running a B&B is a tough business;

although a place is delightful, it may not be a financial success, and the demise of a good bed-and-breakfast—although lamentable—is not altogether unusual.

Here are a few elements worthy of your consideration:

Beds. Some antique beds have been outfitted with comfortable mattresses, but the lovely Victorian four-poster may not be big enough for two people to sleep in comfortably. Always ask whether beds are double or full-size, queen, king, and so on. If you require feather or down pillows, or are allergic to same, be sure to specify your wants. Couples who seek romance but don't want their neighbors to hear the passion may want to keep in mind that antique beds are frequently squeaky.

Baths. Some bathrooms offer only a shower, but some have both bathtub and shower. In more than a few of the older homes and buildings that have been converted to lodgings, there are claw-foot tubs that may or may not have had a shower system added. It's not unheard of for the bathtub or even toilet to be in the bedroom, hidden behind a screen or partition of some sort. If you like utter privacy, be sure to ask in advance whether your bathroom is separate and enclosed.

Breakfast. Continental may mean juice, coffee, and pastries, but it can also mean cereal, yogurt, banana nut bread, and fruit. A full breakfast can be anything from bacon and eggs to crepes, pancakes, waffles, casseroles, smoked salmon, homemade cinnamon rolls, soft tacos packed with sausage and cheese, baked fruit, and French toast. When booking the room, do ask to avoid unpleasant surprises. Many hosts are happy to accommodate special dietary requirements for guests with diabetes, allergies, or cholesterol concerns, but you'll need to give them plenty of notice.

Drinking. Liquor laws vary significantly, especially from county to county in Texas. Find out if it's OK to bring wine or your favorite beverage into the B&B, or if it's served. Remember that Texas is a big chunk of the Bible Belt, meaning that some B&B owners and innkeepers don't want booze on their property.

Smoking. It's tough to find a B&B that allows smoking indoors, but many will permit it outside on the porch, patio, or otherwise on the grounds. Always be sure to ask.

Business travelers. Many B&Bs offer guests the use of fax machines and computers, and many have data port connections in the rooms so that you can use your laptop. Inquire about these options, as well as meeting space availability; some innkeepers will let you use the dining room for small meetings.

Children and pets. Most B&Bs have strict rules regarding kids, in that none under 16 are allowed. Some places have other age requirements, so be sure to ask. There are a few B&Bs that welcome children, but you may want to think twice before bringing a little one into a B&B that's filled with antiques and collectibles. As for pets, the majority of B&Bs don't welcome them, but it can't hurt to ask. Be aware, however, that some innkeepers have pets of their own that may roam the home or property.

Reservations and cancellations. Nearly every bed and breakfast has a policy that requires a down payment of some form with reservation. Some will ask that you send a check for one night's stay, and others will take a credit card to secure your room. Several B&Bs require a minimum of two nights' stay on weekends. Almost without exception, you will be penalized if you cancel your reservation on short notice; find out what the policy is, and get it in writing whenever possible. Occasionally, you'll find a B&B that will let you book via the Internet, but it's wise to ask for a written confirmation in reply to your reservation.

Rates and Payments. B&Bs generally offer a nightly rate for double occupancy and add an extra charge per person for more than two guests in a room or suite. Midweek rates are often less, particularly if the B&B isn't in a big city. Corporate rates are often available, too. Be sure to inquire at the time of the booking about the credit cards accepted and whether personal checks are OK.

B&B rates are subject to change. Thus the following rate categories have been used to reflect rates per night, double occupancy.

$	up to $79
$$	$80–$119
$$$	$120–$159
$$$$	$160 and up

Television, telephone. Each profile notes whether TVs and phones are within the guest rooms, but it's a good idea to ask when you book your reservation in case the status has changed.

Wheelchair access. Victorian homes and older buildings rarely have been retrofitted to accommodate wheelchairs, but you should always ask in advance. Newer structures built to function as bed-and-breakfast inns are required to be ADA (Americans with Disabilities Act)-compliant, meaning there is usually one bedroom and bathroom equipped to accommodate a wheelchair.

The prices and rates listed in this guidebook were confirmed at press time. We recommend, however, that you call establishments before traveling to obtain current information.

Bed-and-breakfast lodgings included in this book have been personally selected by the author based on her own criteria.

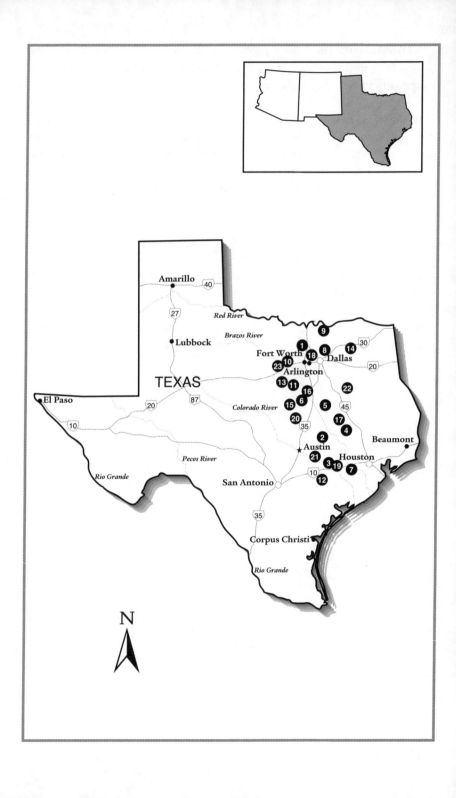

Texas: Praries and Lakes

Numbers on map refer to towns numbered below.

The Country Place at Cross Roads

4000 Historic Lane
Aubrey, TX 76227
Phone: (940) 365-9788; (877) 365-9788

E-MAIL: cntryplc@aol.com

INTERNET SITE: www.countryplacebb.com

INNKEEPERS: Harv and Kay Kitchens

ROOMS: 3 rooms with private bath

ON THE GROUNDS: Twenty-two acres filled with walking paths, ponds, a creek, horses, goats, dogs; rocking chairs on wraparound porch, hammock in yard; shared parlor for guests

CREDIT CARDS: MasterCard, Visa, American Express

RATES: $$

HOW TO GET THERE: From Dallas-Fort Worth go north on I-35 to Denton Loop 288, then east to Highway 380. Turn left and drive 6 miles to Naylor Road; turn right and drive 1 mile to Historic Lane; then turn right again.

Surrounded by century-old oak and cedar trees, the Country Place was built recently, specifically to serve as a bed-and-breakfast. Each of the guest rooms has its own sitting area and private bath, so you're assured of lots of comfort. Harv and Kay designed the house with ceiling fans, transoms, and ten-foot-high ceilings to give it an old-fashioned feel. Each of the guest rooms has French doors which open onto the spacious, wraparound porch.

You can stay in the Harvest Room, with a queen bed, chair, rocker, and a decor filled with bunnies, crocheted tablecloths, and fruits and vegetables; the Floral Room, with queen bed and down comforter, chairs with a countryside view, and antiques; and Kathryn's Room, with a full bed and family antiques and photos.

After a restful night's sleep, you're treated to a full country breakfast, complete with a casserole, fresh fruits, muffins, breads, juices, coffee, and tea.

What's Nearby Aubrey

The Denton County town sits just south of beautiful Lake Ray Roberts, a place well known for outstanding fishing and for excellent dining at Lantana Ridge Lodge. In nearby Tioga you'll get great smoked ribs, meat, and fish at Clark's Outpost and upscale German and European fare at Diverso, a restaurant located inside the executive retreat lodge,

Spirit of the West. Denton's just a quick drive away and a good destination for the cultural events at Texas Woman's University and the University of North Texas. The Denton County Courthouse Square's packed with shopping, galleries, and dining, too.

Other Recommended B&Bs Nearby

Heritage House in Decatur offers four bedrooms with private bath and TV in a 1913 house, constructed from a Sears mail-order kit; full breakfast is served by candlelight; 1002 South Hatcher Street in Decatur, TX; telephone: (940) 627-3736. The *Abbercromby Penthouse Suites* in Decatur has three rooms with private baths, Jacuzzi for two in one suite, and a bookstore on the ground floor; 103 West Main Street, Decatur, TX; telephone: (940) 627-7005. *The Redbud Inn* in Denton offers seven rooms with private baths, porch swing, gazebo, and gardens; 815 North Locust Street, Denton, TX; telephone: (940) 565-6414 or (888) 565-6414.

Pecan Street Inn

1507 Pecan Street
Bastrop, TX 78602
Phone: (512) 321-9504

E-MAIL: pletsch@bastrom.com

INNKEEPERS: Shawn and Bill Pletsch

ROOMS: 5 rooms, 4 with private bath; TV, phone, and dataport available in all, on request; wheelchair accessibility downstairs

ON THE GROUNDS: Verandah, garden, wraparound porch; rear deck

CREDIT CARDS: None accepted

RATES: $-$$; $300 for entire house

HOW TO GET THERE: From Austin drive Texas 71 east to Bastrop, turn left on Loop 150, left on Pecan.

Nearly one hundred years old, this home, listed on the National Register of Historic Places, rests barely more than a block from charming historic downtown Bastrop. Surrounded by a half acre of pecan trees, the home is also just 2 blocks from the breathtaking Colorado River. Combining an eclectic blend of Gothic and Queen Anne designs, the house is filled with period antiques and made more comfortable by fireplaces, parlor areas, and coffeemakers in each guest room.

Shawn does a great job of mapping out sightseeing tours upon request. If you want the entire house for a wedding or reunion, just ask. And be ready for some very special breakfasts, which usually include Shawn's signature pecan waffles with Grand Marnier strawberries, served on china with silver either in the dining room or in your guest room.

Schaefer House Bed & Breakfast

608 Pecan Street
Bastrop, TX 78602
Phone: (512) 303–2734

E-MAIL: schaefferhouse@yahoo.com

INTERNET SITE: www.bedandbreakfast.com/bbc/p613726.asp

INNKEEPER: Mary Ellen Branan

ROOMS: 3 rooms; 2 with private bath, TV/cable/VCR, phone jacks; iMac available for e-mail

ON THE GROUNDS: Deck, garden, spa tub, bicycles, basketball hoop, long-railed front porch, hammock; library

CREDIT CARDS: MasterCard, Visa

RATES: $$–$$$$, including breakfast; AARP discount available

HOW TO GET THERE: From Austin drive 29 miles southeast on TX 71 to Bastrop. From Houston, drive 125 miles west via U.S. 290 and TX 21. Pecan Street is a main street in old downtown area.

Innkeeper Mary Branan, who has Ph.D. in literature and creative writing, found the perfect place in the rolling landscape east of Austin in which to live a quiet existence and explore Texas history. The house she chose was built in 1913 and, Mary says, "lived in for many years by the widow Alma Murchison Schaefer of the prominent, esteemed Schaefer family."

Listed on the National Register of Historic Places, the home's architecture is generally Victorian but, as Mary points out, perhaps more Arts and Crafts in its simple design and farmhouse feel. Thirteen-foot-high ceilings, transoms, longleaf pine floors, original doors, fretwork, three skylights, fireplace, and a private, outdoor full shower are all architecturally interesting. Mary's decor includes some antique and art deco furniture and rugs, and a particularly fine arts collection. She wryly notes that "there's a minimum of kitsch and ruffles."

Guests delve into a full gourmet breakfast that typically features eggs Benedict, or a Southern-style breakfast, with a fresh-fruit course, gourmet coffees, and homemade breads and muffins. The Swedish-French toast sandwiches, which are drizzled with a lingonberry-orange sauce, show creativity and a desire for distinction. Other meals can be arranged with notice and for an extra charge.

Because Schaefer House is situated inside Bastrop's historic district, you're in easy walking distance of charming shops in the renovated downtown, a museum, cafes, and the lovely Colorado River Walk. Chances are, however, you'll just stay put, watching birds at the feeders and basking in the calm of Mary's yard, colored with azalea bushes and blooming beds and shaded by pecan trees, cherry laurels, and the town's oldest crape myrtles.

What's Nearby Bastrop

Take a picnic to the 3,500-acre Bastrop State Park, home to the so-called Lost Pines, and terrific opportunities for hiking, fishing, and golf. In town, the Bastrop County Seat has a charming little Bastrop County Historical Museum, as well as cute shops lining the vintage streets. Quick side trips to consider include one to the town of Lockhart for a big serving of sensational smoked brisket or ribs at Kreuz Market.

Ant Street Inn

107 West Commerce Street
Brenham, TX 77833
Phone: (979) 836-7393; (800) 481-1951

E-MAIL: stay@antstreetinn.com

INTERNET SITE: www.antstreetinn.com

INNKEEPERS: Pam and Tommy Traylor

ROOMS: 14 with private baths, TV, telephone, dataport; 1 downstairs room with wheelchair accessibility

ON THE GROUNDS: Verandah with rocking chairs, garden with fountain; bar

CREDIT CARDS: MasterCard, Visa

RATES: $$-$$$$, including full breakfast

HOW TO GET THERE: From Houston take U.S. 290 west, exiting Business 290 in Brenham. Turn left on Commerce, and it's 3 blocks ahead on the left.

To say that Pam and Tommy Traylor have created a sensation is to make a gross understatement. Their masterpiece lies inside a former mercantile building, erected in 1899, and serving over the years as a grocery, feed store, and saloon. Now a bed-and-breakfast inn, it raises the standards for all throughout Texas.

Tommy, a career antiques dealer and collector, spent three years traveling the nation to gather the proper furnishings for this fourteen-room inn. There are full- and half-tester beds, elaborately carved sofas and chairs, Oriental rugs, and the hilariously odd piece, such as an antique dentist's chair and an umbrella lamp. Pam Traylor also embarked on extensive searches for the handsome, elegant fabrics used in upholstery throughout the inn, and coordinated the paint color and accessory schemes in every room.

Craftspeople were hired to make matching wood trim where the original sections were missing and to build modern bathrooms and incorporate stained-glass windows throughout the building. In the case of the guest room with a freight elevator, the freight elevator was made into part of the attraction.

Pam named each of the rooms for some of the Southern cities—Charlotte, Louisville, Memphis, Galveston, and Natchez—she visited during her tenure with *Southern Living* magazine's cooking school. And as you would imagine, her culinary expertise manifests itself in stunning breakfast spreads that include brie and Canadian bacon quiche, apple strudel with maple cider sauce, rosemary roasted potatoes, fruit kabobs, and angel biscuits.

The Traylors urge guests to sleep late, have a bedtime snack of the locally made Blue Bell Ice Cream, wander the lovely downtown boutiques and antiques shops, or take a drive to the Antique Rose Emporium or the Monastery of St. Clare.

Captain Tacitus T. Clay Home Bed and Breakfast

9445 Farm Road 390 East
Brenham, TX 77833
Phone: (979) 836-1916

E-MAIL: TMZ@alpha1.net

INNKEEPER: Thelma Zwiener

ROOMS: 4 rooms, 3 with private bath, telephone; 2-bedroom suite in Gate House

ON THE GROUNDS: Verandah, garden, hot tub; satellite TV in main house

CREDIT CARDS: MasterCard, Visa

RATES: $–$$

HOW TO GET THERE: Drive to Brenham via U.S. 290. In town pick up Texas

105 north to Farm Road 50 north. Take it to the community of Independence, then turn east on Farm Road 390 and look for sign for Fieldstone Farm. The house is on this farm.

Built in 1852 by Captain Tacitus T. Clay, the one-and-one-half-story frame house was built in the dog-run style that has a grand hall in the center, with porches on each end and spacious bedrooms, a sitting room, and a dining hall. Clay intended to put a ballroom on the second floor, but left Independence to serve in the Confederate Army instead. He returned from the war minus one leg and never completed the upper floor.

When Thelma Zwiener bought the house in 1979, she tried several ways to keep the foundation from crumbling. Eventually she moved the house across the street atop a new foundation. After a fire and lots of restoration, the home became a became a bed and breakfast in the late 1980s. Inside, she's included many of the home's original antique furnishings. Updating included adding central air and heat.

What you'll enjoy as much as Thelma's hard work is the setting. Situated on Fieldstone Farm, the B&B is surrounded by rolling countryside on which adorable miniature horses are raised. The farm sits next to the community of Independence, Texas, which is filled with history pertaining to the beginnings of the Texas republic. Nearby is an amazing garden center called the Antique Rose Emporium.

While away your time roaming the property or soaking in the gazebo's hot tub. Lodging choices include rooms in the main house; a small, cozy room in the Cistern House; and a two-bedroom suite in the Gate House. Thelma's breakfast is a big country affair, including fresh seasonal fruit, eggs, bacon or sausage, a sweet bakery bread, and a yeast bread, such as biscuits.

Far View Estates

1804 South Park Street
Brenham, TX 77833
Phone: (409) 836–1672; (888) FAR VIEW

E-MAIL: farview@phoenix.net

INTERNET SITE: www.bbhost.com/farview

INNKEEPERS: David and Tonya Meyer

ROOMS: 7 rooms with private bath, 4 with TV, telephone, dataport

ON THE GROUNDS: Sunroom, verandah, garden, swimming pool, chipping green, horseshoes, croquet

CREDIT CARDS: MasterCard, Visa

RATES: $$–$$$, including full breakfast

HOW TO GET THERE: From U.S. 290 take TX 36 south into town to Lubbock Street. Turn left (west) onto Lubbock and drive 2.5 blocks to the entrance of Far View.

David and Tonya Meyer have created a place of retreat that's all about chilling out. They would much rather urge guests to settle into a comfy wicker chair with a fat novel than suggest anything else.

But guests who can't sit still will find the Meyers' home surrounded by two lushly gardened acres filled with aged trees, where you can hit some golf balls on the chipping green, pitch some horseshoes, or unwind with a game of croquet. Then there's always riding a bicycle built for two from Far View to nearby downtown Brenham and its charming historic district.

Feeling more reclusive? Fine; you'll have some solitary time on a private balcony overlooking the lawns, watching the squirrels and birds. Or you can ramble around the exquisite Meyer home, a restored 1925 Prairie-style structure that was built by one of the early town doctors and now bears a state historical marker.

Mornings are a time for rejoicing, particularly when you're tucking into a plate of French toast strata, buttermilk-oatmeal pancakes with Maine maple syrup, and baked apples with bacon and brown sugar. And you won't want to miss a special dessert of bread pudding with warm berry sauce and the locally produced, world-famous Blue Bell Ice Cream.

Mostly, you'll want to kick back and do a lot of nothing at Far View. Who can resist a place where the hosts' motto is, "We look forward to greeting you on the front porch"?

What's Nearby Brenham

The seat of Washington County is a seductive hamlet about midway between Austin and Houston. Head to Firemen's Park to see a fabulous antique carousel and leave lots of time to explore the Brenham Heritage Museum and the wonderful downtown shops. If you have a sweet tooth, you can't resist Blue Bell Creameries, a world-famous ice cream maker, founded in 1907. Take a drive to the Monastery of St. Clare to see the miniature horses raised there, and if you're a gardener, check out the Antique Rose Emporium.

Angelsgate Bed and Breakfast

615 East Twenty-ninth Street
Bryan, Texas 77803
Phone: (979) 779-1231; (888) 779-1231
Fax: (979) 775-7024

E-MAIL: stay@angelsgate.com

INTERNET SITE: www.angelsgate.com

INNKEEPER: Nita Harding

ROOMS: 2 suites with sitting rooms with small refrigerators, TV, private bath; 1 room with queen bed and cable TV; telephone and computer connections available

ON THE GROUNDS: Gazebo, sunporch, gardens

CREDIT CARDS: MasterCard, Visa

RATES: $ double; corporate rates available Sunday through Thursday; children over age 12 (well-behaved ones, of course) welcome

HOW TO GET THERE: A two-hour drive from Austin, take Texas (TX) 21 into Bryan, crossing Farm Road 2818, and bearing right onto Farm Road 158, which becomes William J. Bryan. In less than a mile, turn right on Texas Avenue (also TX 6) and stay in left lane. Turn left on Twenty-ninth Street; Angelsgate is in the third block on the right; turn right and park on Baker Street.

Located in one of Texas's most historically rich towns, this very comfortable B&B is housed in a 1909 home built by the Allister Waldrop family. Designed in the American Foursquare style, it bears a National Historic Landmark designation and has been rarely changed from the original plans, obtained by the innkeeper.

She is Nita Harding, a local artist who exhibits her watercolors in the B&B, which opened in 1996 and still displays several of the home's original fixtures. The stained-glass windows are exactly as they were when the home was constructed. The only obvious change is the adding of screens to the verandah.

Obviously, it's a romantic getaway, but Angelsgate is also a favorite of business travelers. The Lord Garrett Suite, outfitted with traditional antiques and a queen bed, has a sitting room, cable TV, and minifridge. The Lady Margaret Room has a queen four-poster and cable TV. Both have computer connections available.

The choice for longer stays, clearly, is the Carriage House, a suite overlooking the garden. The bedroom has a queen bed, the bath has an antique claw-foot tub, and the living area is equipped with a daybed that will sleep two. This separate lodging has a kitchen and cable TV, as well.

If you feel like having a look around, ask Nita for directions to the George Bush Library on the Texas A&M campus in College Station or to the Messina-Hof Winery nearby in Bryan.

What's Nearby Bryan

Half of the pair of towns always called Bryan-College Station, the town is best known for its proximity to the massive Texas A&M University. On the campus, you'll find the outstanding George Bush Presidential Library and Museum and a magnificent bell tower. Do plan on spending time learning about the wine business at Messina Hof Wine Cellars.

Other Recommended B&Bs Nearby

Bonnie Grambrel Bed & Breakfast, with three bedrooms and one private bath; 600 East 27th Street, Bryan, TX 77803; telephone: (409) 779–1022 or (888) 271–7985. *The Villa at Messina-Hof,* ten rooms with private baths at a winery; 4545 Old Reliance Road, Bryan, TX 77808; telephone: (409) 778–9463 or (800) 736–9463.

Calvert Inn Gourmet Bed & Breakfast and Restaurant

406 East Texas Street
Calvert, TX 77837
Phone: (409) 364–2868; (800) 290–1213

E-MAIL: stay@calvertinn.com

INTERNET SITE: www.calvertinn.com

INNKEEPERS: Frank and Sandy Hudson

ROOMS: 3 rooms with private bath

ON THE GROUNDS: Hot tub, porches, gazebo, gardens and three landscaped areas with many large oak and pecan trees, fish pond with fountain in circle driveway

CREDIT CARDS: MasterCard, Visa, American Express, Discover

RATES: $$–$$$

HOW TO GET THERE: From Dallas-Fort Worth drive south on I–35 to Waco, then south on Texas 6 to Calvert. Turn east on Gregg Street, cross railroad tracks, and turn right on Elm Street. Go 1 block and see Calvert Inn on your right.

uilt in 1904 with native cypress, this home belonged to Pete Gibson, whose family owned one of the world's largest cotton gins. Measuring 6,000 square feet, this beauty has enormous galleries, decorated with Waterford and Baccarat crystal chandeliers. There are eight coal-burning fireplaces, as well as a grand piano original to the home.

The home is the centerpiece of a whole city block and is surrounded by enormous oak trees. Stress from life at home seems to melt away quickly in this setting, augmented by porch swings, rockers, lush garden, duck pond, hot tub, and gazebo. Then again, you might not leave your room; each of these has individual heat and air-conditioning, antiques, and terry robes. Some rooms have private porches, too.

Your hosts are known for their special culinary talents, so ask ahead about five-course, candlelight dinners. Three-course breakfast spreads are known to include baked banana with kiwi and mango, cream brown sugar, and warm butterscotch sauce; savory shrimp omelette with hollandaise sauce; and eggs Sardou.

What's Nearby Calvert

Home to the world's largest cotton gin in 1871, Calvert was named for a plantation owner who donated the town site. Look around town and you'll note that many of the Victorian-style structures, which house antiques shops today, are included on the National Register of Historic Places. There's a doll house museum in town, too.

The Rivers Bend B&B

P.O. Box 228
Clifton, TX 76634
Phone: (254) 675-4936

INNKEEPER: Helen M. Hubler

ROOMS: 3-bedroom house, 2 baths, kitchen, telephone

ON THE GROUNDS: Wraparound porch with swing, glider, and chairs and tables; TV in living room; portable phone in house, wood-burning fireplace; all wheelchair accessibility; barbecue and picnic areas

CREDIT CARDS: None accepted

RATES: $$-$$$$

HOW TO GET THERE: From Dallas-Fort Worth drive I-35 south to Hillsboro; take Texas 22 west through Whitney; go south on Farm Road 219 to

Clifton. Host will meet guests in Clifton and accompany them to the bed-and-breakfast, about 4 miles from town.

Helen and her late husband built this home in 1986 when they retired and moved to this woodsy countryside from Corpus Christi. Helen now lives in town and offers this house as a very private B&B. You'll have the entire three-bedroom home to yourself, complete with kitchen, two bathrooms, living room, and big porches overlooking the bucolic Bosque River. Once Helen shows you to the home, you'll be on your own.

Shaded by giant oak, elm, and pecan trees, many of which loom up to sixty feet tall, the farm on which the home sits measures 240 acres. The solitude here is spectacular; your company will be that of some eighty-four species of birds, herds of deer, raccoons, and the occasional train whistle in the distance. If your dogs travel with you, Helen has a half-acre dog pen for your use.

You'll make your own breakfast from the supplies Helen leaves, which usually includes homemade bread, eggs, juices, fruit, milk, cereal, tea, coffee, and hot chocolate.

What's Nearby Clifton

Southwest of Fort Worth on the Bosque River, Clifton was settled in the 1850s and is known as the Norwegian Capital of Texas, thanks to the steadfast traditions of the Norse settlers' descendants. A very short drive from town, you'll find the Norse Settlement, where an old Lutheran church, graveyard, and markers attest to the Scandinavian heritage. A Texas Main Street City, Clifton has several shops within restored downtown buildings, as well as a fine arts conservatory and a local history museum. Lake Whitney and Meridian State Parks, both offering plenty of nature's bounty, are nearby.

Magnolia Oaks Bed and Breakfast

634 Spring Street
Columbus, TX 78934
Phone: (979) 732-2726; (888) 677-0593

E-MAIL: rmstiles@aol.com

INTERNET SITE: www.magnoliaoaks.com

INNKEEPERS: Bob and Nancy Stiles

ROOMS: 8 rooms, 7 with private bath, 6 with TV

ON THE GROUNDS: Library, verandah, garden, bicycles

CREDIT CARDS: MasterCard, Visa

RATES: $$–$$$$

HOW TO GET THERE: Drive east from San Antonio or west from Houston on I-10 to Columbus, taking exit 696. Turn north and bear right on Spur 52. Go 0.7 mile to the courthouse square and turn left on Spring Street. Continue 2 blocks to 634 Spring Street.

Built in 1890, the home serving as Magnolia Oaks was fashioned in the Eastlake Victorian style for Marcus Hervey Townsend and his wife, Annie Buford, by the local contractor, Jacob Wirtz, who deemed it good luck to build the house in the shape of a cross. The West family bought the home from the Townsends in 1906 and held on to it until the Stiles bought it at an estate auction in 1989. In restoring the property, Bob and Nancy put loving effort into preserving the home's architectural integrity and its old-fashioned comforts.

Inside are fourteen-foot-high ceilings, walk-through windows, intricately carved doors. Guest rooms include the Townsend, with a carved fireplace, king bed, sofa, and TV; Texas Room, with king cedar bed, fireplace, and TV; Victorian Room, offering lace curtains and double and twin beds; and a balcony loft apartment, with double and twin beds, kitchen, skylights, and TV. The elaborate sit-down breakfast is sure to fill you up for many hours, and it includes Bob's "Toast to the Morning" song and guitar accompaniment.

Outside, the heavy "gingerbread" detail in the trim takes you back to an utterly different time and mood; the porches are perfect for letting go of everyday stress and catching up on a good book, and the screened summer room is ideal for writing letters and sipping lemonade. The three-quarter-acre grounds are filled with magnolias, oaks, herb and flower gardens, a patio with a tiered fountain, an arbor, swing, chipping green, croquet court, and loads of nature.

What's Nearby Columbus

Built in 1823 on the site of an Indian village called Montezuma, the Colorado County Seat offers a historical marker on the trunk of a live oak tree that's said to have shaded the first court of the Third Judicial District of the Republic of Texas in 1837. There's a town tour you can take on foot or in a car, starting at the 1886 Stafford Opera House, and continuing on to the 1836 Alley Log Cabin, the 1891 Colorado County Courthouse, and a handful of nineteenth-century homes now functioning as museums.

Amelia's Place

1775 Young Street
Dallas, TX 75201
Phone: (214) 651–1775; (888) 651–1775
Fax: (214) 761–9475

E-MAIL: ameliaj@flash.net

INTERNET SITE: www.flash.net/~ameliaj

INNKEEPER: Amelia Core Jenkins

ROOMS: 6 rooms, 4 with private bath

ON THE GROUNDS: Deck, patio; common areas with baby grand piano, library and reading areas, game tables

CREDIT CARDS: MasterCard, Visa, American Express, Discover

RATES: $$

HOW TO GET THERE: In the heart of downtown Dallas.

Amelia has worked hard to make her warehouse loft dwelling a welcoming, warm place for everyone. She couldn't have found a spot with more convenience for travelers and escapists who long for urban pleasures. Her lodging is just a block from the Dallas Public Library's main location and a block from City Hall, where the front plaza is frequently the site of street festivals and outdoor concerts. Amelia's is marvelously close to such downtown delights as the Farmers Market, the original Neiman Marcus store, and the Dallas Museum of Art. A DART trolley bus stops at Amelia's Place every ten minutes, too.

What sets Amelia's apart from many mainstream lodgings is her enthusiasm for a diverse clientele. She says she considers her guests valued family members and invites neither "snobs nor bigots." Amelia emphatically welcomes people of color, same-sex couples, and smokers, the last of whom may indulge in the foyer or one of her living-dining rooms or kitchen. Alas, small children and pets can't be accommodated. She asks guest to feel comfortable storing food and drink in the kitchen and to use the laundry facilities.

A proud feminist, Amelia has crafted an individual style for each of the comfortable guest rooms, naming them for female personalities of color whose work has meant something to Dallas. Amelia loves to tell you that she brings with her Louisiana upbringing a culinary talent that made her "the best cook in three parishes." Among specialties you'll enjoy in her full breakfast are buttermilk biscuits, tomato gravy, fried eggs, and sausage grits; wine and cheese are also included in the room rate. Ask her about special lunch and dinner preparations and about special diet requirements you might have.

Southern House

2625 Thomas Avenue
Dallas, TX 75204
Phone: (214) 720-0845
Fax: (214) 720-4447

E-MAIL: pam@southernhouse.com

INTERNET SITE: www.southernhouse.com

INNKEEPER: Pam Southern

ROOMS: 2 rooms in main house, 1 with private bath; also, a 1-bedroom apartment 1 block away for stays of four-plus nights

ON THE GROUNDS: Deck, patio, common areas with baby grand piano, library and reading areas, game tables

CREDIT CARDS: MasterCard, Visa, American Express, Discover

RATES: $$–$$$$

HOW TO GET THERE: From downtown Dallas drive north on McKinney Avenue; turn right (east) on Thomas Avenue.

A boon for the business traveler is this lovely home, within walking distance of downtown Dallas and dozens of fabulous art galleries. Snuggled into the State-Thomas Historical District and surrounded by a quickly redeveloping and very hip area called Uptown, Southern House is a wonderful alternative to a hotel. Pam Southern has converted her three-story, contemporary Prairie-style home into a small and immensely welcoming B&B.

If you're not relaxing and reading in your room, you can play cards or a game of Scrabble with other guests. Pam can help you arrange a massage or facial in your room, or point you toward the nearby McKinney Avenue Contemporary Gallery. At dinnertime, there are a dozen excellent choices in upscale restaurants within easy walking distance.

Guests who'd like to stay for longer periods can check out the Southern House's one-bedroom apartment, found 1 block away inside an old New Orleans–style four-plex. This unit features antique tiled floors and a private patio with an arbor cover. Apartment guests can enjoy a Continental breakfast on site or walk over to the main house where the full breakfast offerings typically include Pam's special Mexican egg casserole, homemade salsa, and hot tortillas. By special arrangement Pam will serve lunch and dinner. Cocktails, wine, afternoon tea, and nonalcoholic beverages are included with the room rate.

What's Nearby Dallas

Downtown Dallas's offerings alone will keep you plenty busy. There's the Sixth Floor Museum, located in the ill-fated School Book Depository, dedicated to the life and presidency of JFK, and Dealey Plaza, the site of his assassination, which always has its share of curious tourists. The Dallas World Aquarium is within a few blocks, as is the marvelous Dallas Museum of Art. The Neiman Marcus flagship store is downtown on Commerce Street, and afternoon tea is a pleasant treat at the lovely Adolphus Hotel. Immediately north is Uptown, packed with art galleries and fabulous dining. Just a quick drive east of downtown, Fair Park is a collection of art deco buildings, the homes of such worthwhile destinations as the National Women's Museum, the African-American Museum, the Science Place, and the Texas Hall of State.

Other Recommended B&Bs Nearby

Maple Manor, a Victorian inn, offering 6 rooms and suites with private baths in the Dallas Uptown area; 2606 Maple Avenue, Dallas, TX 75205; telephone: (214) 871-0032. *Terra Cotta Inn,* a renovated, three-story motor inn with Mexican and Southwestern decor, ninety-eight rooms with private baths, pool, and business services; 6101 LBJ Freeway, Dallas, TX 75240; telephone: (972) 387-2525 or (800) 533-3591.

Inn of Many Faces

412 West Morton Street
Denison, TX 75020
Phone: (903) 465-4639

INNKEEPERS: Pat Gunter and Judy Johnson

ROOMS: 4 rooms, all with private baths; 2 with working fireplaces; 1 with sitting room; 1 with whirlpool tub

ON THE GROUNDS: Garden with pond; club room with TV, board and card games; wraparound porch

CREDIT CARDS: MasterCard, Visa

RATES: $$–$$$, including full breakfast; one night's prepaid stay is required with reservation

HOW TO GET THERE: Drive into Denison on U.S. 75, turning east on Farm Road 120, which is also Morton Street. The inn is ahead on the north side of the street.

While it seems this B&B bears an odd name, you get the picture on visiting the place. You'll find throughout the home's interior and exterior the faces of people and animals, rendered in fine detail, as part of the artistic design. Faces are found, too, in artwork, on pottery and ceramics, in knickknacks on tabletops, and in nooks and crannies.

The home itself is a work of art, as well. Built in 1897 by a founding father of Denison, J. B. McDougall, the richly Victorian exterior is noteworthy for the wraparound porch, spired cupola, intricate dormer window, finely crafted columns, and numerous gables. A profound restoration effort in recent years turned the home back into its lovely, original state.

Sisters Pat Gunter and Judy Johnson accomplished this impressive undertaking, turning the home into a sumptuous B&B lodging. Period pieces of furniture and accessories, such as mantle clocks and paintings, add to the home's richness, and a lovely garden pond with lily pads and goldfish transport you to a far more serene state than the one you may have left behind in the city.

The inn's rooms are named for Pat's four sons. Kev's Room is subtitled The Romantic Adventurer; it's a suite with a queen bed, working fireplace, whirlpool tub, and full shower. D's Room: The World Conqueror is the inn's largest, with a king bed and sitting area, a view of the east gardens, and a fireplace. Kenneth's Room: Loved by All is a setting for contemplation and reflection, with a queen bed and a view of the west gardens. Timothy's Room: World's Greatest Sportsman has two doubles and a shower.

If you're a fishing enthusiast, Pat and Judy will add on a Fisherman's Package, an $80 deal that includes lunch and a fishing guide for your trip to Lake Texoma, a few miles away on Farm Road 150.

What's Nearby Denison

Known as the birthplace of President Dwight D. Eisenhower, Denison offers his home as a tiny museum for exploration. Other places to poke around in town include the restored 1909 Old Katy Depot and the Red River Railroad Museum. Within easy striking distance are the 450-acre Eisenhower State Park on popular Lake Texoma, Hagerman National Wildlife Refuge, Grayson County Frontier Village, and Munson Vineyards.

Other Recommended B&Bs Nearby

Hart's Country Inn, in a restored historic home facing Austin College with four guest rooms and four private baths; 601 North Grand Avenue, Sherman, TX 75090; telephone: (903) 892-2271. The *Durning House Bed & Breakfast,* in a vintage cottage with two bedrooms and two private baths, adjacent to a charming restaurant; 205 West Stephens Street, Van Alstyne, TX 75495; telephone: (903) 482-5188.

Miss Molly's Hotel

109½ West Exchange Avenue
Fort Worth, TX 76106
Phone: (817) 626-1522; (800) 99-MOLLY (996-6559)
Fax: (817) 625-2723

E-MAIL: missmollys@travelbase.com, and markhancock@email.msn.com

INTERNET SITE: www.missmollys.com

INNKEEPERS: Mark and Alice Hancock

ROOMS: 8 rooms, 1 with private bath; 3 with phone/dataport on request

ON THE GROUNDS: Parlor area upstairs; downstairs is Star Cafe, a casual steakhouse and watering hole

CREDIT CARDS: MasterCard, Visa, American Express, Discover

RATES: $$-$$$$; $$-$$$ extended stay

HOW TO GET THERE: From downtown Fort Worth drive 2.5 miles north on Main Street.

Built in 1910, this historic hotel was operated as prim and proper rooming house until the mid-1940s, when it became a popular bawdy house. Restored and opened as bed-and-breakfast in 1989, Miss Molly's occupies the second floor of a turn-of-the-twentieth-century brick building in the heart of the Stockyards National Historic District, which was once the center of the north-central Texas cattle industry. On the same street are saloons where gunfighters shot each other over games of cards and horse deals gone wrong. Guest rooms are outfitted with shutters, lace curtains, iron beds, handmade quilts, and oak furniture. Bathrobes are provided for all guests, which is especially handy for trotting down the hall to one of three bathrooms. Among the attractive rooms is Miss Josie's, the only one with a private bath, named in honor of the madam who ran the house in the 1940s. Miss Amelia's is a pretty room with handworked linens; Cattlemen's is more masculine, as are the Rodeo, Gunslinger, Oilmen, and Cowboy rooms.

A breakfast buffet is served in the parlor daily under the stained-glass skylight. Specialty bread items, hot egg dishes, fresh fruit, juice, and coffee are the typical offerings. Ask Mark and Alice about special trips on the Tarantula Steam Train, whose station is just up the street.

Texas White House

1417 Eighth Avenue
Fort Worth, Texas 76104
Phone: (817) 923-3597; (800) 279-6491
Fax: (817) 923-0410

E-MAIL: txwhitehou@aol.com

INTERNET SITE: www.texaswhitehouse.com

INNKEEPERS: Grover and Jamie McMains

ROOMS: 3 rooms, all with private bath, lavish bath products, thick towels, TV, telephone, dataport

ON THE GROUNDS: Off-street parking, wraparound porch

CREDIT CARDS: MasterCard, Visa

RATES: $-$$$, one night's stay is required with reservation

HOW TO GET THERE: From I-30, exit Henderson Street and travel south to Pennsylvania Avenue, turning right on Pennsylvania and left on Eighth Avenue. The house is on the left (east) side of the street.

The McMains are understandably proud of their stately bed-and-breakfast home. Designated a Fort Worth Landmark in 1994, the Bishop-Newkirk House—operating as a B&B under the name, Texas White House—was awarded the Historic Preservation Council of Tarrant County Award in 1995 to honor this outstanding restoration of a historic structure.

The couple tells guests that the house was built in 1910 by a man named Bishop but was sold to the Newkirk family without a Bishop having lived there. The Newkirks raised four sons in the home, all of whom served in World War II and returned to their home to marry. Over the years the Newkirk children—one serving as mayor of Fort Worth, and another a prominent attorney in town—have brought their children and grandchildren to visit the home and savor the memories. In 1994 five Newkirk generations held a family reunion in the home, with grandsons sleeping in the rooms where their fathers grew up.

Even without the warm history, the home is a winning offering of style and taste. The design is a classic edition of the hipped cottage, later called the open plan, for its "inside-outside spatial continuity," to quote Grover. The layout served as an anchor in planning entire neighborhoods and was found in both one- and two-story designs.

Guest rooms include the Land of Contrast, with an antique brass bed; Lone Star, with antique wardrobe; and Tejas, with antique writing desk. Guests share a spacious living room with fireplace, parlor, formal dining room, and a wraparound porch for watching sunsets. Breakfast pleasures range from fresh, seasonal fruits or baked fruit in compote to baked egg casseroles and homemade breads and muffins, served on heirloom china with sterling silver and crystal.

What's Nearby Fort Worth

Downtown's Sundance Square is an exciting destination day and night, thanks to lots of shops, art galleries, restaurants, and saloons, as well as a handful of movie theaters, three legitimate theater companies, a world-class opera hall, and horse-drawn carriage rides. Just north of downtown, the Stockyards National Historic District begs you to strut down the wooden sidewalks, wearing your boots and cowboy hat; just west of downtown, the Cultural District offers extraordinary art museums and a science museum.

Other Recommended B&Bs Nearby

Azalea Plantation Bed & Breakfast, a 1940s home and cottage with four rooms and four private baths; 1400 Robinwood Drive, Fort Worth, TX 76111; telephone: (817) 838–5882 or (800) 687–3529. *Bed & Breakfast at the Ranch,* a ranch-style country house on ten acres with five rooms and five private baths; 933 Ranch Road, Fort Worth, TX 76131; telephone: (817) 232–5522 or (888) 593–0352. *Etta's Place,* an inn in downtown Fort Worth with ten rooms/suites with private baths, full business services, and dry cleaning; 200 West Third Street, Fort Worth, TX 76102; telephone: (817) 654–0267.

Inn on the River

205 Southwest Barnard Street
Glen Rose, TX 76043
Phone: (254) 897-2929; (800) 575-2101
Fax: (254) 897-7729

E-MAIL: inn@innontheriver.com

INTERNET SITE: www.innontheriver.com

INNKEEPERS: Shirley and Ernest Reinke

ROOMS: 22 rooms with private bath and telephones; 1 room is handicap accessible

ON THE GROUNDS: Small gift shop; no formal library, but several books available for the guests; chess table and other games available; beverage bar available twenty-four hours a day; immaculately groomed garden that slopes down to the Puluxy River; outdoor fireplace; regulation horseshoe pits; fly fishing schools and guided fishing tours; bicycles available for guests; outside swimming pool

CREDIT CARDS: MasterCard, Visa, American Express, Discover, Diners Club

RATES: $$-$$$$

HOW TO GET THERE: From Dallas-Fort Worth, drive southwest on U.S. 377 to Granbury, then follow Texas 144 to Glen Rose. In Glen Rose follow signs directing you to historic district; turn left on Barnard Street and follow it until you see the courthouse and the inn.

At the turn of the century, Glen Rose was a popular destination, a health resort where thousands of people would come "take the waters" from the area's natural springs and artesian wells. Among those offering treatments was Dr. George P. Snyder, a Californian whose "drugless" sanitarium hosted 3,000 guests annually to enjoy curative mineral baths, freshly grown food; and regimented schedules. In 1919 Dr. Snyder built this two-story structure alongside the lovely Paluxy River. His property had seven buildings, a banana grove, sleeping pavilion, a carbide plant for lighting, and a small zoo, with an ostrich named Judy. So successful was his sanitarium that Dr. Snyder's deposits saved the Glen Rose bank from bankruptcy during the Depression.

The business operated until the 1970s, and the building reopened as a B&B in the 1980s. It's been renovated a few times, and in 1993 a massive overhaul was done and landscaping additions were completed. Now a Texas Historical Landmark, the inn's two-story appearance matches that of seventy-five years ago. In back are three massive live oak trees thought to be centuries old; in the 1950s a guest wrote a song about them called "The

Singing Trees." It was recorded by Elvis Presley in 1965.

Not only is the luxurious Inn on the River a designated Texas Historical Landmark, it is an elegant retreat as well. Each of its rooms is decorated differently, but all have antique armoires, authentic or reproduction period furnishings, European linens, feather beds and down comforters. If you can pull yourself away from your room, you'll relax in the mineral water swimming pool, take a spin around town on the mountain bikes provided for guests, or lounge in an Adirondack chair next to the gentle Paluxy River.

The Reinkes change the breakfast menu daily, but typically you'll be treated to freshly squeezed orange juice, Colombian coffee, fruit, pastries straight from the oven, and a main course that could be anything from eggs Benedict to Belgian waffles with hot maple syrup. If you reserve dinner ahead ($35 per person, not including tax and gratuity), expect a four-course affair that might include tomato-basil soup, fresh greens with raspberry vinaigrette, grilled beef tenderloin, sautéed vegetables, and white chocolate cheesecake.

What's Nearby Glen Rose

Varying perspectives on the past are examined in and around the Somervell County Seat, a lovely little village sitting where the Paluxy and Brazos Rivers meet. At Dinosaur Valley State Park, there are footprints of gargantuan sauropods, duck-billed dinosaurs, and theropods in the limestone riverbeds; at Creation Evidences Museum, exhibits include artifacts and fossils. And at the outdoor Texas Amphitheatre, a historical musical drama called *The Promise* tells the story of Jesus of Nazareth. Some folks come to Glen Rose simply to enjoy the exquisite, rough spread called Fossil Rim Wildlife Center, a sensational preserve that's home to some of the world's most endangered animals.

Another Recommended B&B in Glen Rose

Country Woods, a forty-acre retreat (owned by a former mayor) next to the Paluxy River, with cottages and cabins, private baths, TV/VCR, kitchen, and generous breakfast; 420 Grand Avenue, Glen Rose, TX 76043; telephone: (888) 849-6637.

The Houston House Bed and Breakfast

621 St. George Street
Gonzales, TX 78629
Phone: (830) 672-6940; (888) 477-0760
Fax: (830) 672-6228

E-MAIL: houstonhouse@gvec.net

INTERNET SITE: www.houstonhouse.com

INNKEEPERS: Eugene and Diane Smith

ROOMS: 5 rooms with private bath, TV, telephone, dataport; 1 with wheelchair accessibility

ON THE GROUNDS: Wraparound porches, parlor, and dining areas

CREDIT CARDS: MasterCard, Visa, Discover, Diners Club

RATES: $$-$$$; $$ corporate rate

HOW TO GET THERE: From San Antonio drive east on I-10 and south on U.S. 183; drive into town and turn east from 183 onto St. George Street and watch for home at number 621.

Renowned cattleman and Chisholm Trail driver William Buckner Houston built this sensational mansion in 1895. The Queen Anne masterpiece makes a giant impression with its turrets, wraparound porches, columns, peaks, spires, and ornate trim. Its magnificence already seems straight from a fairy tale, and the effect multiplies a thousandfold when decorated inside and out at Christmas.

Each of the bedrooms is done in elaborate antique furnishings from about 1830 through 1900, and each is a retreat unto itself with its own fireplace, telephone, cable TV, and VCR, AM/FM clock radio, and coffeemaker. Want to watch classic movies? Check out Eugene and Diane's collection on video.

Hand-painted murals in the dining room depict views of a European countryside from a century past; one of the murals dates to the original owners. It's in this setting that you'll have a breakfast set to candlelight and classical music. Always prepared from scratch, this meal starts with orange juice and a special organic coffee and continues with either a large bowl of fruit or a smaller fruit sundae. Entrees always include bacon or sausage and may feature eggs or a puff pastry filled with apples or another fruit, or there might be Belgian waffles with fresh fruit and clotted cream.

St. James Inn

723 St. James Street
Gonzales, TX 78629
Phone: (830) 672-7066

E-MAIL: email@stjamesinn.com
INTERNET SITE: www.stjames.com
INNKEEPER: Ann Covert
ROOMS: 5 rooms with private bath, TV, fireplace
ON THE GROUNDS: Sitting room and porches
CREDIT CARDS: MasterCard, Visa, American Express
RATES: $-$$$
HOW TO GET THERE: Drive east from San Antonio via U.S. 90A; turn south on U.S. 183 in Gonzales. Turn right (west) on St. James Street.

Enveloped by century-old pecan trees, this beautiful Greek Revival masterpiece was the home of Walter Kokernot, son of David Levi Kokernot, a cattleman and an unsung Texas hero, who was a personal confidante to General Sam Houston. Designed by noted San Antonio architect James Phelps, the home was completed in 1914. Renovated in 1989, the home's exquisite original woods and design detail are easily as impressive today as they were eighty years ago.

Your breakfast is accompanied by candlelight. Expect such dishes as chilled fruit in honey cream, egg and ham crepes in sherry sauce, pineapple or cranberry bread, and a surprise dessert.

What's Nearby Gonzales

Nicknamed the "Lexington of Texas," the seat of Gonzales County is where the first battle of the Texas Revolution took place. In front of the town's history museum, there's a wonderful memorial to those who fought in that conflict and to the thirty-two loyalists who went down with Travis at the Alamo. A driving tour is marked with eighty-six historical points of interest; ask about it at the chamber of commerce, located inside an 1887 jail building. Ten miles away, Palmetto State Park is a boon for botany fans and a good place to swim, fish, hike, and picnic.

Angel of the Lake

606 East Bridge Street
Granbury, TX 76048
Phone: (817) 573-0073

E-MAIL: arbor@itexas.net

INTERNET SITE: www2.itexas.net/~arbor

INNKEEPERS: Keith and Angie Tipton, Aletha Ball

ROOMS: 3 rooms with private bath, TV, telephone, dataport

ON THE GROUNDS: Garden, deck with lake view; formal dining room

CREDIT CARDS: MasterCard, Visa, American Express, Discover

RATES: $$$$; discount on Sunday–Thursday

HOW TO GET THERE: From Dallas-Fort Worth drive south on U.S. 377; take Business 377 into Granbury, then turn right on Cleburne Street and right on Bridge Street.

Like the Arbor House, which has the same innkeepers, this house is a recent construction. Built specifically as a B&B in a Queen Anne–like design, the home's function is all about comfort. King beds, cable TV, oversized Jacuzzi tubs, and marble details in every bedroom and bathroom are just the start. The home's sizable wooden deck leads to pretty gardens, through which you stroll en route to the beach on Lake Granbury. You can also walk 4 blocks to the adorable courthouse square, where you're sure to spend a few hours browsing in shops.

The guest rooms are Raphael's, with a mahogany bed and private deck access; Gabriel's, with a cherry wood bed, sofa, and private deck access; and Angel's Loft, with sensational views of Lake Granbury and Comanche Peak, private balcony, cathedral ceiling and church window, and leaded rose window in the bath.

The hosts want you to help yourself to snacks from the well-stocked guest refrigerator. The large breakfast, served in the dining room, includes quiche, fruit, homemade muffins, toast and jelly, orange juice, and coffee.

Arbor House Bed & Breakfast

530 East Pearl Street
Granbury, TX 76048
Phone: (817) 573-0073; (800) 641-0073

E-MAIL: arbor@itexas.net

INTERNET SITE: www2.itexas.net/~arbor

INNKEEPERS: Keith and Angie Tipton, Aletha Ball

ROOMS: 7 rooms, including 2 suites, with private bath, TV, telephone, dataport; 1 with wheelchair accessibility; 3 bathrooms with marble Jacuzzi tubs

ON THE GROUNDS: Verandah, rose garden, gazebo; parlor with fireplace

CREDIT CARDS: MasterCard, Visa, American Express, Discover

RATES: $$–$$$$, discount Sunday–Thursday

HOW TO GET THERE: Go southwest of Dallas-Fort Worth via U.S. 377. Follow Business 377 into town; 377 becomes Pearl Street. Drive directly to number 530.

A new home built to be a B&B, Arbor House has a Queen Anne look with its arbors, porches, and balconies. Guests share the roomy downstairs parlor, where there are oodles of brochures and restaurant menus to help you figure out what Granbury adventures lie ahead of you. The house has terrific views of Lake Granbury, with its swimming beach and boat ramp, right across the street.

Guest rooms include Victoria's Suite, a big spread with queen cherry wood canopy bed, wraparound windows, crystal chandelier, sitting room, and a Jacuzzi tub; Albert's Hideaway, with a queen bed, comfy sofa, lake views, and Jacuzzi tub; and the Garden Room, a first-floor suite with wheelchair accessibility, views of the rear garden, and an oversized, double-headed marble shower.

You won't be hungry after breakfast. The morning feast includes such goodies as a ham quiche, fresh fruit, homemade muffins, orange juice, toast and jelly, coffee, and tea.

The Captain's House on the Lake

123 West Doyle
Granbury, Texas 76048
Phone: (817) 579–6664

E-MAIL: captain@itexas.net

INTERNET SITE: www.virtualcities.com/ons/tx/d/txd2801.html

INNKEEPERS: Bob and Julia Pannell

ROOMS: 2 suites, 1 room, all with private bath

ON THE GROUNDS: Library, large balcony overlooking lake, front Victorian garden; TV in upstairs common room, stocked with books and magazines; all guests welcome to use common phone

CREDIT CARDS: None accepted

RATES: $$–$$$

HOW TO GET THERE: Drive southwest from Dallas-Fort Worth via U.S. 377 to Granbury, about 35 miles from Fort Worth. Ask for specific directions with reservations.

uilt in the 1870s by James H. Doyle, this Queen Anne beauty is a couple of blocks from Granbury's charming, historic town square. Kathleen's Room has an extended double-canopy bed, furniture carved from the distinctive "tiger" oak, and views of the square. Trenholm's Suite offers a queen bed and a separate sitting room with antiques, old dolls, and vintage clothing in the decor. The Mary Kate Doyle Suite contains period furniture, a king bed, a sitting area with a refrigerator, and a very large bathroom.

Bob and Julia are as hospitable as any innkeepers can be. They bring a lavish Continental breakfast tray to rooms each morning and provide gift certificates for brunch or lunch at the cute Nutshell Bakery on the square. Homemade desserts are served to guests daily, and you're given fresh flowers when you arrive. If you'd like a special gift basket for your guest, ask Bob and Julia to arrange it. They're also good in helping with dinner plans, tickets to the Opera House, and offering ideas for shopping and sight-seeing, and they'll point you to the best fishing spots a few steps away on Lake Granbury.

Dabney House Bed & Breakfast

106 South Jones
Granbury, TX 76048
Phone: (817) 579–1260; (800) 566–1260

E-MAIL: safe-dabney@flash.net

INTERNET SITE: www.flash.net/safe-dabney

INNKEEPERS: Gwen and John Hurley

ROOMS: 4 rooms with private bath, 2 with TV

ON THE GROUNDS: Porch swings, fish ponds, outdoor hot tub; living room TV/VCR with a selection of movies

CREDIT CARDS: MasterCard, Visa, American Express

RATES: $–$$

HOW TO GET THERE: Drive southwest from Dallas-Fort Worth on U.S. 377; in Granbury take Business 377 downtown to historic district; go past the square 7 blocks to traffic light. Go through traffic light 1 block and turn left on South Jones. House is at West Pearl Street and South Jones Street.

his delightful B&B occupies a home built in 1907 by local prominent banker Dan Cogdell, a wedding present for his daughter Zuma and W. F. Juliff. They sold it in 1918 for a whopping $4,000, and less than a year later Dr. Thomas H. Dabney, a local physician, bought it for $6,000. Dabney was the consummate community man, working as a town doctor until he was ninety-four, as well as serving as mayor, coroner, founder and elder for the Church of Christ, and supporter of the local Thorp Springs Christian College. Because he lived in the home until he was one hundred, the Hurleys chose to keep his name on the house when they opened it as a B&B.

The home's solid Craftsman style survives, as does original woodwork, copper-and-beveled glass windows, and a wood-beam wagon wheel on the dining room ceiling. It's in this dining room that you'll enjoy a bountiful breakfast of baked blueberry French toast with ham or an egg-sausage casserole with homemade biscuits, fruit, juice, and coffee. Gwen also does a pretty candlelight dinner by reservation. Guests are crazy about her baked Parmesan chicken breast, as well as the fresh flowers and quiet music she adds to the setting.

Doyle House on the Lake

205 West Doyle Street
Granbury, TX 76048
Phone: (817) 573-6492

E-MAIL: doylehse@hcnews.com

INTERNET SITE: www.doylehouse.com

INNKEEPER: Linda D. Stoll

ROOMS: 2 suites, 1 cottage with private bath and TV

ON THE GROUNDS: Swimming pool, fishing dock, volleyball, basketball, horseshoes, covered deck

CREDIT CARDS: MasterCard, Visa, American Express, Discover, Diners Club

RATES: $$–$$$; $ corporate rate during week

HOW TO GET THERE: From Dallas-Fort Worth drive southwest on U.S. 377 to Granbury, taking Business 377 through the downtown square. Stay on 377, which becomes Pearl Street. Turn left on Houston Street, then right on Doyle Street.

Doyle House is named for its original owner, a Civil War surgeon named John N. Doyle, who built the house around 1880. Another of the town's original civic-minded leaders, Dr. Doyle served as a physician, mayor, and finance manager for the public schools. Building a home on a street named for him, which also was on a bluff overlooking the Brazos River, Dr. Doyle's spread measures nearly two acres today.

The two-story, Colonial-style white house has been a bed and breakfast since the summer of 1990. Guest rooms are Emily's Suite, outfitted with elegant cherry and mahogany woods, a king bed, private bath with Jacuzzi, and a separate sitting area with TV and coffeemaker; Carriage House, a suite with a queen bed and a day/trundle bed, Shaker-design furnishings, bath with Jacuzzi, coffeemaker, microwave, refrigerator, and TV; and Pool Cottage, offering a queen bed, double futon, large living area with lodge-style furniture, covered deck, coffeemaker, microwave, refrigerator, TV, and a shower in the bathroom.

All guests are treated to a full breakfast, which includes hot egg and meat entrees, fresh bakery goods, fruits and juice, tea and coffee. If you're traveling on business and want a lighter meal, just tell Linda. If you'd like to dine privately in your room or suite, say so. Ask her also about tickets to the Opera House, Fossil Rim Wildlife Ranch, and Granbury Live, as well as for dinner recommendations in town.

The Iron Horse Inn

616 Thorp Spring Road
Granbury, TX 76048
Phone: (817) 579–5535

INTERNET SITE: www.theironhorseinn.com

INNKEEPERS: Robert and Judy Atkinson

ROOMS: 7 rooms with private bath, 1 with TV, telephone, dataport; cottage with fireplace

ON THE GROUNDS: Large front porch wicker chairs; gardens spreading over more than one acre, shaded by massive, 400-year-old oak trees; huge goldfish pond and waterfall; two living rooms for guests to share

CREDIT CARDS: MasterCard, Visa, American Express, Discover

RATES: $$–$$$$

HOW TO GET THERE: Drive southwest from Dallas-Fort Worth via U.S. 377; take Business 377 into town, drive 2 blocks past courthouse square, turn right on Travis Street. The Iron House Inn is on the right just 4 blocks.

Named for the place in history made by Daniel C. Cogdell, who brought the railroad to Hood County in the late 1800s, and who built his home a block from the train station, the Iron Horse is a magnificent construction in the Craftsman style. Designed by famed architect Wyatt Hedrick, the 7,000-square-foot home features maplewood floors, beamed ten-foot-high ceilings, beveled leaded windows, built-ins for the extensive library, a huge fireplace in one of the large living rooms, and an impressive hand-milled staircase. In front, an expansive porch is filled with wicker furniture, a perfect place for whiling away a morning or afternoon. At Christmastime the home is a fairyland, decorated with 20,000 tiny white lights, and there's a tree in each guest room.

Among guest room choices are the Cogdell Suite, with an antique tub and French doors leading to a large solarium; the Wine Cellar Suite, with a private entrance and limestone walls; the Baron's Balcony, with French doors opening onto a balcony; and the Nantucket Cottage, a very private escape with a fireplace.

Bob and Judy serve an elegant breakfast spread. Specialties include quiches, homemade muffins and breads, Belgian waffles, and lots of fruit. They also prepare sinful, homemade desserts, like chocolate cake or bread pudding, for the afternoon. When it's time for dinner, they'll make good recommendations.

What's Nearby Granbury

Straddling the banks of the Brazos River, which is dammed here to create Lake Granbury, the Hood County Seat is a favorite escape hatch for Fort Worth residents. The delightful courthouse square is a chockablock collection of antiques and home furnishings shops, and there's good dining, too, at Hennington's Cafe, Pearl Street Pasta, the Nutt Shell, and Merry Heart Tea Room. Also downtown are well-received productions at the Granbury Opera House.

Saline Creek Farm Bed and Breakfast

182 Van Zandt County Road 1316
Grand Saline, TX 75140
Phone: (903) 829–2709; (800) 308–2242

E-MAIL: lollyf@flash.net

INTERNET SITE: www.bbhost.com/salinecreekfarm

INNKEEPERS: Karen and Bob Franks

ROOMS: 7 rooms with TV, 5 with private bath, 4 with VCR; 3 private cabins

ON THE GROUNDS: Lots of trees, walking paths, fishing in private bass- and catfish-stocked lake

CREDIT CARDS: MasterCard, Visa, American Express, Discover

RATES: $$–$$$

HOW TO GET THERE: From Dallas take I–20 East to Farm Road 1255 (which is two exits past Canton exit). Go north on FR 1255 approximately 5.5 miles to intersection VZCR 1316; then right on 1316, turning at first drive on the right. Look for sign.

ocated only one hour east of Dallas, this inn and its additional, private cabins serve as a retreat with utter quiet and solitude. Inside the two-story, redbrick main house, which was built in the 1980s, are three upstairs guest rooms with either king or queen beds, quilts, antiques, and rockers. Honeymooners and couples like the Garden House, a two-room cottage with a queen bed, TV/VCR, microwave, small refrigerator, coffeepot, and access to a barbecue grill.

More rustic is the Cowboy Cabin, offering similar amenities as the Garden House. If you need two guest rooms, book the Lodge, a barnlike building with private baths and a full kitchen. Bedrooms here have queen-size, lodgepole beds and compatible wood furniture. Included with the price is a fabulous view of the private, stocked fishing lake from the Lodge's second-story deck. Downstairs, you'll find a TV and VCR.

You're served sumptuous breakfasts in a dining room overlooking the lake, and you're given porches and decks on which to relax and read or nap, as well as enjoy the evening campfires. Ask Karen and Bob to point you toward paths for nature walks, the best drives for spring wildflower or fall foliage views, or to the bargain-hunting grounds known as Canton First Monday Trade Days.

What's Nearby Grand Saline

Head over to the Grand Saline Museum-Salt Palace to understand the town's heritage. Sprung from an 1845 salt works, the town is home to one of the nation's largest salt plants, thanks to an underground salt dome thought to be 1.5 miles across and 16,000 feet thick. The prevailing theory is that this site could supply the world's salt needs for 20,000 years. Other diversions include a restored 1920 railroad depot, now serving as the library and civic center, and Lake Holbrook, with swimming and fishing.

Hamilton Guest Hotel

109 North Rice Street
Hamilton, TX 76531
Phone: (254) 386–8977; (800) 876–2502
E-MAIL: hamiltonguesthotel@juno.com
INTERNET SITE: www.bedandbreakfast.com
INNKEEPER: Christian Roff
ROOMS: 6 rooms, all sharing two full baths
ON THE GROUNDS: Sitting room; dining room; lobby shops selling imported

and domestic lotions, oils, soaps, powders, and beauty products; Egyptian cotton linens, down comforters, Battenburg lace items, quilts, and shams; gourmet flavored and roasted coffees; antique furniture, art, and kitchen accessories; silk wearables, cards, and pins; and the Tea Garden, serving coffees and teas, light lunch, and evening cappuccino, espresso, and specialty desserts

CREDIT CARDS: MasterCard, Visa, American Express

RATES: $ or $$$$ for entire hotel

HOW TO GET THERE: From Dallas-Fort Worth drive south on U.S. 67 to Glen Rose, then south on Texas 220 to Hico, where you'll take U.S. 281 south to Hamilton.

Hamilton Guest Hotel is the first historical bed-and-breakfast lodging in town, offering six rooms overlooking the historic town square. Each of the rooms has individual period decor, and each has its own eclectic brand. The antique lock and key in each room came from the historic Texas Hotel in Fort Worth; guests are also given a separate key for the downstairs door. The dining area, with its rosy skylight, is where you'll sit to enjoy your self-served Continental breakfast of juices, coffee, and pastries.

Guests share two full bathrooms, in which are antique, claw-foot tubs, equipped with handheld shower fixtures. A nice touch is the assortment of handmade, hand-cut soaps crafted just for the hotel, as well as shampoos and large towels. If you'd like a therapeutic or sports massage, inquire ahead of time. The hosts will also arrange catering, flowers, entertainment, fax, and e-mail services if you'd like to plan a party or a business function at the hotel.

What's Nearby Hamilton

The seat of Hamilton County is a scenic courthouse square right on U.S. 281, not far from the pretty Leon River. Established in 1885, the town's centerpiece is a native limestone courthouse; inside the local historical society has preserved various artifacts. Look on the courthouse lawns for a memorial to Anne Whitney, a frontier school teacher who was killed while defending her students during a Comanche attack, and another to Elsie Warenskjold, a pioneer writer whose letters back home drew several settlers to Texas from Norway. Several good shops fill the buildings on the square. Other downtown sites include the county museum, the county genealogy society library, and the Texan Theatre, for live stage performances.

The Countess Rose House 1910

301 East Franklin Street
Hillsboro, TX 76645
Phone: (254) 582–ROSE (7643); (877) 582–ROSE (7643)

E-MAIL: countessrose1910@hillsboro.net

INNKEEPER: Nancy Laman Countess

ROOMS: 6 rooms with private bath, TV, telephone, dataport

ON THE GROUNDS: Sunroom, rose garden, lily pond, balcony, wraparound front porch

CREDIT CARDS: MasterCard, Visa, American Express

RATES: $–$$$$

HOW TO GET THERE: From Dallas-Fort Worth take I–35 south to Hillsboro; take first exit, drive to courthouse, turn left on Franklin Street, and drive 2 blocks.

Nancy really wants you to stop and smell the roses, because she has thousands to sniff. Rose gardens surround the home, a ninety-year-old beauty, built in the four-square Prairie style. In her utter remodeling effort, Nancy furnished the home with period antiques and trimmed the decor with rose accents. Each of the guest rooms is painted a different shade of rose. Stress is guaranteed to melt away in one of her claw-foot bathtubs.

In the afternoon Nancy serves high tea. For breakfast you'll have a country feast of eggs and bacon or sausage, with plenty of lovely breads. On Sunday it's a champagne brunch with eggs Benedict and her special rose cookies. You'll need the fortification for exploring the neighborhood, a historic district, as well as nearby antiques shops.

Tarlton House B&B Retreat Center

211 North Pleasant Street
Hillsboro, TX 76645
Phone: (254) 582–7216; (800) 823–7216

E-MAIL: lovelace@hillsboro.net

INTERNET SITE: www.triab.com/tarlton

INNKEEPERS: Pat and Bill Lovelace

ROOMS: 8 rooms with private bath, 7 of the rooms with TV

ON THE GROUNDS: Wraparound porch, stained-glass windows, parlor, game room, dining room

CREDIT CARDS: MasterCard, Visa

RATES: $–$$

HOW TO GET THERE: From Dallas and Fort Worth, drive south on I–35 to the 370 exit, turning right onto Spur 579. Continue on to the courthouse square, and turn left at Franklin Street. Drive two blocks to Pleasant Street and turn left.

Green Duke Tarlton, as real estate lawyer and cotton farmer, built his family home in 1895, shortly after building the town's land and title office near the courthouse. A Louisiana native, Tarlton used termite-resistant cypress to build his masterpiece, but used oak for his mantles and longleaf pine in floors and other areas. He imported tiles from Italy to adorn the seven fireplaces, all of which boast different designs. Four stained-glass windows are found in the home, as well as a front door transom made up of more than 200 pieces of beveled glass. Sparing no expense, he also installed a dumbwaiter and a speaking tube to communicate with the house servants. Today the structure bears state and national historical markers.

Bill and Pat Lovelace bought the home in 1998 and have continued running it as a bed-and-breakfast, as did its previous owners. They frequently host murder mystery weekends—appropriate, as it's said that Mr. Tarlton's ghost haunts the home—in which you bring friends, family, and co-workers to participate in a two-night party. The hosts package the deal with Friday night hors d'oeuvres, rooms for two, breakfast on Saturday and Sunday, and a buffet dinner on Saturday. The hosts also offer "pampering" packages that include massage, manicure, pedicure, aromatherapy, and meals.

Their B&B retreat, as they call it, includes second-floor rooms, such as the Blue Room, with its king bed, bay window, hand-carved fireplace, and a fainting couch, which is perfect for reading and napping. On the third floor there's Abby's Attic, with a daybed and a king bed, as well as a claw-foot tub behind a fabric room partition; and the Gables Honeymoon Suite, furnished with a king bed, sitting nook, a reading area for two, and a gabled bathroom with shower and footed tub.

What's Nearby Hillsboro

Crowned by an architectural masterpiece, the Hill County Courthouse Square is a good place to spend a day prowling shops and cafes. On the campus of Hill College, you'll find the Confederate Research Center, dedicated to Civil War history. Regional history, complete with Native American artifacts, is on display at the Hill County Cell Block Museum. Nearby, the tremendous expanse of Lake Whitney provides hiking, fishing, waterskiing, and picnicking options.

Woodbine Hotel and Restaurant

209 North Madison Street
Madisonville, TX 77864
Phone: (936) 348-3333
Fax: (409) 348-6268

E-MAIL: woodbinehotel@aol.com

INTERNET SITE: www.woodbinehoteltexas.com

INNKEEPERS: Susan and Reinhard Warmuth

ROOMS: 7 rooms with private bath, TV, telephone, modem; 6 with whirlpool tubs; suites available

ON THE GROUNDS: Gazebo, wraparound covered porches upstairs and down, at front and rear of house; four acres, two of which are landscaped

CREDIT CARDS: MasterCard, Visa, American Express

RATES: $-$$$

HOW TO GET THERE: From Houston drive north on I-45 to Texas 21; take Texas 21 west into town to third light. Turn left at town square on Madison Street and drive 2 blocks.

A blend of Queen Anne and Eastlake styles, this wonderful hotel was originally called the Shapira Hotel when it opened in 1904. Listed as both national and state historic sites, the Woodbine offers rooms with either king or queen beds, Victorian decor, individual heat and air-conditioning, and endearing hospitality. The Parten Suite is the largest, with a king-size sleigh bed and a sunny turret with loveseat; the suite perfect for sunset watching is the Wills Suite, with an Eastlake king bed, writing desk, and windows on two walls, overlooking the gazebo and backyard; and the ultimate suite for privacy is the Shapira, situated in the tower of the front upstairs porch.

Both Susan and Reinhard Warmuth have extensive backgrounds in the hotel and entertainment industry. Susan has managed a number of hotels, and Reinhard—a German native with European culinary training—has been a chef in several hotels in the United States and in France and England. Breakfast, which is included with your stay, ranges from waffles, French toast, fruit plates, and omelettes to eggs Benedict and pastries. Reinhard also offers a full menu at lunch and dinner, with such offerings as grilled chicken Alfredo, pork tenderloin sandwich, Caesar salad, grilled salmon, and rib eye.

What's Nearby Madisonville

Located just north of Houston, the seat of Madison County was named for President James Madison and lies on historic Texas 21, also known as El Camino Real. From Madisonville it's an easy reach to the outstanding golf courses around Lake Conroe, and it's an easy drive to Davy Crockett and Sam Houston National Forests, both of which offer excellent hiking and nature study in thick, gorgeous woods.

Barton on Boydstun

505 East Boydstun Street
Rockwall, TX 75087
Phone: (972) 771-4350

E-MAIL: ebarton@bartononboydstun

INTERNET SITE: www.bartononboydstun.com

INNKEEPERS: Lindy and Edie Barton

ROOMS: 3 cottage suites with private bath, TV, telephone, dataport, wheelchair accessibility

ON THE GROUNDS: Garden; private, screened porches; original art and art gallery; chapel

CREDIT CARDS: MasterCard, Visa, American Express

RATES: $$–$$$

HOW TO GET THERE: From Dallas drive I–30 east to Rockwall, exit 205; drive north three traffic signals, turn right on Boydstun; B&B 3 blocks on left.

This spread on two wooded acres is less than a decade old, but it was built to have a vintage cottage look and appeal. Each of three cottage suites is particularly homey, cozy, and private, and each has its own design. The Browning Suite, for instance, is furnished with an oak china cabinet, comfy sofa and chair, and a pretty, old oak bed. The Avila Suite contains hand-carved Mexican table and chairs, armoire and dresser, hardwood floors, iron bed, and a great sofa for napping. When you're not curled up with a book in your suite, roam the sculpture garden with its bronzes or explore the chapel with its paintings and bronzes. There's an art gallery on the premises, too.

Breakfast is usually a full feast of cereals, fresh fruit, quiche, sweet breads, juices, milk, coffee, and tea.

Heart of My Heart Ranch

403 Florida Chapel Road
Round Top, TX 78954
Phone: (979) 249-3171; (800) 327-1242

E-MAIL: heart17@cvtv.net

INTERNET SITE: www.heartofmyheartranch.com

INNKEEPERS: Bill and Frances Harris

ROOMS: 12 rooms with private bath, TV, phone, dataport; 7 with fireplaces; 1 with wheelchair accessibility; in 3 modern and 3 historic houses

ON THE GROUNDS: Library, verandah, garden, porches with rockers, hot tub, swimming pool, golf driving range, horseback riding, fishing lake; conference room

CREDIT CARDS: MasterCard, Visa, American Express, Discover

RATES: $$$-$$$$

HOW TO GET THERE: From Austin drive east on U.S. 290 to Farm Road 237, then southeast on Florida Chapel Road.

This family ranch contains three historic houses and three modern houses, so you have your pick of lodging styles. At the core of the ranch is an 1836 log cabin, the most popular of all options. Inside is a queen bed, a double bed, and a twin bed in the loft, a full kitchen, bath with a view from the tub. The cabin also has central heat and air. Other choices are the honeymoon suite in the main house, with a queen-size four-poster, French doors opening onto a private porch, a private parlor, fireplace, library, and queen sleeper sofa; and a poolside cottage with two bedrooms, Jacuzzi tub, and walk-in shower.

The hosts are the very sweet Bill and Frances Harris, who knock themselves out providing hospitality. Bill's ancestors settled in Round Top in the 1830s, so the area is close to his heart. They built a home on this ranch in

1985 and have gradually expanded construction to accommodate travelers flocking to the town's antique fairs and to concerts at the nearby music conservatory.

Guests like to swim, hang out in the hot tub, get a Swedish massage, go fishing, hiking, and bicycling, and watch TV. Experienced riders can saddle up on one of the ranch's horses, and kids can enjoy the ranch's pony, donkey, dogs, and cats.

At breakfast time you can dig into plates of waffles, French toast, freshly baked muffins, sausage, fresh fruit salads, yogurt and granola, and an assortment of pastries. Groups can inquire about lunch and dinner arrangements.

Outpost @ Cedar Creek

5808 Wagner Road
Round Top, TX 78954
Phone: (409) 836–4975; (888) 433–5791

E-MAIL: lenorew@pointecom.net

INTERNET SITE: www.outpostat cedarcreek.com

INNKEEPER: Lenore Winston

ROOMS: 5 rooms, 3 with private bath, 2 with TV, telephone, dataport, in main house, log cabin, and barn-cottage conversion

ON THE GROUNDS: Library, verandah, garden; conference room with wheelchair accessibility

CREDIT CARDS: MasterCard, Visa, American Express

RATES: $$–$$$

HOW TO GET THERE: From Austin drive U.S. 290 east to Farm Road 1457, and drive 5.6 miles to Newmann Road, which you'll follow to Wagner Road.

The original house on this German farmstead dates to the 1880s, as do log cabins and barns on the grounds. All are filled with vintage Texas artifacts and antiques and are surrounded by native plant gardens and hay meadows. Pick a room either in the main farmhouse, one of the double log cabins, or in the barn-cottage conversion. You can't go wrong, and you can't argue with an escape that offers such solitude: Don't be surprised if all you can hear way out in this thirty-acre spread of countryside is the trill of cicadas in the trees and the thwack of an old screen door.

Plan on doing some bird-watching, going on a hay ride, and roasting marshmallows. Bring your bicycle and hiking boots if you think you'll be energetic, or a trashy novel to curl up with. At breakfast time get your appetite ready for Lenore's goodies, which can range from Southwestern egg dishes to giant country feasts.

The Settlement at Round Top

2218 Hartfield Road
Round Top, TX 78954
Phone: (979) 249-5015; (888) ROUNDTOP

E-MAIL: stay@thesettlement.com

INTERNET SITE: www.thesettlement.com

INNKEEPERS: Karen and Larry Beevers

ROOMS: 10 rooms with private bath in restored log cabins, house, cottages

ON THE GROUNDS: Library, sunroom, verandah, garden, hot tub, rocking chairs, games; video cassette selection

CREDIT CARDS: MasterCard, Visa, American Express

RATES: $$–$$$$, single or double occupancy

HOW TO GET THERE: Located halfway between Austin and Houston, Round Top is 8 miles south of U.S. 290. Continue south on Texas 237 1.5 miles, then west on Hartfield Road 0.5 mile to ranch located on the right. The second gate is the guest entrance.

Restored 1800s log cabins, houses, and cottages are scattered around this thirty-five-acre haven, populated also by wildflowers, deer, antique roses, and miniature horses, and decorated with split-rail fences and giant, ancient oaks. Your hosts enjoy giving you background on such buildings as the Lone Star House, an old newspaper building, and the Little House, a railroad ticket house, and on the struggles of the family that originally settled this homestead.

Although the accommodations seem rustic, look a little more closely: Each accommodation has a private bath, individual heat and air, porches with rockers, and fine linens. Some have very cozy whirlpool tubs for two and/or fireplaces. You can hide out, or you can play croquet or Scrabble, watch a movie, hike or bike, or wander into town to hunt for antiques. Nearby are the music institute, Shakespeare festival shows, and a restored pioneer settlement.

Breakfast is an event, served inside the restored barn. The magnificent spread, which includes casseroles, pancakes, and pastries, even warranted coverage in *Country Living* magazine.

The Settlement is closed Thanksgiving and Christmas Days.

What's Nearby Round Top

With a population hovering close to 100, this is easily one of the smallest incorporated towns in Texas. People love it for that and for the sensational shopping and good dining at Klump's and Royer's Round Top Cafe. Established in 1835 under the name of Jones Post Office, Round Top is close to Brenham, about halfway between Houston and Austin. You can easily while away a day or two exploring the historical buildings at Henkel Square and at the Winedale Historical Center. For musical interludes you can't do better than enjoy the programs at the International Festival Institute, where orchestral, chamber, and solo performances keep crowds happy at the Festival Concert Hall.

The Rose Mansion

One Rose Way
Salado, TX 76571
Phone: (254) 947-8200; (800) 948-1004

E-MAIL: nhunter@vvm.com

INTERNET SITE: www.touringtexas.com/rose

INNKEEPERS: Neil and Carol Hunter

ROOMS: 2 houses with 3 bedrooms, fireplaces; 2 log cabins with 1 and 2 bedrooms; 2 cottages; private baths and TV

ON THE GROUNDS: Two acres of landscaped grounds; sunroom, parlor, dining room, verandah, garden, hammocks

CREDIT CARDS: MasterCard, Visa, American Express

RATES: $–$$$

HOW TO GET THERE: From Dallas-Fort Worth drive south on I-35 to Salado. Take exit 284 and follow Main Street; turn east on Royal Street and watch for Rose Mansion.

The main house of this B&B is a Greek Revival mansion built in 1870 by Major A. J. Rose that bears national and state historical markers. Filled with Rose family memorabilia, the main house has three bedrooms—two of which have fireplaces—a grand parlor, elegant dining room, and a cozy kitchen. Also on the property are Chester House, with three bedrooms, one of which has a fireplace; the historic Garrison Log Cabin, with a bedroom, fireplace, and loft; George's Log Cabin, an 1800s structure with two bedrooms, fireplace, and swing; Austin Cottage, with stone walls, fireplaces, and two bedrooms; and Summer Kitchen Cottage, a cozy outbuilding that was once the kitchen and is now a one-bedroom hideout.

If you're not heading into the village of Salado to shop, you can lose yourself in the old-fashioned spirit of this spread. The grounds also have a windmill with a cypress storage tank, a rock smokehouse, and an old wagon. You can easily find your own little corner for writing letters and reading in one of the swings or hammocks. Breakfast is a different affair each day, but you can expect goodies like an egg casserole, quiche, French toast, pancakes, biscuits and gravy, or muffins, cereal, and fruit.

Katy House Bed & Breakfast

201 Ramona Street
Smithville, TX 78957
Phone: (512) 237–4262; (800) 843–5289

E-MAIL: thekatyh@onr.com

INTERNET SITE: www.katyhouse.com

INNKEEPERS: Bruce and Sallie Blalock

ROOMS: 5 rooms in suite and carriage house, with private bath, TV, phone, dataport

ON THE GROUNDS: Porch with rockers; common rooms with antiques and railroad memorabilia

CREDIT CARDS: MasterCard, Visa, American Express

RATES: $–$$

HOW TO GET THERE: Drive east from Austin on Texas 71; exit Loop 230, which becomes Third Street. Follow Third east to Ramona Street.

Named for the M-K-T (Missouri, Kansas & Texas) Railroad, this beautiful home was built in 1909 by J. H. Chancellor. Old-timers still refer to it as Dr. Stephens's house, as it belonged to the railroad division surgeon who moved here in 1937. For many years the first floor of the home was his clinic, and the half-bath under the stairs was his lab.

Lovingly restored to its original splendor, the home features an arched portico, bay-windowed living room, Georgian columns, longleaf pine floors, pocket doors, Battenburg lace, and a gorgeous staircase. Main house accommodations include the large Texas Special Suite, with a private balcony. Most private of all is the Carriage House, decorated with Western tack and trimmings.

The main dining room is the setting for a big country breakfast, which typically includes homemade breads and goodies, like jalapeño cheese grits.

What's Nearby Smithville

Just east of Austin, this charming hamlet on the Colorado River banks is simply a perfect place to leave the rushed, modern world behind. The historic downtown is filled with shops, and the Railroad Historical Park and Museum is a fine place to examine the histories of the old Union Pacific and Missouri, Kansas & Texas, with their cabooses, photos, and other train memorabilia. Like Bastrop State Park, Buescher State Park is an irresistible place to revel in the outdoors, populated by the mysterious Lost Pines, as well as thickets of live oak, draped dramatically with Spanish moss.

The Rosemary Mansion on Main Street

903 West Main Street
Waxahachie, TX 75165
Phone: (972) 923-1181
Fax: (972) 923-1199

E-MAIL: denwcross@aol.com

INTERNET SITES: www.texasguides.com /rosemarymansion.html; www.hat.org

INNKEEPERS: Dennis and Judy Cross

ROOMS: 5 rooms with private bath; 1 with TV, telephone, dataport; cottage with kitchenette

ON THE GROUNDS: Library, sunroom, verandah, garden, lily pond, greenhouse, bell tower, conservatory

CREDIT CARDS: MasterCard, Visa, American Express

RATES: $$-$$$$

HOW TO GET THERE: Drive from Dallas-Fort Worth south on I-35 or U.S. 287; exit Business 287, which becomes Main Street. Follow this 2 miles to number 903.

Built in 1916 by Texas oilman, banker, and rancher, P. A. Chapman, the 5,000-square-foot, Georgian-style home has been restored to its original grandeur and elegance. Dennis and Judy have filled the arts-and-crafts interior with the eclectic antique and art collection they've spent thirty years amassing.

Guest rooms to choose from include the French Lavender Bridal Suite, which has a hand-carved fireplace mantle from France, a sitting room with Louis XVI furnishings, candelabras, mantel cases, hardwood floors covered with Oriental rugs, and a bed that Judy designed; the Victorian Rose, a cozy room with period furniture such as an Eastlake chest of drawers with copper hardware; and the Garden View Guest House, a cottage with a fireplace, sitting room, and kitchenette.

Judy and Dennis serve cocktails and hot and cold appetizers at 6:30 P.M. Complimentary drinks include beer, wine, and other liquors, as well as soft drinks. It's a good time to meet other guests and have your hosts recommend places to go in town. Breakfast is a three- to five-course, sit-down affair. The gourmet spread changes all the time, but it always involves some of the 200 herbs grown on the mansion grounds. Served on antique china, crystal, and sterling silver, the meal is unforgettable.

What's Nearby Waxahachie

The state's most photographed courthouse is the sensational red-sandstone creation crowning the Ellis County Courthouse Square. Look closely to see some of the elaborate detailed faces on the façade, carved by artisans brought from Italy to do the fine detail work. At the Ellis County Museum, explore a collection of artifacts, and at the nearby Sims Library, have a look at the carved gold leaf and Carrara marble used in the interior design. Plenty of shopping in the restored downtown will occupy you for a day or two; in late spring the renaissance festival called Scarborough Faire will amuse you for at least a weekend.

St. Botolph Inn B&B

808 South Lamar Street
Weatherford, TX 76086
Phone: (817) 594-1455; (800) 868-6520

E-MAIL: buttolph@mesh.net

INTERNET SITE: www.bedandbreakfast.com

INNKEEPERS: Dan and Shay Buttolph

ROOMS: 6 rooms with private bath, TV/VCR; 1 with hot tub; 2 with wheelchair accessibility; 1 bedroom Carriage House

ON THE GROUNDS: Ballroom, wraparound verandah, five-acre hilltop to roam, swimming pool

CREDIT CARDS: MasterCard, Visa, American Express, Discover

RATES: $$–$$$$; discounts for clergy and military

HOW TO GET THERE: From Dallas-Fort Worth take I-20 west to exit 408; at fourth stoplight turn left on Russell, then at second stop sign turn right on South Lamar. Go past B&B and turn left on Norton Street and come up rear drive to park.

Crowning a five-acre hilltop is this 1897 mansion built from a Queen Anne design by William E. Tate, a local mercantile dealer. Giant at 5,500 square feet, the home features extensive gingerbread detailing on the front porch, a two-story tower, an ornate ballroom on the second floor, Tudor-style wainscoting, elaborately carved woodwork, fretwork, and transoms on doorways, carved mantels on five fireplaces, sliding pocket doors, gas light fixtures, and a wraparound porch.

Dan and Shay have painted the exterior in a tasteful scheme, using twelve historically accurate colors. Inside they've furnished rooms with antiques they've collected in Europe, Asia, and the United States. Among rooms in the main house are the King David Suite, with French walnut bedroom pieces, a turret breakfast room and a commanding view of downtown, a balcony, and a Jacuzzi tub in the bath; and St. Luke Room, with a queen bed, European water closet, and a footed tub. The Carriage House has a poolside entrance through French doors, a king brass bed from England, and a hot tub.

Although Weatherford offers much to enjoy, you'll have a hard time pulling yourself away from this retreat. The grounds covering the peaceful hilltop are home to more than twenty-six bird species and a handful of wild animals. Plan a long swim in the beautiful pool, then plenty of hang time on the verandah with a good book. On a clear night, look for the downtown Fort Worth night lights.

Dan and Shay serve a full gourmet breakfast that usually features four types of juices and three hot entrees from which to choose. Served on Victorian-era dishes with crystal and gold ware, you can enjoy breakfast either in your guest room, the dining room, or on the porch.

What's Nearby Weatherford

Take plenty of film to capture the marvelous Parker County Courthouse, an 1886 work constructed from locally quarried limestone. Mosey over to the Farmers Market for wonderful produce, vegetables, and bedding plants, and if you time the visit right, you can wander through the giant swap meet grounds at First Monday Trade Days. See the grave of renowned trail driver Oliver Loving in the town's Greenwood Cemetery, then explore the exquisite grounds of Chandor Gardens, a spread of landscaping, pathways, fountains, and falls that cover the estate created by the late, famous portrait artist Douglas G. Chandor.

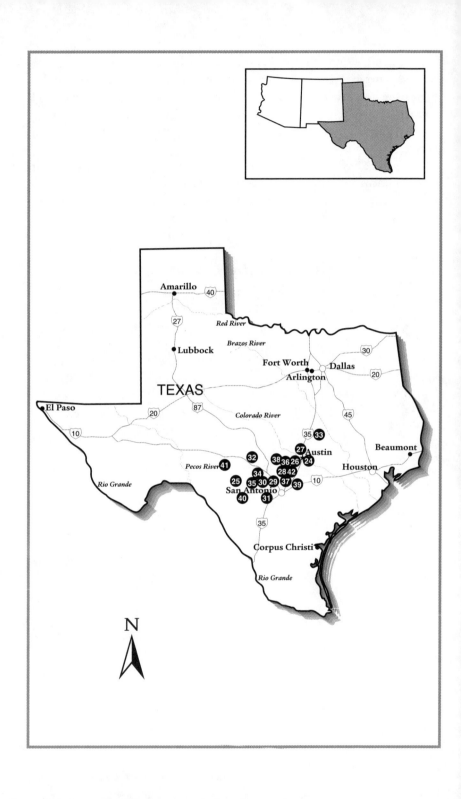

Texas: Hill Country

Numbers on map refer to towns numbered below.

Carriage House Inn and Ranch House Inn

1110 West 22½ Street and 1114 West 22½ Street
Austin, TX 78705
Phone: (512) 472-2333

E-MAIL: dcarriagehouse@aol.com

INTERNET SITE: www.carriagehouseinn.org

INNKEEPER: Tressie Damrom

ROOMS: 5 rooms in 2 buildings with private bath, TV, phone

ON THE GROUNDS: Gazebo, lily pond, fish pond, swings, deck, and porches

CREDIT CARDS: MasterCard, Visa, American Express, Discover

RATES: $$–$$$

HOW TO GET THERE: From I-35, exit at 19th Street/Martin Luther King Boulevard, driving west on MLK to San Gabriel Street. Turn right on San Gabriel and left on 22nd Street.

Here's a heck of deal, two B&Bs situated next door to each other and under the same ownership. The Carriage House Inn, about sixty years old, is a two-story, wooden Colonial design; the Ranch House Inn, about ninety years old, is a single-story home covered in lava rock. Both homes have original hardwood floors, plenty of windows, and wonderfully thoughtful details. Guests love the elegance of beautiful furniture and fine linens. All bedrooms are furnished either king or queen beds and television with cable and private telephone line.

Every morning brings a full breakfast. A typical meal will be a bowl of fresh fruit—strawberries, melons, grapes, and bananas—homemade waffles with freshly whipped cream, bacon, juice, coffee, and tea. Guests are served at individual, handmade cedar tables. If you have special dietary needs, just say so, and you'll get special treatment.

Lake Travis Bed & Breakfast

4446 Eck Lane
Austin, TX 78734
Phone: (512) 266-3386; (888) 764-5822

E-MAIL: ltbinnb@aol.com

INTERNET SITE: www.laketravisbb.com

INNKEEPERS: Judy and Vic Dwyer

ROOMS: 4 suites with private bath, TV, refrigerator, CD player; 1 with telephone, dataport by request

ON THE GROUNDS: Swimming pool, hot tub, sauna, boat dock with bar, dining table, sundeck, fitness deck with exercise equipment, game room, pool table, library, gift shop

CREDIT CARDS: MasterCard, Visa

RATES: $$$$

HOW TO GET THERE: From Austin follow Ranch Road 2222 to Ranch Road 620, and turn left, continuing 1 mile past Mansfield Dam. Turn right on Eck and drive 1 mile to the B&B's blue gate.

If your idea of heaven is a lakeside retreat where you'll be pampered, this is your destination. Once retired from the Texas Department of Health, Vic Dwyer, and travel agent wife, Judy, decided to buy this gigantic executive retreat perched on the limestone bluffs over Lake Travis from a Dallas oil company and turn it into a dream B&B. Suffice to say, they've done everything under the sun to make this a reality.

What's your pleasure? How about a session on a treadmill or with free weights, while looking at the blue waters of Lake Travis? Follow that with a sauna and a hot tub soak before settling into a couple of hours of reading on a chaise beside the swimming pool. You can easily while away the day in one entertaining way or another, shooting a game of pool, watching videos, or snuggling in front of the stone fireplace. Ask Vic and Judy about extras, such as a massage on the deck, a boat tour, or fishing or sailing trip. And if your escape is a celebratory one, ask ahead for a vase of roses, picnic basket, lavender-scented sheets, or a teddy bear-balloon bouquet.

And then there's the matter of which room to choose: Heart's Delight Suite offers a heart-shaped tub, fireplace, living room, kitchen, deck patio with table, love seat, and hammock; Eagle's Nest Suite provides a 180-degree view of the lake, hills, and sunset; Sunset Suite has its own private deck; and Lago Vista Suite, hidden among cedar and mountain laurel, has immediate access to the main deck, pool, and hot tub. All rooms have a half-canopied king-size bed, private bath with tub and shower, refrigerator, hair drier, CD player, and terry robes.

And what about this breakfast: Delivered to your door each morning will be a tray laden with such delights as an egg soufflé, a specialty pastry, jams, orange juice, and flavored coffee. Enjoy it in bed, if you're so indulgent, or take it onto your deck to greet the morning.

Woodburn House Bed & Breakfast

4401 Avenue D
Austin, TX 78751
Phone: (512) 458-4335; (888) 690-9763

E-MAIL: woodburn@iamerica.net

INTERNET SITE: www.woodburnhouse.com

INNKEEPERS: Herb Dickson and Sandra Villalaz-Dickson

ROOMS: 5 rooms with private baths, phones, dataports, and desks; 1 with TV

ON THE GROUNDS: Living room common area where guests watch TV and read

CREDIT CARDS: MasterCard, Visa, American Express

RATES: $$–$$$, including full breakfast

HOW TO GET THERE: Driving into Austin on I-35, take exit 237A, Airport Boulevard. Go west on Airport Boulevard and turn left at 45th Street. Follow 45th Street almost 1 mile to Avenue D; turn left and find house at corner of 44th and Avenue D.

Deep in the heart of Texas's capital city, not far from the University of Texas, Woodburn House was built in 1909 in the style of old southern plantation homes. Its builder was John Headspeth, whose work in Austin over a forty-year period crossed over from the nineteenth to the twentieth centuries. Woodburn's history is as rich as its design.

In 1920 a couple named Frank and Bettie Hamilton Woodburn moved into the home with their three daughters. The daughter of Andrew Jackson Hamilton, the provisional governor of Texas during Reconstruction, Bettie was credited with writing many of her father's speeches. Woodburn family members stayed in the home until 1973, but it fell into terrible disrepair by the late 1970s.

Plans were made for demolition, but the Hyde Park Neighborhood Association saw the importance of preserving this masterpiece—where once there had been many, Woodburn had the last remaining double-wrap porches in the neighborhood. The association prevailed, and the home was moved a few blocks to a new location, within a setting of mature trees on a lot similar to the original to preserve the home's integrity. The impressive restoration effort makes the home a source of understandable pride for owners Herb and Sandra, who have made their home an addition to the Hyde Park National Register Historic District.

Inside are lovely period furnishings. Combined with the graceful neighborhood setting, Woodburn is a place you'll feel privileged to visit. Breakfast is a full affair that typically includes fresh fruit and a hot dish, such as a broccoli-cheddar frittata, waffles, or pancakes, with bacon or sausage, juice, and coffee and tea.

What's Nearby Austin

Right downtown, the State Capitol Building is an exquisite pink granite creation, with a lovely rotunda to explore. Next door the Capitol Complex Visitors Center and the Texas History Museum occupy the 1857 General Land Office Building. The Governor's Mansion is within a couple of blocks, too, and should also be toured. On the University of Texas campus, find the Jack S. Blanton Museum of Art, with a permanent collection of more than 13,000 works that span the history of Western civilization. Take your own great photos in front of the dramatic Littlefield Fountain on the campus, which makes a perfect end to a long walk on The Drag, that stretch of Guadalupe Street that fronts the main campus and holds a wealth of unusual, unforgettable shopping opportunities. When the weather's fine—and it almost always is in Austin—enjoy the trails and beaches lining Town Lake; the cool, clear waters of Barton Springs in Zilker Park; and the magnificent Lady Bird Johnson Wildflower Center.

Other Recommended B&Bs Nearby

Adams House, a 1911 Colonial Revival home with an extensive art collection, custom-designed linens, baby grand piano, sunroom, plenty of books, four bedrooms and four private baths; 4300 Avenue G, Austin, TX 78751; telephone: (512) 453-7696; Internet site: www.theadamshouse.com. *Ragtime Ranch Inn,* a newly built country inn 23 miles from Austin, with donkeys, chickens, wildflowers, stocked fishing pond, reading/video libraries, screened porches, breakfast burritos, and four rooms with private bath, TV, phone; 203 Ragtime Ranch Road, Elgin, TX 78621; telephone: (512) 285-9599 or (800) 800-9743; Internet site: www.ragtimeranchinn.com. *Carrington's Bluff,* an 1877 home with English and American antiques, eight rooms with private bath, TV, and phone, and

Hill Country Equestrian Lodge

1580 Hay Hollar Road
Bandera, TX 78003
Phone: (830) 796–7950
Fax: (830) 796–7970

E-MAIL: lovettor@aol.com

INTERNET SITE: www.hillcountryequestlodge.com

INNKEEPERS: Dianne Tobin and Peter Lovett

ROOMS: 4 cabins and 5 suites with full kitchens and private baths

ON THE GROUNDS: Horseback riding, hiking paths, small pool, hot tub

CREDIT CARDS: MasterCard, Visa

RATES: $–$$$$

HOW TO GET THERE: Drive through Bandera and exit the town square going south on Texas 173. Turn east on Ranch Road 1077 and drive 9.5 miles; then turn right on Hay Hollar Road and watch for signs. At fork, take the ranch entrance with the cattle guard on the left.

Lifelong equestrienne Dianne Tobin enjoyed a successful career with her fitness business in Dallas before the call of home became irresistible. The Bandera native and her companion Peter Lovett bought this ranch and moved into its century-old house. Upon building cabins and suites, barn, paddock, and training pen, they opened their ranch to horseback-riding fans in early 2000.

Dianne's expertise in horse training, kinesiology, and riding instruction make her an unusual and valuable host. Easily as noteworthy is the work she and Peter have put into crafting lodgings made cozy with Texas limestone fireplaces and comfortable with porches that offer dramatic views of the scrubby hillsides.

In each of the cabins, which sleep six, are living and dining areas, as well as full kitchens with range, oven, microwave, refrigerator, dishwasher, toaster, and coffeemaker. There are sunrooms with game booths, plus two bathrooms. The suites sleep four each, and each offers a bath and kitchen, as well as front porches and rear decks. In your refrigerator find eggs, bacon, bread, margarine, milk, and orange juice for your breakfast, as well as a big basket of fresh bananas, pears, nectarines, oranges, and apples.

Guests are welcome to bring their own horses, as Dianne and Peter have built first-class stable facilities for their horses and yours. Whatever your horseback riding level, Dianne will take you with a small group to enjoy the 40-plus miles of trails in the adjacent, 6,000-acre Hill Country State Park. Dianne provides private riding lessons, as well.

Dianne and Peter will help you plan a round of golf at the nearby Flying L Ranch; a day of fishing, tubing, or kayaking on the Medina River; or a dinner at one of Bandera's restaurants. Between outings, cool off in their little pool, converted from an old stock tank and filled with spring water brought up by a working, antique windmill. The choices are completely up to you. As Dianne says, "We want to give our guests the chance to reconnect with nature or maybe with a part of themselves they've forgotten. We want them to leave rejuvenated and ready to enjoy life."

Other Recommended B&Bs Nearby

Bandera Creek Guest Cottage, with two bedrooms and one bath, full kitchen, patio, antiques, creekside setting; 148 Robindale West, Bandera, TX 78003; telephone: (830) 460–3517. *Hackberry Lodge,* a pretty limestone mansion built in 1880—with a carriage house—six rooms and two suites, kitchenettes, laundry facilities, living and dining rooms; 1005 Hackberry Street, Bandera, TX 78003; telephone: (830) 460–7134.

Green Gables Bed & Breakfast

401 Green Gables
Blanco, TX 78606
Phone: (830) 833–5931; (888) 833–5931

E-MAIL: mcfarlin@moment.net

INTERNET SITE: www.greengables-tx.com

INNKEEPERS: Glen and Sue McFarlin

ROOMS: 1 stone cabin with private bath, kitchen, fireplace; 1 suite with private bath and balcony

ON THE GROUNDS: Hot tub, fireplace

CREDIT CARDS: MasterCard, Visa

RATES: $$–$$$

HOW TO GET THERE: Drive U.S. 290 west from Austin to the intersection of U.S. 281 north of Blanco. Turn south on U.S. 281 to Blanco. From the stoplight in Blanco continue south approximately 7 miles to Rural

Route 473 (just before U.S. 281 crosses the Little Blanco River); turn left (east) on RR 473 approximately 3.3 miles. Turn right through the gate with Texas flag and white fence posts.

You can't help but feel renewed after spending a couple of nights on this fifteen-acre spread with centuries-old pecan and cypress trees and sensational Hill Country views alongside the crystal-clear, spring-fed waters of the Little Blanco River.

Choose between two lodgings, starting with the Morning Star Suite, found in the Colonial-style main house. The oversized suite has elegant detail, such as designer linens, and features a king-size bed, private bath, and separate balcony that overlooks the Little Blanco River and surrounding countryside. McBride's Retreat is a stone cabin built around (or possibly, before) 1943. Fully renovated, it offers a rustic queen-size cedar post bed, a full-size futon for extra guests, private bath with rock-enclosed shower, and a fully equipped kitchen with microwave, as well as a fireplace on the porch and one inside the cabin. Outside a spa adds to the relaxation and romance factors.

Either way you'll get a full country breakfast, including breakfast meat, fruit, homemade breads, juice, coffee, and eggs.

What's Nearby Blanco

Originally the seat of Blanco County when the area was settled in the mid-1800s, Blanco boasts a pretty courthouse built in Second Empire style in 1886. Sadly it was abandoned just four years later when the county seat moved 14 miles north to Johnson City, but the town's tireless residents raised money recently for an impressive restoration project. Today it's one of the most attractive period buildings in the state. Around the square are charming limestone buildings filled with antiques shops, cafes, and a timeless general store. A few blocks from the square is Blanco State Park, one of the state's oldest and smallest, but certainly one of the most appealing, thanks to its position on the Blanco River.

Lakeside Lodge

201 Lakewood Drive
Burnet, TX 78611
Phone: (512) 756-4935

E-MAIL: lakesidelodge@281.com

INTERNET SITE: www.lakesidelodge.com

INNKEEPERS: John Trainor and Virginie Caruso

ROOMS: 2 three-bedroom houses with private bath, TV, cable, telephone; 1 with fireplace

ON THE GROUNDS: Patio with 5-mile lake view, sandy beach, fishing dock

CREDIT CARDS: MasterCard, Visa

RATES: $–$$

HOW TO GET THERE: In Burnet turn west from U.S. 281 onto Texas 29 and drive to Ranch Road 2341. Drive north on RR 2341 as it curves along the banks of Lake Buchanan. It will become Lakewood Drive.

Supercasual and laid-back, this sixties fishing lodge turned bed-and-breakfast is bursting with retro charm. John and Virginie like to say that they cater to the mature traveler who is budget-minded. You'll find it to be an especially quiet place, shaded by century-old oak trees and perfect for groups traveling together.

Sitting on the banks of gorgeous Lake Buchanan, the lodge consists of two three-bedroom houses, one of which has a fireplace and screened porch; both have a Southwestern decor theme, as well as TV with cable and telephone. There are VCR/video rentals, and you can arrange for massage therapy and seaweed wraps.

Guests enjoy a full country breakfast with eggs and meat, fresh fruits, homemade muffins and breads, and freshly ground coffee. You'll need the energy for the days of fishing, swimming, bird-watching, and wildflower hunting.

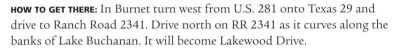

What's Nearby Burnet

When visiting the seat of Burnet County, you'll have to do like the locals and pronounce their town "BURN-it." Founded on the site of the old pioneer Fort Croghan, Burnet is a good jumping off place for exploring Longhorn Caverns State Park, a giant maze of underground rooms formed over a million years—give or take. Tour opportunities are varied, from easy to slightly challenging. Be sure to check out also Inks Lake State Park, located about 8 miles from town and one of the prettiest of all parks in Texas.

Landmark Inn State Historical Park

402 Florence Street
Castroville, TX 78009
Phone: (830) 931-2133; (512) 389-8900

INTERNET SITE: www.tpwd.state.tx.us/park/landmark/landmark

INNKEEPER: June Secrist

ROOMS: 8 rooms, 4 with private bath; 1 with wheelchair accessibility

ON THE GROUNDS: Historical resource center, museum and museum shop, library; river, fishing, hiking, butterfly refuge

CREDIT CARDS: MasterCard, Visa, Discover

RATES: $

HOW TO GET THERE: From San Antonio drive west on U.S. 90 to Castroville. Stay on U.S. 90, turn left on Athens Street and drive to Florence Street.

Once a nineteenth-century stage stop, this hotel was built near a ford on the serene Medina River along the San Antonio–El Paso Road. Inside each room are furnishings that range from the late 1800s to the 1940s, when a Miss Ruth Lawler owned the place and called it the Landmark Inn. Listed on the National Register of Historic Places, the inn is part of the Texas Department of Parks and Wildlife.

In keeping with traditions of its period furnishings, there are no televisions or telephones, but there are exceptions—all rooms do have air-conditioning (turned on April 15 through October 15) and ceiling or wall fans, as well as panel heaters. Each has either two single beds or a double bed. There's a spacious verandah on the second floor of the main building where you'll likely want to hang out to read or write letters.

Among the rooms perfect for a couple is Room 1, with a double Victorian bed, Alsatian wall hanging, private bath with shower, and high ceilings; and the very cozy, tiny Room 8, with a private porch and a private bath. Breakfast is Continental, with cereals, pastries, juice, and coffee.

Do bring your rod and reel to fish for catfish, bass, and panfish in the Medina River, where you can swim and wade, too. The park's office can provide information on places to canoe and kayak. After a day of bicycling (bring your own wheels), you'll want to kick back and play games, which you can check out at the park's kitchen. Bring a camera, too, to photograph the old buildings, as well as the 1850s grist mill and dam on the property. If you're a history buff, you won't be able to resist the inn's museum and historical research center.

What's Nearby Castroville

Known as the "Little Alsace of Texas," this charming burgh some 20 miles west of San Antonio was settled in 1844 when an immigrant named Henri Castro brought a bunch of his fellow Alsatians with him from that distinguished area of France. You'll find bits of that sturdy heritage at St. Louis Cathedral Church, built from 1868 to 1870; the Moye Center, built in 1873 as a Sisters of Divine Providence convent; and Mount Gentilz Cemetery, which offers a marvelous view of the Medina Valley. And don't miss a wonderful dinner of French food at La Normandie.

La Luna Linda Bed & Breakfast

Route 1, P.O. Box 127
Comfort, TX 78013
Phone: (830) 995-5062

E-MAIL: laluna@hctc.net

INTERNET SITE: www.bbonline.com/tx/laluna

INNKEEPERS: Melinda and Roman Luna

ROOMS: 2 rooms with private bath, phone; 1 with TV

ON THE GROUNDS: Creek, views, wildlife

CREDIT CARDS: None accepted

RATES: $$

HOW TO GET THERE: From San Antonio drive west on I-10 to the Cypress Creek Road exit. Turn right and drive 4.5 miles to Allerkamp Road (Route 1). Turn right and drive 1 mile.

No question about it, friends, this is how to get away from everything. Out on this century-old, seventy-acre farm—once a German immigrant homestead—your troubles seem to melt away when you take in the creek setting, filled with wildlife, farm animals, exceptional views, and utter tranquility. Couples love the solitude, but families enjoy this retreat, too. Whatever your age, you'll enjoy spotting wild turkey, porcupine, fox, deer, and hummingbirds, and it's a kick to sit outside on warm evenings and watch the bats come out to feed. Children love gathering eggs, milking the cow, feeding the horses, playing in the creek, and hunting for fossilized seashells.

The hundred-year-old guesthouse is built of solid stone, but it has been updated and renovated to offer a king bed, full kitchen, air-conditioning, and telephone. Everyone loves the full breakfasts, all made from scratch, right down to the jams and jellies made from fruit grown right on the farm. A sample breakfast would be blueberry pancakes, eggs from the farm's chickens, biscuits with homemade mulberry, peach, or mustang grape jelly, and homemade venison sausage.

What's Nearby Comfort

Never did a name suit a town more perfectly, both in the past and present tenses. When settled in 1854, it was by a group of free-thinking German intellectuals who wanted a place where they'd be unlimited in their philosophies. They chose this bucolic settlement, which remains one of the most relaxed, simple, and pleasant places in the state. Some very nice shops line the main drag, High Street, and there's good, home-style cooking at Cypress Creek Inn. Nature lovers enjoy taking a trip out to the Hygieostatic Bat Roost, about 14 miles north of town, where several thousand bats live in an abandoned railroad tunnel. In town take note of the Treue Der Union Monument, a testament to the settlers' Union sympathies during the Civil War.

Another Recommended B&B in Comfort

Comfort Common, an 1880 limestone building made over into a country inn with double porches, luxurious furnishings, nine bedrooms with private baths, and a full breakfast; 717 High Street, Comfort, TX 78013; telephone: (830) 995–3030.

J. M. Koch's Hotel Bed & Breakfast

Main Street
D'Hanis, TX 78850
Phone: (830) 363–7500; (800) 460–8481

E-MAIL: kochhotel@hi-tex.net

INTERNET SITE: www.kochhotel.com

INNKEEPERS: Candy and Hilo Del Bosque

ROOMS: 5 rooms with private bath, TV

ON THE GROUNDS: Landscaped yard with flower garden, pond, and waterfall

CREDIT CARDS: MasterCard, Visa

RATES: $

HOW TO GET THERE: Drive 37 miles west of San Antonio on U.S. 90; the inn is on the main road, which is U.S. 90.

uilt in 1906 to serve as a railroad hotel, the inn had a Texas Historical Marker placed in 2000. The exterior is covered with some of the first brick to come from the D'Hanis Brick Factory. Just inside the front door is an old lamp fixture that was one of the early electrified models, and throughout the inn are beautifully restored original wood floors.

Each of the five large guest rooms is outfitted with period antiques, and each has its own grace. One downstairs bedroom, which has four large windows that allow plenty of refreshing light, has a sink set in an antique sideboard, as well as a quilt-covered queen bed. Another of the downstairs rooms has a high Eastlake wood double bed, antique wardrobe, and a dresser topped with two candle-style lamps. Upstairs, where there's a roomy sitting area in the hallway, you'll think there are eight bedrooms, but remodeling has turned eight small rooms into three large guest quarters. One suite occupies half of the upper floor and has a big bathroom with a claw-foot tub. Each room has its own bathroom and air-conditioning.

Each morning you'll enjoy a home-cooked country-style breakfast. Don't be surprised if your dining mates are travelers from as far away as Guatemala, Alsace, Italy, or Alaska, who are likely on their way to hike at Lost Maples State Park or do some tubing along the Frio River in Garner State Park.

What's Nearby D'Hanis

Positioned on U.S. 90 almost midway between San Antonio and Uvalde, this tiny Medina County town was settled in 1847. Some of the oldest folks in town might call it New D'Hanis, because the original town site lies about a mile east of the present place; it moved, you see, to be where the railroad tracks were laid. The town's most famous site might be the old brick plant; all over Texas bricks are labeled "D'Hanis." Perhaps a dozen miles west of town is the pretty Sabinal River, a good place to picnic and enjoy the quiet.

Ab Butler's Dogtrot at Triple Creek

801 Triple Creek Road
Fredericksburg, TX 78624
Phone: (830) 997–8279; (877) 262–4366

E-MAIL: abbutler@fbg.net
INTERNET SITE: www.fbg.net/tce/abbutler.htm
INNKEEPERS: Robert and Nan Mosley
ROOMS: 2 rooms with private bath

ON THE GROUNDS: Wood-burning fireplaces, private living rooms, Jacuzzi tubs

CREDIT CARDS: MasterCard, Visa, Discover

RATES: $$$

HOW TO GET THERE: Drive from Austin west on U.S. 290, or from San Antonio drive west via I-10 and turn north on U.S. 87 at Comfort. Ask for detailed directions at time of booking.

Talk about making a commitment: This hideout is a 200-year-old cabin that was built in Kentucky and used as a hospital during the Civil War. The Mosleys moved it to Fredericksburg in 1997 and transformed it into a B&B the following year. You don't have to be an expert to recognize a master craftsman's beautiful finishing job, and you can't help but appreciate the use of designer fabrics to showcase the primitive furnishings you see throughout.

Found 4 miles from the center of town, Ab Butler's sits in a serene, rural setting surrounded by oaks and visited by deer and squirrel. If you need to forget the hectic world at home, you'll find solace by exploring the property's creeks, napping in a hammock, sitting in a swing, or tossing some horseshoes. When it's time to take a scenic drive, you'll be pleased to know you're only ten minutes from the famed Willow City Loop.

A nice treat to find in each of the two suites—besides your own living room, fireplace, and Jacuzzi tub—is a sampling of variously scented soaps made on the premises. And your full breakfast will be ready whenever you decide to face the day. Expect pleasures such as vegetable frittata, tomato pie or quiche, along with cereals, milk, coffee, teas, juices, fruit plate, and homemade breads.

The Cook's Cottage, Elizabeth's on Austin Street, and Patsy's Guest House

703 West Austin Street
Fredericksburg, TX 78624
Phone: (210) 493–5101

E-MAIL: patsy@aisi.net

INTERNET SITE: www.bed-inn-breakfast-tx.com

INNKEEPER: Patsy Swendson

ROOMS: 1 cottage with private bath, kitchenette; 2 suites with private bath, 1 with kitchen, 1 with kitchenette

ON THE GROUNDS: Whirlpool, spa, garden spa room, gardens, verandah

CREDIT CARDS: MasterCard, Visa, American Express, Discover

RATES: $$$–$$$$

HOW TO GET THERE: Drive into town on U.S. 290 (Main Street from Austin) and turn right on Acorn Street, then left on Austin Street. From San Antonio drive I-10 west and exit U.S. 87 at Comfort. Drive north on U.S. 87 to Fredericksburg; turn left on Main Street, right on Acorn Street, then left on Austin Street.

San Antonio food maven Patsy Swendson decided to add to her plate—already full with her duties as a cookbook author and cooking personality on TV and radio—by becoming an innkeeper. But like all of her endeavors, she executes this new career with style and substance, offering guests equal doses of comfort and romance. Results have been impressive: In 1999 *Travel & Leisure* magazine included The Cook's Cottage among the top twenty-five most romantic places in the United States, and the trio of B&Bs at this single address are frequently noted in such publications as *Texas Highways.*

The Cook's Cottage was built in 1987 behind the main house at 703 West Austin Street; it's reached by walking through a pretty little garden busy with butterflies, flowers, and herbs. Past the peaceful little screened porch with primitive Texas furniture is the cottage's spacious room. Here Patsy has put a pine table for two in front of a bay window and a wonderful, custom-made cypress pole bed that incorporates an antique Irish garden gate in the headboard. Other elements include a slate gray floor, stained-glass windows, a copper sink, whirlpool tub for two, and a kitchenette with minifridge, microwave, and coffee bar. When you check into The Cook's Cottage, as well as the other two B&Bs here, Patsy will have a chilled bottle of wine and appetizers waiting.

Patsy split the main house into two separate lodgings. Downstairs is Elizabeth's on Austin Street, where you can really spread out. In addition to the bedrooms, one with a queen four-poster and the second with twin beds, there's a spacious bathroom, big living and dining area, and a full kitchen. Decor tends toward laces and country touches, but men won't feel like it's too frilly, thanks to big wooden tables and comfortable couches and chairs. The back part of the house has a luxurious garden spa room, which is exclusively for Elizabeth's guests. As in the other two B&Bs, there are herbal bath salts, snacks, pastry platter, juices, fruits, coffee, tea, bedside chocolates, and desserts to enjoy.

Upstairs is Patsy's Guest House, a two-room suite with a private entrance. In addition to the bedroom with its queen bed is a sitting room with an iron daybed, so this B&B actually sleeps three. Some of the remarkable elements Patsy has added here include a kitchenette sink made from an antique copper mixing bowl and a bathroom sink crafted from an antique angel food cake pan. If you'd like to book both Elizabeth's and Patsy's, you'll have accommodations for nine.

None of three guest quarters has a phone or TV; Patsy's a big believer that a trip to Fredericksburg means escaping not just the concrete freeways of city life, but finding pure relaxation, too. You certainly won't go hungry, between the goodies Patsy provides and the complimentary brunch/light lunch she serves at the Oak House. At check-in you'll be given a voucher to redeem at this lovely restaurant.

Creekside Inn

304 South Washington Street
Fredericksburg, TX 78624
Phone: (830) 997–6316; (888) 997–6316

E-MAIL: creekside@fbg.net

INTERNET SITE: www.fbg.net/creekside

INNKEEPER: Helen Lane Smith

ROOMS: 7 rooms with private bath, TV/VCR, telephone, dataport

ON THE GROUNDS: Video library in house, patios; fish pond by creek, rose garden

CREDIT CARDS: MasterCard, Visa, American Express, Discover

RATES: $$

HOW TO GET THERE: Drive from Austin west on U.S. 290, or from San Antonio drive west via I–10 and turn north on U.S. 87 at Comfort. U.S. 87 is Washington Street; you'll find the inn just south of U.S. 290/Main Street.

This 1905 house was built in the design style called Basse Block and is a pretty, solid work in stone. The front part of the house holds the office, where guests check in; there's also a living room where you can borrow books and videos.

Alongside Baron's Creek you'll find the newer, modern guest rooms. Each of these has a large interior with a kitchenette and roomy whirlpool tubs for that long, luxurious soak most people only manage on vacations. Helen tries to provide just about everything in each room, from baskets brimming with coffees, teas, flavored creamers, cocoas, and cappuccino mixes to tea kettle, toaster, dishes, wineglasses and corkscrew, iron and ironing board.

Each morning at 9:00 A.M., you'll sit down in the dining room at the main house for a full spread. Helen's morning meal typically includes a casserole combining meat, eggs, and cheese, served alongside biscuits, pancakes, juice, and coffee. You won't go hungry.

What's Nearby

Ask well-traveled Texans what they know about Marble Falls, about 60 miles northeast of Fredericksburg, and the first thing they're likely to tell you is that there are no better homemade pies anywhere than at the Bluebonnet Cafe in that very town. The friendly and usually crowded dining room is also a good spot for home-cooked stuff like meat loaf, fried chicken, and catfish. In spring you'll find roads crowded with bluebonnet watchers; Ranch Road 1431 is an especially popular route to look for spring colors.

Das Garten Haus Bed & Breakfast

604 South Washington Street
Fredericksburg, TX 78624
Phone: (830) 990-8408; (800) 416-4287

E-MAIL: mac@hctc.net

INTERNET SITE: www.dasgartenhaus.com

INNKEEPERS: Kevin and Lynn MacWithey

ROOMS: 2 suites with separate entrances, cable TV, kitchen, and private bath; 1 with telephone

ON THE GROUNDS: New Orleans–style courtyard and flower gardens

CREDIT CARDS: MasterCard, Visa, Discover

RATES: $$–$$$

HOW TO GET THERE: Drive from Austin west on U.S. 290, or from San Antonio drive west via I-10 and turn north on U.S. 87 at Comfort. Washington Street is U.S. 87, just south of Main Street (U.S. 290).

Within this fifty-year-old home, noted for pretty pine and oak floors and beautiful crown molding, are two private suites. These have separate, private entrances and cable TV. The upstairs quarters sleeps as many as four guests—traveling together, of course—in two bedrooms, each furnished with queen beds. If that's not enough, there's also a queen sleeper sofa in the suite's living room, as well as a full-size kitchen with a refrigerator and microwave and a bathroom with a shower.

The downstairs suite, which sleeps two, is situated just off the courtyard. There's a queen-size bed, a private bath, and a separate sitting/kitchen area, which has a refrigerator and microwave. Across the courtyard find the cottage, where a king-size bed, full bath, and bar kitchen await.

Each of the accommodations overlooks the MacWithey's lovely, flowering courtyard, bursting with colorful annuals and perennials. Kevin, the resident, professional horticulturalist, is always at work changing and perfecting these views. In the mornings you're treated to a generous, homemade breakfast, such as omelettes and casseroles that incorporate the plentiful garden vegetables. Like many of Fredericksburg's B&Bs, this one is in easy walking distance to plentiful shopping.

The Delforge Place

710 Ettie Street
Fredericksburg, TX 78624
Phone: (830) 997–6212; (800) 997–0462

E-MAIL: info@delforgeplace.com

INTERNET SITE: www.delforgeplace.com

INNKEEPERS: Sandy and Lee Seelig

ROOMS: 2 suites and 2 rooms with private bath, TV, telephone; 3 with wheelchair accessibility

ON THE GROUNDS: 2 patios; membership at swim and racquet club

CREDIT CARDS: MasterCard, Visa, American Express, Discover

RATES: $$

HOW TO GET THERE: Drive into town on U.S. 290 west from Austin, or from San Antonio take I–10 west and U.S. 87 north. From U.S. 87, turn west on Live Oak and continue to Ettie Street.

Built as a Sunday House in 1898, the home was expanded in 1923, restored in 1975, and opened as a B&B in 1985. What you'll find is graceful Victorian details, including original beaded board paneling, twelve-foot ceilings, original wood floors, ornate chandeliers, and windows and doors with beveled, stained, and etched glass. Furnishings range from American and European antiques to home touches, such as colorful braided throw rugs, footlockers functioning as luggage stands, and dried flower decorations.

Two of the accommodations are suites and two are rooms, and each has its own historical theme. One of the bathrooms has a Jacuzzi tub, and another has a claw-foot antique tub. Guests share the large front porch, a patio, and a deck. At breakfast time everyone sits down to an eye-popping spread that's merited mention in the pages of *Gourmet* and *Bon Appétit* magazines. Expect your plate to be piled with such treats as German sour cream twists, Belgian pastries, egg creations, sausages, fruits, and homemade jellies and jams.

Hoffman Haus, Inc.

608 East Creek Street
Fredericksburg, TX 78624
Phone: (830) 997–6739; (800) 899–1672

E-MAIL: watkins@ctesc.net

INTERNET SITE: www.hoffmanhaus.com

INNKEEPERS: Ted and Joy Ciereton, owners; Betty O'Connor, manager

ROOMS: 7 buildings, including a log cabin with 2 suites, cottage, and main lodge, with private bath, TV, VCR

ON THE GROUNDS: Library, sunroom, verandah, garden, lily pond

CREDIT CARDS: MasterCard, Visa, American Express

RATES: $$–$$$$

HOW TO GET THERE: Drive from Austin west on U.S. 290, or from San Antonio drive west via I–10 and turn north on U.S. 87 at Comfort. In Fredericksburg turn left (south) on Elk Street and left (east) on East Creek Street.

More than a century ago, Hoffman Haus was a private country estate. Now a two-acre compound, the retreat consists of seven buildings on wonderfully scenic grounds that include a Texas native plants garden. The four nineteenth-century buildings date from 1835 to 1890.

Opened in 1995 with three rooms and expanded recently to offer eleven rooms, this lodge bears the title, "Fredericksburg's most beautiful guest house." And certainly it may be, given all the elegant accoutrements found here: Within various rooms are claw-foot tubs, designer linens, elaborately canopied beds, antiques from the eighteenth and nineteenth centuries, and chandeliers. Each guest room has its own private entrance, porch, and butler's pantry, the last stocked with coffees, teas, fruit juices, and water.

Each suite and room offers individual style and decor. Among the appealing choices are the Bluebonnet Suite, done in blue and white, with a queen-size bed and queen sleeper sofa, kitchen and footed tub with shower; the Morning Star Suite, inside the 1835 log cabin, with eighteen-foot ceilings, a queen-size iron bed, loft with twin beds, and Jacuzzi tub; and the similar Evening Star Suite, also in the old cabin. The latter two can be connected to sleep a party of ten.

More intimate are the Calico Cottage, Emily Morgan Room, Crockett Room, and Violets & Ivy Room. All guests can visit the Main Lodge, an 1840s log barn, where offerings include a 1,200-volume library, cozy parlor, and conservatory. The site, as you'll find, is perfect for weddings and other parties. Each morning, guests are pampered with a big breakfast that includes an egg dish, fresh fruit, freshly baked goods, French toast, local peaches, and fresh berries—all delivered to rooms in picnic baskets.

Kiehne Kreek Farm

c/o Gastehaus Schmidt
Texas Highway 16 North
231 West Main Street
Fredericksburg, TX 78624
Phone: (830) 997–5612

E-MAIL: gasthaus@ktc.com

INTERNET SITE: www.fbglodging.com

INNKEEPERS: Bill and Nancy Wareing

ROOMS: 4 rooms; 1 with private bath; 3 with shared half-bath

ON THE GROUNDS: Patio and porch with tables and chairs; duck pond, acreage to roam

CREDIT CARDS: MasterCard, Visa

RATES: $$–$$$$

HOW TO GET THERE: Drive from Austin west on U.S. 290, or from San Antonio drive west via I–10 and turn north on U.S. 87 at Comfort. In Fredericksburg head 9 miles northeast of town via Texas 16 and Knopp School Road; specific directions provided by Gastehaus Schmidt.

This charming old rock-and-wood house was built by a family named Kiehne (pronounced "kinny") around 1850 and was lovingly restored by the Wareing family, who lived here for several years before restoring and moving into the old house next door. The guest home is a comfortable, rambling assemblage of eight rooms, including a master bedroom, which has an attached bath with shower and a big, footed tub. There are three small bedrooms, too, which share a half-bath. An ample living room opens onto a dining room and onto the covered porch, but you'll be tempted to hang around the homey kitchen, which opens onto a patio, shaded by a mulberry tree.

Furnished with period antiques, the old farmhouse is great if your group is a family or a bunch of good pals hanging out for the weekend. You're 9 miles from the shopping and dining hubbub of adorable Fredericksburg and about 20 miles from extraordinary hiking at Enchanted Rock State Park. The hosts stock the refrigerator with orange juice, farm-fresh eggs, country bacon, sausage, bakery breads, and fresh fruit for you to whip up your own spread each morning.

The Wareings are particularly friendly but not a bit intrusive. If you want restaurant suggestions, they'll oblige—but mostly they'll leave you to your own devices. Their sweet Labrador dogs will ask for love and attention, but they're not pushy, either. Bring children by special arrangement only.

The Luckenbach Inn

3234 Old Luckenbach Road
Fredericksburg, TX 78624
Phone: (830) 997–2205; (800) 997–1124

E-MAIL: theinn@luckenbachtx.com

INTERNET SITE: www.luckenbachtx.com

INNKEEPERS: Matthew and Eva Carinhas

ROOMS: Log cabin with 2 bedrooms and bath; cottage with private bath; farmhouse with 1 suite with full kitchen, 2 rooms with whirlpool tub and fireplace

ON THE GROUNDS: Twelve acres with creek

CREDIT CARDS: MasterCard, Visa, American Express, Discover

RATES: $$$–$$$$

HOW TO GET THERE: Drive from Austin west on U.S. 290 and turn south on Ranch Road 1376, just east of Fredericksburg. Follow this road, which becomes Old Luckenbach Road, to the inn. From San Antonio drive west via I–10 and turn north on U.S. 87 at Comfort. In Fredericksburg turn east on U.S. 290 and follow it east to Ranch Road 1376.

Some people are so taken with Luckenbach after just a short visit that they don't want to ever go anyplace else. Luckily for them this delightful inn can make such wishes come true. At the heart of the inn is an 1860s log cabin, which was one of the town's original structures, dating back to its founding. Here, two bedrooms share a full bath, which is an ideal situation for families or two couples traveling together. Behind the cabin is the Old Smokehouse, a very private cottage with a private bath, sunflowers, picket fence, and period decor.

And attached to that is a farmhouse of native limestone, whose longleaf pine floors and picture-perfect rock porches make it an easy place to love and a tough place to leave. Inside, the Grape Suite, with its spacious bedroom and a full kitchen, is decorated with family heirloom paintings of grapes. The porch out front is a perfect place to sip wine in the evening after visiting area wineries. The Cypress Room, named for the 200-year-old cypress trees that overhang the creek, has a whirlpool tub, limestone fireplace, and botanical colors. The Coral Room, with the same floor plan as the Cypress Room, is decorated with seashells and soft colors.

In addition to the rustic beauty of the place, a measure of appeal is found in its country purity—twelve acres along South Grape Creek, where hiking, swimming, and bird-watching are there for the doing. And what's not to love about the simplicity of a rooster's crow, a friendly family dog, and a pot-bellied pig called Rooter? This is one of the rare B&Bs that allows pets and children, too.

Be prepared for a big breakfast from the inn's own farm-fresh eggs, used in a house omelette called eggs Luckenbach. Applewood-smoked bacon, juices, seasonal fresh fruit, banana nut pancakes, and hash browns are part of the pleasure.

What's Nearby Luckenbach

This legendary little town, found about ten minutes east of Fredericksburg, has been called a Texas-style Brigadoon: popularized by a writer-humorist in the 1970s named Hondo Crouch—who said this was a place where "everybody's somebody"—Luckenbach, population twenty-five, became somewhat famous in a song by Willie Nelson and Waylon Jennings. Essentially it consists of a general store, beer bar, dance hall, barbecue shack, and big doses of good humor. An unofficial party is usually in progress, and then there also are terrific special bashes of the organized variety. There are all kinds of celebrations for every holiday, as well as Saturday night concerts and dances and the annual chili cook-off in early October. Expect a spirited crowd and a good time, any time.

The Magnolia House

101 East Hackberry Street
Fredericksburg, TX 78624
Phone: (830) 997-0306; (800) 880-4374
Fax: (830) 997-0766

E-MAIL: magnolia@hctc.com

INTERNET SITE: www.magnolia-house.com

INNKEEPERS: David and Dee Lawford

ROOMS: 2 suites, 3 rooms with private bath, TV

ON THE GROUNDS: Porches, stone patio with fishpond and waterfall; kitchen

CREDIT CARDS: MasterCard, Visa

RATES: $$-$$$

HOW TO GET THERE: Drive from Austin west on U.S. 290, or from San Antonio drive west via I-10 and turn north on U.S. 87 at Comfort. From U.S. 290/Main Street, turn north on Adams Street, then right on East Hackberry Street.

In 1923 Edward Stein designed and built this stately home for his family, choosing each piece of lumber and brick for the construction. As designer of the Gillespie County Courthouse in historic downtown Fredericksburg, Stein had a lofty reputation to uphold. As witness to his hard work and careful planning, the house bears a Texas Historical Commission designation as a recorded Texas Historic Landmark.

Restored in 1991, the home has been converted to a B&B with two suites and three rooms, all filled with antiques and family heirlooms. Inside the Magnolia Suite, there's a marvelous living room with gas-log fireplace and oak floor, as well as a bedroom with a queen bed, a bath and shower, and a private entrance. The Bluebonnet Suite, also with a private entrance and a living room with fireplace, has a small kitchen with an antique refrigerator in working order and a bedroom with a mahogany king-size bed. The other guest rooms—the American Beauty, Peach Blossom, and Lilli Marleen—feature things like antique dressing tables, antique tubs, and longleaf yellow pine floors.

Guests begin every Magnolia House morning with an elaborate breakfast in the dining room. Expect to fill up on fresh fruit, homemade muffins, juice, and a buffet spread that typically includes waffles or crepes, bacon, sausage, an egg entree, sweet rolls, and biscuits and gravy. The whole production is prepared from scratch and served on antique china with silver settings.

Orchard Inn

1364 South U.S. 87
Fredericksburg, TX 78624
Phone: (830) 990-0257; (800) 439-4320

E-MAIL: orchard@fbg.net

INTERNET SITE: www.orchard-inn.com

INNKEEPERS: Annette and Mark Wieser

ROOMS: 3 suites with private baths, 1 with Jacuzzi; 1 room in main house; separate 1870 cabin with kitchen, private bath; all with TV, VCR, telephone, dataport; 1 with wheelchair accessibility

ON THE GROUNDS: Library, antiques; lake, paddleboat, canoe, fishing, and hiking

CREDIT CARDS: MasterCard, Visa, American Express, Discover

RATES: $$–$$$

HOW TO GET THERE: Drive from Austin west on U.S. 290, or from San Antonio drive west via I-10 and turn north on U.S. 87 at Comfort. The inn is south of U.S. 290/Main Street on U.S. 87/Washington Street.

Texas travelers well acquainted with Fredericksburg history are aware of the town's well-earned heritage, and Orchard Inn has a storied background that offers a fitting timeline for the town. The property stands on farmland that was part of the 1846 purchase by the multinamed German immigration agent Baron Ottfried Johanns Friedherr von Meusebach, who sold to a New Orleans speculator named M. A. Dooley, who sold to Oscar Basse, who lost it to a bankruptcy sale. The farm changed hands again and again until a German farmer named Peter Bonn bought it and built a wedding house for his daughter in 1904.

Additional sales went on from 1921 until 1928, when German immigrant and judge J. B. Wieser bought it and began peach farming. In the ensuing years Wieser kept growing enormous crops of peaches, apples, and pears; preserving these fruits had an impact on his child, Mark, whose cottage business is that of selling fresh fruits and marketing locally made jams and jellies at his shop, Das Peach Haus.

Chances are, you're already familiar with Mark and his wife Annette, who own this charming retreat. They, of course, are the "Wieser" in the Fischer & Wieser Specialty Food Company, whose products—such as sauces, jams, and preservers—are sold throughout the nation. Their B&B is an accurate reflection of the style and good taste (no pun intended) found in their sophisticated gourmet gift food line.

Mark, who's also a judge, and Annette have turned the original 1904 farm house into an inn. Three suites are connected at the north wing of the house, and another bedroom is inside the older section. The German Suite is decorated with Oriental rugs; lighting fixtures from Konstany, Germany; antique artwork; and a library of German and American literature. Another worth noting is the Texas Suite, decorated in Ralph Lauren fabrics, with an antique mission oak sofa, Texas artifacts and paintings, and a bright red Jacuzzi tub, and a Texas-shaped sink.

A separate lodging on the property is the 1870 Konig Cabin, done in Timberlake linens and quilts, with an overstuffed chenille sofa and chairs and a homey feel. There's a fully equipped kitchen here, too. A full breakfast is served to all guests in the main house, where Mark and Annette are happy to help you plan your explorations of Fredericksburg shopping, museums, and historic sites.

The Schandua Suite

205 East Main Street
Fredericksburg, TX 78624
Phone: (830) 990-1415; (888) 990-1415

E-MAIL: sharla44@hctc.net

INTERNET SITE: www.schandua.com

INNKEEPERS: Sharla and Jonathan Godfrey

ROOMS: 1 room with private bath, TV, telephone

ON THE GROUNDS: Library, kitchen, private porch, private courtyard, rooftop cactus garden

CREDIT CARDS: MasterCard, Visa, American Express

RATES: $$$-$$$$

HOW TO GET THERE: Drive from Austin west on U.S. 290, or from San Antonio drive west via I-10 and turn north on U.S. 87 at Comfort. In Fredericksburg turn west (left) and go 2 blocks.

Built in 1897 the Schandua Building is a wonderful, eye-catching structure made in the handhewn limestone fashion called *fachwerk*. Easily one of Fredericksburg's downtown landmarks, this important piece, located within the town's National Historic District, once housed a hardware store on the street level, while the owners lived upstairs. A century later owners Sharla and Jonathan have seen fit to bring back this tradition and restore the upstairs as a one-bedroom suite for guests.

Travelers who want absolute convenience in their Fredericksburg stay can't possibly beat this location: Smack in the middle of the historic and shopping district, Schandua Suite is the easiest walk possible to restaurants, taverns, and museums, too.

But when you feel like being alone, your privacy is complete inside the suite, which has twelve-foot ceilings and gorgeous crown molding. Your bedroom has a four-poster, king-size bed, covered with elegant bedding; your large bathroom and dressing area has a skylight and walk-in closet, as well as plush cotton robes. The sitting area has TV, games, books, and there are fresh flowers in each room. Pampering is part of the deal, too. Guests are treated to Godiva chocolates at bedtime and a tray of hors d'oeuvres at check-in. There's also a marvelous fully stocked library and sitting area on the premises, as well as a kitchen, all of which you're welcome to use.

In the morning the Godfreys will treat you to a Continental-plus breakfast, which includes fresh juices, cereals, specialty coffee, fresh fruit, and just-baked goodies from the German bakery across the street.

Schildknecht-Weidenfeller House

c/o Gastehaus Schmidt
231 West Main Street
Fredericksburg, TX 78624
Phone: (830) 997–5612

E-MAIL: gasthaus@ktc.com

INTERNET SITE: www.fbglodging.com

INNKEEPERS: Carter and Ellis Schildknecht

ROOMS: 3 rooms; 2 with private baths, phone, cable TV

ON THE GROUNDS: Kitchen, parlor, sitting room, dining gallery, large yard, porch with rockers, cellar, fireplace

CREDIT CARDS: MasterCard, Visa

RATES: $$

HOW TO GET THERE: Drive from Austin west on U.S. 290, or from San Antonio drive west via I–10 and turn north on U.S. 87 at Comfort. Located 1 block off Main Street in historic district; directions are given when booking.

Historically known as the Johann Weidenfeller House, this wonderful limestone cottage dates from the 1870s and has been owned by Carter and Ellis since 1994. Because Carter's law practice keeps her particularly busy and Ellis's agricultural business is demanding, the two spend most of their time in their Texas Panhandle home in Lamesa. They love visiting this cozy escape when they can make the 285-mile trek south, but they like knowing that guests are enjoying it when they can't.

That means that you'll have utter privacy while staying here. The main floor, which has a parlor and a front bedroom, is noted for thick rock walls; wide, deep-set windows; pine plank flooring, and high ceilings. You'll particularly like the cozy sitting room and full bath that was converted from a rock-floored kitchen. Upstairs there's a roomy bedroom, a quaint lav with a shower, and a charming little "grandchildren's" room tucked under the eves in an original loft.

An expansion that was true to the home's original style added a delightful kitchen and spacious dining gallery, which provide lovely views of the big yard. Follow stone steps from the kitchen, and you'll wind up in the two-room cellar. Throughout the house are thoughtfully chosen primitive antiques and period pieces that reflect the area's pioneer origins and complement the comforting setting. Gentle afternoons are splendid on the porch; winter evenings are dreamy in front of the fireplace.

When you're hungry, there is a Continental breakfast spread—including breads, fruit, cereals, milk, juice, coffee, and tea—left for you to enjoy, and there's a plate of German meats and cheeses awaiting you on arrival. And you can head to a nearby grocery store to get goodies to prepare in the home's full kitchen.

Schmidt Barn Bed & Breakfast

c/o Gastehaus Schmidt
231 West Main Street
Fredericksburg, TX 78624
Phone: (830) 997–5612

E-MAIL: gausthaus@ktc.com; schmidtbarn@fbg.net

INTERNET SITES: www.fbglodging.com; www.b-and-b-schmidt-barn.com

INNKEEPERS: Charles and Loretta Schmidt

ROOMS: 1 room with private bath, telephone

ON THE GROUNDS: Countryside setting, wildlife, porch, flower and herb garden, swing beneath giant oak trees; kitchenette; CD/tape player; antiques

CREDIT CARDS: MasterCard, Visa, Discover

RATES: $$–$$$

HOW TO GET THERE: Drive from Austin west on U.S. 290, or from San Antonio drive west via I–10 and turn north on U.S. 87 at Comfort. In Fredericksburg head to 231 West Main Street to check in at Gastehaus Schmidt service. Directions will be given there.

Here's one of the original Fredericksburg B&Bs, opened in 1982. Remnants of this 1860s limestone barn were faithfully restored to the structure's original look and turned into a guesthouse. A stay here gives you a real sense of the period, thanks to stone walls, brick floor, and milled timber beams in the living and dining rooms. A romantic addition is a sunken tub in the bathroom, perfect for erasing stress piled on by city life.

The loft bedroom recalls the nineteenth-century Fredericksburg's Sunday House tradition and style, with a sleeping space that's cozy with quilts, antique linens, and samplers. Two can sleep there, and two more can take the downstairs sleeper sofa. The barn is centrally cooled and heated throughout.

Early mornings and late afternoons usually hold the promise of deer, roadrunner, bird, and squirrel activity, which you can watch from the table and chairs on the porch or on quiet walks. Swing under the ancient oaks and savor the starry nights.

Charles and Loretta, who live in the main house next door, will leave you goodies for a German breakfast of meats, cheeses, pastries, breads, coffee, and tea. A microwave, toaster, and coffeemaker are provided, as is a bouquet of fresh flowers, a CD player, and a selection of music.

What's Nearby

The town of Llano is about 40 miles north of Fredericksburg and is worth a side trip. The seat of Llano County is small and comfortable, with a good dose of historic architecture. Check out the courthouse downtown, as well as charming shops surrounding it. Be sure to make a lunch stop at Cooper's, widely considered one of the best barbecue places in the whole state. Go north via Texas 261 and visit the very popular and successful Fall Creek Vineyards on the northwestern shore of beautiful Lake Buchanan. Follow the Colorado River a bit north from there and visit the new lodge called Canyon of the Eagles, a wildlife lover's haven and the new home to the Vanishing Texas River Cruise.

Settlers Crossing

104 Settlers Crossing Road
Fredericksburg, TX 78624
Phone: (800) 874–1020

INTERNET SITE: www.settlerscrossing.com

INNKEEPERS: David and Judy Bland

ROOMS: 7 guesthouses with private bath and fireplace, 1 and 2 bedrooms; 4 with Jacuzzi tubs

ON THE GROUNDS: Porches, fireplaces; thirty-five acres with creeks, oak groves, wildlife, and pets

CREDIT CARDS: MasterCard, Visa

RATES: $$$–$$$$

HOW TO GET THERE: Drive from Austin west on U.S. 290, or from San Antonio drive west via I-10, then turn north on U.S. 87 at Comfort. Precise directions given at booking.

Alavish country estate, Settlers Crossing is one you may have read about in such magazines as *Country Home, Country Living,* and *Country Inns.* That's largely because there really isn't anything else like it in Texas.

The B&B is a collection of seven historic guesthouses scattered over the expansive grounds. The buildings date from 1787 but have been exquisitely renovated and extensively decorated by an interior designer whose touches include eighteenth- and nineteenth-century country antiques and appropriate artwork, chandeliers, rugs, draperies, bedding, and tabletop items for each of the themed cottages. Some of the dwellings have full kitchens, living, and dining areas, and all have delightful outdoor seating areas where you can't resist watching sunrises or sunsets, wandering deer, the resident sheep, and the unforgettable Buster, the donkey.

Each cottage is a wonderfully cozy, romantic retreat for two, complete with a fireplace, but some can accommodate up to four or six people traveling together. Indiana House, for example, has two bedrooms and one bathroom, two fireplaces, a kitchenette, and an outdoor arbor. The Kusenberger Cabin, built in 1850, has one bedroom and a bathroom with a Jacuzzi, a coffee bar with refrigerator and microwave, and a living room with a fireplace. The log-and-rock Pioneer Homestead, built in 1865, has three bedrooms—two of which have fireplaces—a bathroom with a claw-foot tub, and a full kitchen.

The two-story rock Kusenberger Barn, built on the property around 1865, has two bedrooms, a bathroom with a Jacuzzi, a full kitchen, and a fireplace in the living room. The Baag Farm House is a 1925 home with two bedrooms, one bath, and a wood-burning stove in the parlor, as well as a full kitchen. Then the Bohl Log Cabin, circa 1850, is a structure that was moved from Missouri and authentically restored to offer two bedrooms, a living room with a fireplace, a bathroom with a Jacuzzi tub, and a kitchenette. The Von Heinrich Home is a remarkable 1787 structure brought here from Pennsylvania. Inside this home are two bedrooms, a bath with a Jacuzzi tub, a living room with fireplace, a queen-size sleeper sofa, and a full kitchen.

At breakfast time, David and Judy will bring you a Continental breakfast basket of pastries to go with the juices, cereals, coffees, and teas already stocked in your cottage.

What's Nearby Fredericksburg

One of the Hill Country's richly German towns, Fredericksburg has emerged in the past decade as the burgh with the most shopping and better dining, not to mention a wealth of bed-and-breakfast lodgings. At last count there were more than 300 B&Bs in and around this town, with selections ranging from quaint, nineteenth-century stone houses and ornate Victorian homes on or within walking distance of Main Street to log cabins, elegant ranch houses, and creaky-but-charming rock farmhouses 10 or so miles out in the countryside. Fredericksburg devotees have found that they'd rather avoid the heavy weekend crowds by visiting during weekdays or by choosing a weekend when special events aren't planned. No matter when you plan your stop in Fredericksburg, do make time to visit Fredericksburg Herb Farm for gardening needs, lovely herbs, and a divine lunch; Wildseed Farms, for wildflower seeds; Admiral Nimitz State Historical Park, for World War II Pacific history; and various wine-tasting rooms, for samples of Texas's vineyards.

Other Recommended B&Bs Nearby

Yellow House Bed & Breakfast, a pretty little cottage 2 blocks from Main Street with one bedroom and bathroom, TV, telephone, antique furnishings and linens, porch, and giant oak trees; c/o Gastehaus Schmidt, 231 West Main Street, Fredericksburg, TX 78624; telephone: (830) 997-5612. The *Garden Path,* a late-nineteenth-century house with two separate and private suites with king-size beds, Jacuzzi tubs for two, fireplaces, patio, porches, and flower beds; c/o Gastehaus Schmidt, 231 West Main Street, Fredericksburg, TX 78624; telephone: (830) 997-5612. *Palo Alto Creek Farm,* with two historic guesthouses outfitted with fireplaces, TV/VCR, whirlpool tubs for two, king-size beds, porches and swings; 90 Palo Alto Lane, Fredericksburg, TX 78624; telephone: (800) 997-0089. Other reservation services include *Bed & Breakfast Accommodations of Fredericksburg/Sunnyside Properties,* (830) 997-3049; *Bed & Breakfast of Fredericksburg,* (830) 997-4712; and *Fredericksburg Traditional Bed & Breakfasts,* (800) 494-4678.

Inn on the Square

104½ West Eighth Street
Georgetown, TX 78628
Phone: (512) 863-8562; (888) 718-2221

INTERNET SITE: www.bedandbreakfast.com/bbc/ p603445.asp

INNKEEPERS: JoElla and Joel Broussard, Mary Katherine and Garett Koch

ROOMS: 4 rooms with private bath, TV, phone

ON THE GROUNDS: Library, parlor, rooftop terrace, antiques and art, fireplaces, formal dining room

CREDIT CARDS: MasterCard, Visa, American Express

RATES: $$-$$$

HOW TO GET THERE: From I-35 exit University Avenue at Georgetown (also Texas 29) and head east. At Main Street turn left (north) and drive to Eighth Street.

Built in the 1890s, the inn was actually two structures, one of which housed a general store, and the other, a pharmacy and barber shop, with a blacksmith in the rear. Initially it was a single-story building, but a second floor was added at the turn of the last century to bring Georgetown its first professional offices.

Reopened as an inn in very recent years, the B&B is beautifully restored to show off fine hardwood floors and extensive woodwork, as well as exquisite stained-glass and leaded-glass windows, doors, and wonderfully crafted mantels and mirrors. Both parlors have fireplaces, and the lovely formal dining room is decorated with an Italian tapestry and a built-in china closet with etched glass doors.

Guest rooms include the San Antonio Rose, a romantic retreat with a lacy, high-back iron bed, cable TV, refrigerator, Victorian writing desk, and a private bath; the Chisholm Trail room, with a carved pine bed, cowboy theme, and private bath; Noche de Paz, with an antique brass bed, footed tub, and a terrace view; and the San Gabriel Suite, with a terrific view of the courthouse square, king bed, love seat, and elegant bathroom. If you book ahead, you can reserve the parlor that attaches to this room and has a queen-size sleeper sofa.

Breakfast is certainly not an afterthought at this inn: Your Texas-size morning meal usually consists of Garett's Eggs, a mix of cheese, tortillas, tomatoes, onions, and potatoes with Mary's own salsa, or you might have the baked French toast, corn pudding, or Inn-on-the-Square quiche. Rest assured, you won't leave hungry.

What's Nearby Georgetown

The Williamson County Seat offers an exemplary courthouse square, recognized as one of Texas's distinguished Main Street projects. Fine restoration work has gone into pepping up the period buildings surrounding the square, where shopping and dining can easily fill a day for wanderers. A firefighters' museum is worth exploring, as is the campus of Southwestern University. Founded in 1840, the college is Texas's oldest private higher learning institution, and it boasts an impressive spread of ornate architecture. Within a half-hour drive of Georgetown is the town of Taylor, home to two renowned barbecue joints, Louie Mueller's and Mikeska's.

River Oaks Lodge

Texas 39
Ingram, TX 78025
Phone: (830) 367–4214; (800) 608–2596
Fax: (830) 367–3545

INTERNET SITE: www.riveroakslodge.com

INNKEEPER: Gilda Wilkinson

ROOMS: Lodge with 7 rooms, all with private baths; 2-bedroom River House with full kitchen; guesthouse with 2 suites

ON THE GROUNDS: Large common area on main floor; living room, kitchen, dining room, library with TV/VCR; porches, river

CREDIT CARDS: MasterCard, Visa

RATES: $$–$$$

HOW TO GET THERE: From San Antonio drive north on I–10; take exit 508 to Kerrville; turn south on Texas 16 and continue to Texas 27. Go west on Texas 27 to Texas 39. Stay on Texas 39 about 3 miles. River Oaks Lodge will be on the right.

This sensational retreat along the lovely, restorative Guadalupe River is a collection of guesthouses and a lodge. Within moments of arrival, you'll have a clear understanding of why people speak in dreamy tones about this pocket of the Texas Hill Country. You'll soon begin plotting ways to move here so that you can canoe or float in an inner tube on the glassy Guadalupe for the rest of your days.

Lodging choices here vary, but the biggest building is the River Oaks Lodge, a 1950s stone structure with plenty of windows and good views from seven rooms, all with private baths. On the main floor is a solarium with couches and chairs, a library, and a dining room, where all guests are served a large breakfast. Outside are two large porches and expansive grounds shaded by nineteen giant oak trees.

The River House is surrounded by two screened porches, which offer great river views. Inside there are two bedrooms, a living room, and a full kitchen and dining room. This dwelling sleeps six people, as the living room is furnished with twin daybeds. The Ivy House, a snug guesthouse next door to the River House, offers two suites, each with a bedroom, bath, and living room; one of the suites has a kitchen, and both overlook the river.

What's Nearby Ingram

Following Ranch Road 1340 west from Kerrville, you'll pull into this minute town that rests on the exquisitely beautiful banks of a particularly gentle stretch of the Guadalupe River. Take the drive very slowly and soak in the lovely surroundings of river, trees, and twisting roadway. It's a picture to keep in your mind and pull out when life's daily stresses make you eager for something simple and serene.

River Run B&B Inn

120 Francisco Lemos Street
Kerrville, TX 78028
Phone: (830) 896–8353; (800) 460–7170
Fax: (830) 896–5402

E-MAIL: riverrun@ktc.com

INTERNET SITE: www.riverrunbb.com

INNKEEPERS: Ron and Jean Williamson

ROOMS: 6 rooms with private bath, TV, telephone, dataport; 1 with wheelchair accessibility

ON THE GROUNDS: Library, antique pharmacy artifacts, large porches, whirlpool tubs

CREDIT CARDS: MasterCard, Visa, American Express, Discover

RATES: $$–$$$

HOW TO GET THERE: From San Antonio drive north on I-10; take exit 508 to Kerrville and follow Texas 16 into center of town. At Water Street turn right. At first light, turn left on Francisco Lemos Street.

Years of traveling across the United States and Europe, staying at B&Bs along the way, showed Ron and Jean exactly what they wanted in their own inn. They studied, researched, and planned, then chose a spot in downtown Kerrville as the perfect place to build their new inn. In doing so, they captured the look of the hallmark Hill County architecture—specifically, using native limestone and high-pitched tin roof—found in German-settled towns. A giant porch hugs the front of the house and offers a fine place for sipping morning coffee or reflecting on the day's feats.

Inside there's the charming spirit of a country home, but one with all the contemporary comforts: central air and heat, whirlpool tubs, TVs, and telephones with dataports. Each guest room has a queen-size bed, shower, ceiling fan. Guests collectively enjoy a cavernous great room, a restored 1892 pharmacy fixture exhibiting medicinal antiquities, a 400-year-old mirror from Germany, a 2,000-volume library, and several porches with rockers. Behind the inn is Town Creek, and next door is Riverside Nature Center.

Ron, a pharmacist whose nickname is "Honest Doc," is also an accomplished cook who's had a recipe published in a national cookbook. His big country breakfast offerings have merited mention in statewide and national travel publications. Ron and Jean, a registered nurse, are delightful guides who can point you toward shopping bargains, bicycle tour routes, swimming holes, and good dining.

What's Nearby Kerrville

The Guadalupe River runs through the middle of this town, which is larger than most others in the Hill Country. Art galleries, boutiques, and restaurants are booming these days in Kerrville, which is home to the distinguished Cowboy Artists of America Museum. Dedicated to the work of living painters and sculptors who are also working cowboys, this art center has a healthy permanent collection and offers special exhibits, too. Plan to spend at least a day exploring the Y.O. Ranch, nearly 30 miles west of town and a true Texas treasure. Founded in 1880, the ranch is home to one of North America's largest collection of exotic wildlife, such as wildebeest, sika deer, aoudad sheep, black buck antelope, zebra, and Watusi cattle. In late spring there's an annual longhorn trail drive.

Inn Above Onion Creek

4444 Farm Road 150 West
Kyle, TX 78640
Phone: (512) 268-1617; (800) 579-7686

E-MAIL: innkeepers@innaboveonioncreek.com

INTERNET SITE: www.innaboveonioncreek.com

INNKEEPERS: Jean and Scott Taylor, Janie and John Orr

ROOMS: 9 rooms with private bath, phone, dataport, TV/VCR, stereo, fireplaces, including 2-story suite; 1 with wheelchair accessibility

ON THE GROUNDS: Library; swimming pool, 500 acres with miles of hiking trails

CREDIT CARDS: MasterCard, Visa, American Express

RATES: $$$–$$$$ (includes dinner)

HOW TO GET THERE: Located halfway between Austin and San Antonio; exit Farm Road 150 from I-35 and drive ten minutes west.

There's a very solid argument made by experienced Texas travelers that this is the most luxurious B&B in the entire Lone Star selection. Built in 1995 to the style of an 1860s Hill Country homestead, the nine-bedroom inn measures 10,000 square feet and overlooks a 500-acre spread that wins the scenery sweepstakes.

Your toughest choice may be figuring out which room will best pamper you. The Tom Martin Room is done in pale moss and has a library theme, a bronze bed, and antique claw-foot tub with shower; the Schlemmer Room has a queen-size spindle bed and an additional twin, a galley kitchen, and an antique tub; the Captain Fergus Kyle Room is a downstairs room with wheelchair accessibility, a king bed, tub for two, and a private porch with a marvelous northward view; and the two-story Kuykendall Suite has a downstairs sitting room and powder room, an iron king-size bed, and an oversized bath with a whirlpool and double shower. The other choices are easily as impressive.

In addition to the hiking and exploring the inn's 500 acres, dining is a big part of the stay at Inn Above Onion Creek. Breakfast—which usually includes such delights as oven-baked French toast with applewood-smoked bacon and seasonal fruit—and dinner are included with your stay. Because the inn lies in one of Texas's infamous "dry" districts, alcohol can't be served; you are welcome to bring your own, however. And if you still need more de-stress efforts, ask in advance for the innkeepers to book a massage therapist for you.

Going Wild for Spring Flowers

The Hill Country wildflower season is as tough to predict as the stock market, but one thing is certain, there will be carloads of people searching the region's highways for a palette-filled vista and the ultimate photo opportunity. Typically the hunt begins in early April and can last as long as late May; everything depends on rainfall, temperatures, and the whims of Mother Nature. The best news is, the state highway department offers help for wildflower wanderers at (800) 452–9292; travel counselors will tell you which roadways are currently offering blooms, and they'll also fill you in on special events happening the weekend you're traveling. Some of the best roads to seek out are U.S. 281 from Lampasas to San Antonio; Texas 16 from Llano to Medina; U.S. 290 from Austin to Fredericksburg; Texas 71 from Austin to Llano; Texas 46 from New Braunfels to Bandera; and U.S. 87 from Mason to Fredericksburg. A particularly popular drive is called the Willow City Loop, just 12 miles north of Fredericksburg via Texas 16; turn east on Farm Road 1323 and watch for the signs that will take you on a memorable, 13-mile route.

Acorn Hill Bed & Breakfast

250 School House Road
New Braunfels, TX 78132
Phone: (830) 907–2597; (800)
525–4618

E-MAIL: acornhill@netscape.net

INTERNET SITE:
www.acornhillbb.com

INNKEEPERS: Richard and Pamela
Thomas

ROOMS: 2 suites with complete kitchen, TV, telephone

ON THE GROUNDS: Hot tub, swimming pool, horseshoes, washer pit; antique/gift shop

CREDIT CARDS: MasterCard, Visa, American Express

RATES: $$–$$$

HOW TO GET THERE: Drive north from San Antonio or south from Austin on I–35 and exit at Farm Road 306. Drive west on FR 306, which turns into School House Road, for 7.5 miles and find inn on right.

While away a morning or afternoon on the porches overlooking hills and fields, take a swim in the pool or a late-night soak in the hot tub, and you'll be hooked on this place. Your lodging choices here include a log house, originally a school, and a 1910 house that was the school mistress's home.

If you want the luxury of space, you'll check into one of the two suites, each of which offers a complete kitchen, living room with queen-size sleeper sofa, and a separate bedroom with a king-size bed. Whatever your quarters, you'll be surrounded by antiques, family heirlooms, quilts, and an easy warmth and friendliness.

Mornings bring a big sit-down breakfast affair of fresh fruit, baked goodies, two hot entrees, juice, coffee, tea, and milk. This is a B&B that accommodates pets, so bring your furry baby if you'd like.

Aunt Nora's Countryside Inn

120 Naked Indian Trail
Canyon Lake, TX 78132
Phone: (830) 905–3989; (800) 687–2887

INTERNET SITE: www.texasbedandbreakfast.com/auntnoras

INNKEEPERS: Alton and Iralee Haley

ROOMS: 3 cottages with kitchen and private bath, 2 guest rooms in main house; TV available

ON THE GROUNDS: Porches, swings, hot tub, gazebo with ponds/waterfalls; in-room Jacuzzi

CREDIT CARDS: MasterCard, Visa, American Express

RATES: $$–$$$

HOW TO GET THERE: From New Braunfels drive Texas 46 west and turn right onto Farm Road 2722 and continue 7.8 miles. Turn left on Farm Road 2673 and left again onto Naked Indian Trail. Split rail fence lines the front of the inn's acreage.

In the rugged countryside north of New Braunfels and along the south shore of Canyon Lake, you'll find a compound of cottages that are guaranteed to give you a sense of relaxation. Each of the private cottages is spacious and decorated to the nines, and they're surrounded by pretty grounds, courtyards, and views of the legendary shaded hills. On site are a meadow, gazebo, and a bridge-crossed goldfish pond.

Alton and Iralee built the cottages and filled them with handhewn wood furniture that suits the period styling. Your lodging choices include Adam's

Country Cottage, with a beaded-board cathedral ceiling, 1940s mahogany dining table and buffet, charming kitchen, private deck, master bedroom, large bath, and a loft with a twin bed; it sleeps five in all. Joshua's Cottage was built to resemble an early Texas dwelling, but with luxuries like a hand-built maple bed, a living room with a love seat, a private deck, full kitchen, washer and dryer, and a TV.

In the Victorian cottage, you'll find Suite Shari, with a covered porch with a swing, a stained-glass window, a handmade pine four-poster bed, frilly bedding, a large bath, and a full kitchen. You can sleep five in Bethany's Bedroom, upstairs in the Victorian cottage, which has a living room that flows into a large bedroom, a dining room, and a full kitchen, as well as a large bath with Jacuzzi tub. There are also two guest rooms in the main house that share a bath.

Each morning, a full breakfast will be brought on a tray to your door. How spoiled can you get?

Castle Avalon

10900 Texas 46 West
New Braunfels, TX 78132
Phone: (830) 885-4780; (877) 885-4780

E-MAIL: auther@gvtc.com
INTERNET SITE: www.castleavalon.com
INNKEEPERS: Ron and Elaine Bigbee
ROOMS: 5 rooms with private bath, 1 with wheelchair accessibility
ON THE GROUNDS: Hot tub, garden, library, nature
CREDIT CARDS: MasterCard, Visa, American Express
RATES: $$$
HOW TO GET THERE: From San Antonio drive north on U.S. 281, exit at Texas 46 and drive east 8.5 miles.

Rarely will you find an English Tudor style inspired by those built in the sixteenth century in this part of the world, but that's exactly what awaits you just 10 miles west of the German-settled town of New Braunfels. The castlelike home was built in 1996 specifically to serve as a romantic getaway for travelers who need to forget about city life, and who want something much more personal than a motel and more luxurious than a cabin.

Ron and Elaine's aim is to make you feel like royalty when you're staying in their quiet castle. And in the event you love the place so much you'd like to host a party, reunion, or wedding there, you can book Castle Avalon's restaurant, ballroom, and/or garden for your event.

Each of the five guest rooms is individually decorated. Two of these have hand-painted ceilings, as does the ballroom. You'll also find special touches in the breakfast spread each morning, which typically includes coffee, juice, and muffins or fruit, followed by plates of scrambled eggs with cheese, potatoes, bacon, and toast, or pancakes or waffles with whipped cream, fruit, and bacon. When booking your stay, ask Ron or Elaine about packages that include champagne and elegant dinners for two.

Karbach Haus B&B Inn

487 West San Antonio Street
New Braunfels, TX 78130
Phone: (830) 625-2131; (800) 972-5941

E-MAIL: Khausbnb@aol.com
INTERNET SITE: www.texasbedandbrakfast/karbach.htm
INNKEEPERS: Kathy and Ben Jack Kinney
ROOMS: 6 rooms with private bath, TV, phone/dataport, includes suite and separate apartment; 1 with wheelchair accessibility
ON THE GROUNDS: Library, sunroom, pool, verandah, garden, hot tub
CREDIT CARDS: MasterCard, Visa, Discover
RATES: $$-$$$$
HOW TO GET THERE: Drive north from San Antonio or south from Austin on I-35 and exit Business 46. Drive west on Business 46 to San Antonio Street and turn right.

Built in 1906 by a wealthy merchant, this Plains-style home was bought by Dr. H. E. Karbach (Kathy's father) in 1936 and has been a Karbach family residence for more than sixty years. She and Ben Jack were married in the home in 1956 and have made it into a lovely inn for guests. Throughout you'll find antiques and special items the couple collected during Ben Jack's thirty-year naval career.

Each of the guest rooms has its own private bath, a sitting area, cable TV, VCR, bathrobes, down comforters, designer linens, queen or king bed, and ceiling fan. The Doctor's Suite is impressive, roomy and sun-filled, with antiques and Texas handmade furniture, including a walnut, four-poster bed. French doors lead to a screened porch that overlooks the pool, spa, and gardens. If you're in need of a romantic escape, think about the Hayloft, a separate apartment with a full kitchen, imported rugs on cypress floors, and absolute privacy.

Your morning gets off to a solid start, as Kathy and Ben Jack serve a multicourse, German-style breakfast of eggs, meat, cheese, and breads. You're sure to skip lunch.

The Lamb's Rest Inn

1385 Edwards Boulevard
New Braunfels, TX 78132
Phone: (830) 609-3932; (888) 609-3932

E-MAIL: lambsbb@aol.com
INTERNET SITE: www.bbhost.com/lambsrestbb
INNKEEPERS: Judy and George Rothell

ROOMS: 6 rooms, 5 with private baths, TVs

ON THE GROUNDS: Swimming pool and hot tub, two large decks with swings overlooking the Guadalupe River, fireplaces, verandah with rockers overlooking the river, terraced gardens, pond, and fountain

CREDIT CARDS: MasterCard, Visa, Discover

RATES: $$-$$$$

HOW TO GET THERE: Drive north from San Antonio or south from Austin on I-35 and exit Loop 337 toward Boerne. Drive approximately 3 miles west on the loop and turn right on River Road, then turn right on Edwards Boulevard.

Quiet and secluded, this spacious country inn on the Guadalupe River was purchased and remodeled by the Rothells in 1996. You can enjoy a morning cup of coffee on a porch overlooking the river, and if you're an early riser, you'll see a magical sunrise and watch deer feeding on the Guadalupe's banks. In the afternoon after a day of floating in tubes or rafts on the river or shopping in the village of Gruene—which is just a mile away— you can review the day in the pool or hot tub and end your evening by watching fireflies in the yard or snuggling in front of the living room's crackling fire.

Judy and George have created an atmosphere of comfort and hospitality for their guests through close attention to quality and detail, such as luxurious linens and lovingly tended herb and flower gardens that sit on terraces down to the river. One of the couple's signature design elements prominent throughout the house is their extensive collection of a Dickens Village series.

Mornings get off to a happy start with extraordinary breakfasts served on the verandah or in the formal dining room. Menus usually include such wonders as Vancluse eggs, pork tenderloin, pumpkin biscuit with cranberry butter, strawberries zabaglione, frappes, and specialty teas and coffees, or stuffed French toast with fresh lean sausage, cinnamon rolls, honey cinnamon butter, poached pears in wine, and orange coolers.

What's Nearby New Braunfels

Still another Hill Country town bursting with German heritage, the Comal County Seat was settled in 1845 by a German prince and 200 immigrants. The entire story of the settlement is detailed at the Sophienburg Museum, but you'll want to leave time to see the historic buildings downtown, collectively known as Conservation Plaza. There are several good bakeries downtown, as well, and Krause's Cafe is one of the more popular German restaurants. On the north side of town is a charming old community called Gruene (pronounced "green"), home to several rafting companies that will put you on the Guadalupe's usually small rapids. Within the historic district of Gruene, which was settled in 1870, also find several cafes, boutiques, and—best of all—the oldest dance hall in Texas.

Other Recommended B&Bs Nearby

Gruene Homestead Inn, a countryside setting with twenty-three rooms or suites with private baths in various, completely restored historic buildings near shopping and Guadalupe River recreation; 832 Gruene Road, New Braunfels, TX 78130; telephone: (830) 606-0216; Internet site: www.gruenehomesteadinn.com. *The Old Hunter Road Stagecoach Stop*, with three rooms and private baths, TV, and telephone in an old stagecoach stop, Amish pioneer homestead, and handhewn log cabin of German *fachwerk* construction; 5441 Farm Road 1102, New Braunfels, TX 78130; telephone: (830) 620-9453 or (800) 201-2912.

Crystal River Inn

326 West Hopkins Street
San Marcos, TX 78666
Phone: (512) 396-3739; (888) 396-3739
Fax: (512) 353-3248

E-MAIL: info@crystalriverinn.com

INTERNET SITE: www.crystalriverinn.com

INNKEEPER: Cathy Dillon

ROOMS: Collection of 4 buildings, includes 2 suites, 2 guest rooms, an executive apartment; 12 guest rooms, all with private bath

ON THE GROUNDS: Gardens, topiary, fountains, verandah, fireplaces

CREDIT CARDS: MasterCard, Visa

RATES: $$–$$$

HOW TO GET THERE: From I–35 in San Marcos, exit at Ranch Road 12/Hopkins Street (exit 205) and drive west. You'll find the inn on the right side of the street.

Easily one of the finest, pace-setting B&Bs in Texas, this inn is a collection of historically important buildings, surrounding a lovely rose garden. Your room might be in the columned Main House, San Marcos's first Victorian structure, built in 1883, or it could be in the Young Building, built in 1885 as the town's first apartment building. The latter is particularly appealing to business travelers, who love the rooms with phones, TVs, and a far more personal appeal than the average hotel or motel.

Newest is the Rock House, a single-story, 1930s rock bungalow, containing two elegant suites and two individual guest rooms. The fourth historic building in the Crystal River complex houses a fully furnished executive apartment. In all there are twelve guest rooms which, in total, make up a graceful lodging that has earned the inn features in such publications as *Country Inns, Southern Living,* and *USA Today.*

Cathy and her husband, Mike, also offer their delightful river house, two hours west in the Hill Country reaches near Bandera. The 1930s rustic rock lodge, with an attached guest apartment, has a total of three bedrooms and a four-bed sleeping porch. Tucked away on three acres above the clear and sparkling Medina River, it has fireplaces in the kitchen and living room, a long stone patio overlooking the river, an outdoor barbecue pit, swings, and sandbox.

You'll never forget the lavish breakfast served at Crystal River Inn. Treasures include the eggs Benedict, bananas Foster crepes, and raspberry French toast. You'll need the fortification to handle the sensational shopping at the local factory outlet, where big name draws include Donna Karan and Coach Leather.

Special events are frequent at this inn. On the first Friday of every month, you can join in the gourmet dinner extravaganza, when resident chef Sam Evans and catering coordinator Sonya Kibby present seven elegant courses and complementary wines, accompanied by live piano music. Murder mystery weekends are big here, too.

Weinert House

1207 North Austin Street
Seguin, TX 78155
Phone: (830) 372–0422
Fax: (830) 303–0912

INTERNET SITE: www.texasbedandbreakfast.com/weinerthouse

INNKEEPERS: Tom and Lynna Thomas

ROOMS: 1 suite, 3 rooms, all with private bath

ON THE GROUNDS: Grape arbor, gardens, yard; front porch, fireplaces, antiques, music room, formal dining room, sunroom

CREDIT CARDS: MasterCard, Visa

RATES: $$

HOW TO GET THERE: From San Antonio drive east on I-10; exit at New Braunfels Street and continue north to North Guadalupe Street; turn right on North Guadalupe and take a left on East Kingsbury Street. Turn right on North Austin Street.

One of Seguin's premier Victorian homes is the serene setting for a lovely B&B. The downstairs of this grand house features a music room with a hand-cranked Victrola and records, as well as a sunroom where afternoon tea is served on the second and fourth Thursday afternoons of each month. The moment you have a look around Weinert House, you'll understand why small weddings and receptions are hosted here in the dining and sunrooms and on the grounds, which are surrounded by a picket fence. Behind the 1895 home there's an old smokehouse and plenty of grounds on which to take up a game of croquet.

Guest quarters start with the Senator's Suite, which has a king-size bed, fireplace, screened sunporch, an alcove with a twin bed, and a private bathroom. Tanta Clara's Room is furnished with a white iron bed, fireplace, stained-glass windows, and an antique claw-foot tub in the private bath. Kathinka's Quarters offers a king bed of white iron and brass, a fireplace, antique tub, and detailed columns. Finally, there's Ella's Chambers, which has a king-size mahogany bed, private bath, and view of the grape arbors.

Before you set off in the morning, Tom and Lynna will pamper you with an elegantly set, elaborate breakfast. At the end of your busy day, if you arrange in advance, you can enjoy a special dinner in the formal dining room.

What's Nearby Seguin

Originally called Walnut Springs at its 1838 founding, the town was later named for Juan N. Seguin, a Mexican-Texan who served under Sam Houston in the fight for Texas's independence. A bevy of historic places in town include the Magnolia Hotel (1824), the Los Nogales Museum (1823), and the lauded Sebastopol House State Historic Site (1850s). Just southwest of town is Lake Placid, a popular water-ski spot created from the Guadalupe River.

Casa de Leona Bed and Breakfast

1149 Pearsall Highway 140
Uvalde, TX 78802
Phone: (830) 278-8550

E-MAIL: bednbrek@admin.hilconet.com

INTERNET SITES: www.virtualcities.com; bluebonnet.texasrural.org/

INNKEEPER: Carolyn Durr

ROOMS: 2 suites with private bath; 3 guests rooms, 1 with private bath; cottage with kitchenette and private bath; TV, telephone

ON THE GROUNDS: Sundeck, balcony, fishing pier; gazebo, fountains

CREDIT CARDS: MasterCard, Visa, American Express

RATES: $–$$$

HOW TO GET THERE: Drive west from San Antonio via U.S. 90; turn south in Uvalde onto U.S. 83 to Farm Road 117. Continue on FR 117 to Ranch Road 140, turning east toward Pearsall. Cross Leona River Bridge and watch for inn on the right.

Built in the style of a Spanish hacienda, Casa de Leona sits next to historic Fort Inge. The land was once roamed by native American and Mexican Indians from the Coahuiltecan, Apache, Comanche, and Tonkawa tribes before the fort was built in 1849. Once you've had time to do your own exploring, you'll see the surprisingly lush hills and flatlands along the spring-fed Leona River that were clearly the gathering, hunting, and prospecting sites of the natives, as well as soldiers, pack trains, buffalo hunters, and cattle ranchers.

Between your rock and arrowhead hunting, hiking, and bird-watching expeditions on the inn's seventeen acres, you'll enjoy hanging out on the sundeck or the gazebo. Or maybe you'll just yearn to curl up in your room to while away the afternoon reading.

Among the lodgings to choose from are the Oriental Suite, with a king-size bed, sitting room, sundeck, balcony, fireplace, refrigerator, and private bath; the Picasso/Art Studio Suite, with a queen-size bed, sitting room with a queen-size sleeper sofa, small dining area, window seat, and private bath; the Doll Room, with its private bath and a doll collection; and the Fort Inge and Victoria Rooms, which share a bath. The separate guest cottage offers twin beds, kitchenette, dining area, private bath, and a porch overlooking the river. In the mornings you'll have a Continental breakfast of pastries, cereals, juices, fruits, coffee, and tea.

Shared areas include the home's music room, courtyard, art studio, and formal living room. There's a gift shop on the grounds, too.

What's Nearby Uvalde

"Cactus Jack" was the nickname given John Garner, a Uvalde native who served as vice-president to Franklin D. Roosevelt. His former home is a fine little memorial museum, housing various historical items, Garner artifacts, and the occasional art exhibit. Also in the town is the restored Grand Opera House, an 1891 culture center that offers tours. Uvalde is also a good home base for driving tours; check out the lovely scenery along U.S. 83 north to Concan and Leakey, as well as east on Farm Road 337 toward Vanderpool and Farm Road 187 south to Sabinal. Be sure to leave yourself lots of time to stop and take photographs.

Texas Stagecoach Inn

Ranch Road 187
Vanderpool, TX 78885
Phone: (830) 966–6272

INTERNET SITE: www.bbhost.com /txstagecoachinn

INNKEEPER: David and Karen Camp

ROOMS: 2 suites, 2 rooms with private bath

ON THE GROUNDS: Three acres of spectacular views

CREDIT CARDS: None accepted

RATES: $$

HOW TO GET THERE: From San Antonio drive west on I–10 to Texas 46. Exit

Texas 46 and drive west to Texas 16; go west on Texas 16 to Ranch Road 337, which you'll follow west about 20 miles to RR 187 in Vanderpool.

"Miles from nowhere, in the middle of the surrounding country" is the tagline the Camps have put on their ultimate retreat. Actually, they understate the idyllic nature of their inn's setting: Experienced Hill Country wanderers will tell you that this is, by far, the most spectacular corner of the entire beloved region. At the very western edge of the Hill Country, there is precious little development—just scrubby, rugged, tree-carpeted hills, rocky bluffs, and exquisitely serene rivers.

On the banks of the Sabinal River, the Camps have made this stately white mansion, built around 1885, into a hospitable inn. Downstairs accommodations include the Cottonwood Canyon Suite, a pretty and sunny space with a king-size bed, dressing room, and private bath; the Panther Hill Room, with a queen-size bed, an Old West look with a touch of lace, and a private bath; and the Thompson Peak Room, also with a queen-size bed and a private bath. Upstairs, find the Button Willow Canyon Suite, a great place for a family or friends traveling together, thanks to two adjacent bedrooms—one with a king-size bed and one with two double beds—and balcony and bath.

Throughout the house the decor includes original landscapes, custom-made furniture, and thoughtfully executed style. Texana literature is available for your perusal, if you feel like kicking back. But if your passions lie in nature, you're just minutes away from great country for biking and hiking, canoeing, fishing, horseback riding, river tubing, scenic drives, and bird-watching. Plan on seeing breathtaking sunrises and sunsets and a stunning blanket of stars.

The Camp's signature breakfast is bread pudding, baked casserole style, using a raisin bread. The dish is dusted with powdered sugar and topped with sliced strawberries. Accompaniments typically include a German sausage, fresh fruit, and freshly ground coffee.

What's Nearby Vanderpool

Clinging to a particularly scenic spot on the Sabinal River, this town lies in a most beloved part of the Hill Country. Out on this westernmost edge of the region, there are no fast-food chains or discount department stores. There are stunning views from ribbons of highway that rise and fall over these craggy bluffs and hills and plenty of peace and quiet. The town is busiest in fall when hikers flock to Lost Maples State Park to see the vivid colors that paint the hollows and hilltops, thanks to the unusually displaced stands of big-tooth maple trees. Lost Maples Cafe in Utopia is a dandy place to eat, and Garner State Park is a popular place to take a river float in an inner tube.

The Lodge at Creekside

310 Mill Race Lane
Wimberley, TX 78676
Phone: (512) 847–8922; (800) 267–3925

E-MAIL: innkeeper@acountryinn.com

INTERNET SITES: www.acountryinn.com; www.lodgeatcreekside.com

INNKEEPERS: Merry, Sally, and Ashley Gibson

ROOMS: Lodge with 6 cabins, guesthouse with 2 suites; private bath, TV, telephone, dataport; 2 rooms with wheelchair accessibility

ON THE GROUNDS: Porches, fireplaces; six acres along 1,000 feet of Cypress Creek, fishing, tubing

CREDIT CARDS: MasterCard, Visa, American Express, Discover

RATES: $$$

HOW TO GET THERE: From I–35 exit Texas 80 at San Marcos and drive west to Ranch Road 12. Turn north on Ranch Road 12, noting the sign for Wimberley; stay on Ranch Road 12 through the center of Wimberley. Cross the Cypress Creek bridge and turn right immediately onto Mill Race Lane.

Now here's a marvelous retreat for two or a place for a family reunion. The Lodge consists of six individual cabins and a guesthouse that contains two suites. Among these buildings are an 1800s rock cabin and a 1970s log house—the latter having been remodeled to remove the seventies look— that have early Texas design styling.

How in the world anyone can choose the right cabin is something of a mystery, because each has its own certain appeal. The Angler's Cabin has a king-size, handhewn cypress bed, a full kitchen, whirlpool tub, and a wood-burning stove; the Gardener's Suite offers a queen-size iron garden-gate bed, garden antiques, and a sitting area with club chairs; and the Mountaineer's Retreat, on the ground floor of the log house, has two bedrooms, a rock fireplace, a twenty-foot vaulted ceiling, and a bath and a half.

Nautical accessories fill the Boat House, a board-and-batten cottage with a white pine, queen-size bed and an authentic brass porthole. Constructed of log slabs, salvaged windows, and recycled barn tin, the Trapper's Cabin is decorated in Double D Ranchwear plaids and has a queen-size cedar post bed and deep armchairs. The remaining lodgings are Miller's

Cabin, which with the Trapper's Cabin occupies either end of a Texas dog-trot house; the Creek House, a rock cabin; and the Hunt House, built in a German-style stucco.

Typical breakfast menus include tomato-thyme frittata, apricot strudel and banana nut bread, caramel-apple French toast, farm sausage, grilled French toast stuffed with strawberries and cream cheese, maple-smoked bacon, fresh juices and fruits, tea and coffee. Newest to the property is a main lodge with dining hall that's ADA compliant.

Wimberley Lodge at Lone Man Creek

Red Hawk Road
Wimberley, TX 78676
Phone: (512) 847-0544

INTERNET SITE:
www.wimberleylodge.com

INNKEEPER: Siri Hutcheson

ROOMS: 3 suites with private bath, TV, telephone

ON THE GROUNDS: Porches, picnic tables, swimming pool, barbecue pit, tennis court

CREDIT CARDS: MasterCard, Visa, American Express, Discover

RATES: $$$–$$$$

HOW TO GET THERE: Specific directions will be provided by your host at time of booking.

Here's a wonderful hideout if you want to be far from everything except nature. Found just a couple of miles east of what passes for a town square in the burgh of Wimberley, this thirty-three-acre retreat opened in late 1999 and is destined to be one of those places you'll return to time and again, once you've experienced it.

The lodge was built as a hunting lodge in the 1960s by the Moody family of fabulous Galveston Island wealth. By the time Siri got her hands on the place in the late 1990s, it had fallen into utter disrepair—but she could see that the beautiful stonework and the view gained from the porch was worth the headaches and backaches of restoration. The first phase to be reconstructed is a 4,000-square-foot portion of the whole building, which measures 7,000 square feet.

What you'll find (and fall in love with) are three amazingly spacious suites, furnished in chic Texana style, including furniture covered in heavy upholstery and leather and hand-carved Mexican tables and chairs. Nice touches include fabulously expensive bed and bath linens, Aveda hair and body products, and thoughtful lighting. The favorite suite is the one with two bedrooms, each with its own private bath, and a full kitchen, dining area, and living room. After a long day of shopping or hiking, you'll want to come back here, soak in the hot tub, grill a steak, and settle in with a glass of wine and watch *Giant* or another movie on the VCR or just gaze at the stunning spread of stars stretching overhead. If you have family and friends traveling with you, the three suites together will sleep fourteen people.

In the morning a nice, long swim in the giant swimming pool is a great way to get going. Have breakfast outside on your porch: Siri will leave fresh fruit, juice, coffee, milk, and muffins to start your day. Play a set of tennis or just hang out by the pool and drink in the beautiful hillside and valley view.

What's Nearby Wimberley

A bustling artists' community, Wimberley is an ideal place to pick up nice, one-of-a-kind pieces of pottery and sculpture, handmade jewelry, and various home decor pieces. It's also developing into a good town to find a day spa, so book yourself some massage therapy and a facial. Other diversions include floating on an inner tube beneath ancient cypress trees on the Blanco River or Cypress Creek; driving one of the state's most scenic drives, the Devil's Backbone; and tucking into a sensational dessert at Wimberley Pie Company.

Other Recommended B&Bs Nearby

Blair House Inn, 8 rooms with private baths and whirlpool tubs, sauna, massage room, library, video room, decks, ponds, eighty-five acres, and exquisite meals at breakfast and dinner; 100 Spoke Hill Road, Wimberley, TX 78676; telephone: (512) 847-1111 or (877) 549-5450; Internet site: www.blairhouseinn.com. *Southwind Bed & Breakfast Inn and Cabins,* on twenty-five acres with hiking trails, library, decks, hot tub, porch swings; telephone: (800) 508-5277; Internet site: www.southwindbed andbreak.com. Reservation services include All Wimberley Lodging: (512) 847-3909; Hill Country accommodations; (512) 847-5388.

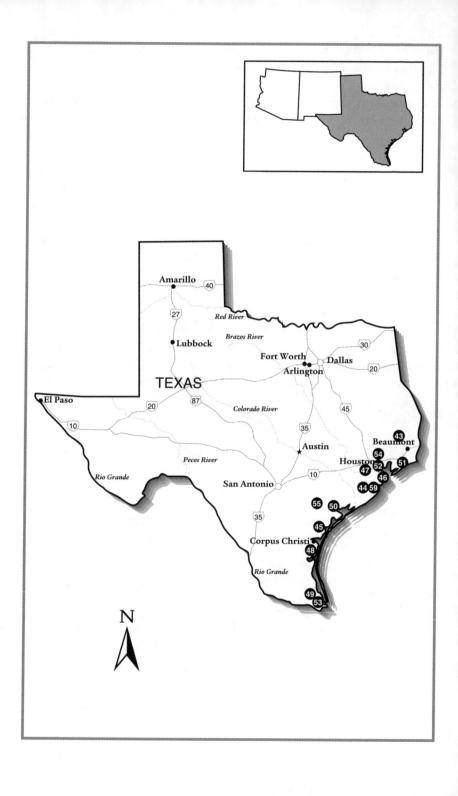

Texas: Gulf Coast

Numbers on map refer to towns numbered below.

Grand Duerr Manor

2298 McFaddin Street
Beaumont, TX 77701
Phone: (409) 833-9600

INNKEEPERS: Karl and Doug Duerr

ROOMS: 5 rooms with private bath

ON THE GROUNDS: Library, sunroom, verandah, garden, courtyard, lawn chairs/table; also huge front porch of main house for sitting

CREDIT CARDS: None accepted

RATES: $$-$$$; a 50 percent deposit is required

HOW TO GET THERE: From Houston drive east on I-10 and exit at Seventh Street. Turn right on Seventh Street and then right on McFaddin.

A graceful home built in 1937 in the Georgian style by U.S. District Attorney and judge Steve King, this two-story inn is a treasure for travelers who love hearing stories. The elder of the father-son innkeeper duo is Karl Duerr, who recently retired from Mobil Oil. Karl loves to reminisce about his father, a German immigrant who worked for the flamboyant oilman, Glenn McCarthy. Karl has entertaining accounts of McCarthy, who built the famous old Shamrock Hotel in Houston, and on whom the character Jett Rink in the novel *Giant*—played by James Dean in the film—was based.

The home is filled with Victorian-era antiques and art; rooms have themes that range from Victorian to Hollywood to Texana. There's a bridal suite, as well as a private cottage—behind the main home—which is good for families traveling with children.

You're fed a full breakfast in the dining room, egg casserole, baked goods, and fruits. Ask about other treats, such as wine or champagne, hot chocolate, and flowers.

What's Nearby Beaumont

Originally a trading post established by French and Spanish trappers and explorers in the early 1800s, this settlement became a boomtown nearly a century later when the world's first giant oil gusher roared to life in January 1901, at a site called Spindletop. You can see the re-created boomtown, along with a replica of the derrick that forever changed the state's economy. Other good stops in town include the Fire Museum of Texas, the ornate McFaddin-Ward House, and the Babe Didrikson Zaharias Museum and Visitors Center, dedicated to the phenomenal all-American and Olympic athlete.

Roses and the River Bed and Breakfast

7074 County Road 506
Brazoria, TX 77422
Phone: (979) 798-1070; (800) 610-1070

E-MAIL: hosack@roses-and-the-river.com

INTERNET SITE: www.roses-and-the-river.com

INNKEEPERS: Dick and Mary Jo Hosack

ROOMS: 3 rooms with private bath, telephone, TV, dataport

ON THE GROUNDS: Long verandahs with rockers and overhead fans, riverside garden, and yard with roses

CREDIT CARDS: MasterCard, Visa, American Express

RATES: $$$

HOW TO GET THERE: From Houston drive south on Texas 288; turn right at Farm Road 523, keep right, and watch for dead end at Farm Road 521. Follow Farm Road 521 to County Road 506 and turn right.

Hugging the San Bernard River in the coastal plains southwest of Galveston, this marvelously relaxing B&B inn was converted from a private home in 1995. Built in a Texas farmhouse style with a metal-seamed roof, the inn just begs you to pass a lazy afternoon on the verandah that wraps the entire house. Roses is surrounded by spreads of rose bushes in every direction that'll probably inspire you to write poetry—or at least a love letter.

The three upstairs guest rooms have queen-size beds and are named for Dick and Mary Jo's favorite roses. New Dawn is decorated in the blush tones of this climbing rose; Rainbow's End—which has bedroom and bathroom window seats—brings out the jewel tones of this rose; and Rise 'n' Shine bears the bright yellow shade found in this miniature rose.

Every morning you can count on an inspired breakfast of blushing orange coolers, lemon ricotta pancakes with sauteed apples, maple syrup, and sausages.

What's Nearby Brazoria

Within the Brazosport area is a cluster of eleven cities sitting at the mouth of the Brazos River. One is Brazoria, but the towns with opportunities for sightseeing are Angleton, Lake Jackson, Surfside, and West Columbia. Your best outdoorsy options are the Brazoria National Wildlife Refuge, with headquarters in Angleton; Wilderness Park, 1 mile west of Lake Jackson; and Surfside Beach at Surfside. Check out local heritage at Brazoria County Historical Museum in Angleton, Columbia Historical Museum in West Columbia, Dr. Freeman's Historical Dental Museum in Lake Jackson, and the Greek Revival plantation home at Varner-Hogg Plantation State Historical Park near West Columbia.

The Habitat

164 Fourth Street
Fulton, TX 78358
Phone: (361) 729-2362

E-MAIL: a.nugent@worldnet.att.net

INTERNET SITE: www.virtualcities.com/vacation/tx/g/txg48v/htm

INNKEEPERS: A. W. and Dr. Robin Nugent

ROOMS: 4 cabins with private bath, air-conditioning, kitchen, screened porch

ON THE GROUNDS: Screened porches, outdoor barbecue pit, picnic tables

CREDIT CARDS: MasterCard, Visa, American Express

RATES: $

HOW TO GET THERE: From Corpus Christi drive north on U.S. 181 to Texas 35, which you will take north through Rockport and Fulton, across the Copano Bay via the Lyndon B. Johnson Causeway, to the community of Lamar.

This two-year-old inn is custom-made for lovers of nature. Inspired by a 1940s lake cabin, which the Nugents have restored, The Habitat now includes four cabins built along the same period design. It's precisely the right look and feel for this environment, a place where you'll lose yourself in the wildlife. The Habitat sits on the edge of the St. Charles Bay and the Aransas Wildlife Refuge, which is famous as the Texas home of the magnificent whooping cranes.

Each of the cabins is equipped with air-conditioning, a kitchen that is completely outfitted, a full bath with shower, and large, screened porches. The Egret cabin has 3 full-size beds in two lofts; the Heron has a queen bed and a king bed in a loft; the Kingfisher has two king beds, one of which is in a loft; and the Sanctuary has two full beds and one bunk bed.

The Nugents will stock your cabin with light breakfast makings, such as homemade banana pecan muffins, milk, and juice, as well as afternoon snack goodies, such as homemade salsa, chips, and fruit. Bring groceries for your other meals, and be sure to include steaks and chicken to cook on the grill outside.

What's Nearby Lamar

The tiny burgh of Lamar lies just across the Copano Bay, via the causeway, from the art and seaside communities of Rockport and Fulton. Be sure to check out the ornate, four-story Fulton Mansion, as well as the Rockport Center for the Arts, and the Texas Maritime Museum at Rockport. At Goose Island State Park, you'll find the Big Tree, a gigantic live oak that's said to the largest in Texas, perhaps 1,000 years old. At Aransas National Wildlife Refuge, you can do some serious birding; in winter, look for the magnificent whooping cranes. And remember your fishing pole and bait: There are piers along the Copano Bay Causeway.

Other Recommended B&Bs Nearby

Ocean House Bed and Breakfast, a 1936 home renovated in a Mediterranean style, with swimming pool, hot tub, sauna, garden, elaborate breakfasts, and five suites with private baths, telephone, TV, and private entrances; 3275 Ocean Drive, Corpus Christi, TX 78404; telephone: (361) 882-9500; e-mail: sshoemaker@interconnect.net; Internet site: www.oceansuites.com. *Anthony's by the Sea Bed and Breakfast,* a 1953 home shaded by live oaks, within walking distance of the beach and Yacht Club, with a swimming pool and lanai, six rooms and suites in the main house and guesthouses; 732 South Pearl Street, Rockport, TX 78382; telephone: (361) 729-6100; (800) 460-2557.

The Coppersmith Inn

1914 Avenue M
Galveston, TX 77550
Phone: (409) 763-7004; (800) 515-7444

E-MAIL: coppersmithinn@worldnet.att.net

INTERNET SITE: www.coppersmithinn.com

INNKEEPERS: Karen and Patrick Geary

ROOMS: 5 rooms with private baths, 1 guest cottage with TV/VCR, CD player; Carriage House with TV, CD player, Jacuzzi

ON THE GROUNDS: Hot tub on deck; gardens

CREDIT CARDS: MasterCard, Visa, Discover

RATES: $$$

HOW TO GET THERE: Follow U.S. 75 into Galveston as it becomes Broadway; turn south on Nineteenth Street and watch for Avenue M.

Karen and Patrick Geary never planned to become innkeepers, but fate decided differently. The couple, who lived in a Dallas suburb, visited Galveston Island frequently to see family members. Next door to their relative's lovely historic home was a B&B, which happened to be for sale; after some prodding, the owner convinced the Gearys this was their calling.

With enthusiasm the pair have taken over this elegantly restored Queen Anne masterpiece, built in 1887 by renowned architect Alfred Muller for the cashier of a steamship and rail firm. (The name actually came from the second owner, who was a coppersmith from Ireland.) The dollhouse of a home is painted yellow and bears green trim, which shows off the plentiful gingerbread trim, double veradah, and turret tower. In front are phenomenal flowering beds; hundreds of plants in dozens of colors. As soon as you step inside and once you roam the gardens, you'll see why this is a favorite for wedding parties and bridesmaid luncheons.

On acquiring the house in 1999, the Gearys put in central air and created private baths for the three guest rooms inside the home. Up the breathtaking staircase crafted from teak, walnut, and curly pine is a sensational stained-glass window. At the top of the stairs is a sitting room with a TV and a self-serve coffee area; grab a paperback from the shelf and if you like it, take it home with you.

Above the doors to the guest rooms are transoms bearing antique, cobalt-blue glass. The Victoria Room has a nickel-plated queen bed, giant windows that open onto the upper verandah, a rocking chair, and a gas fireplace—which may or may not be needed in winter here. A full bath is offered, and all guest rooms are furnished with bathrobes.

In back a private guest cottage occupies what was the home's original kitchen. It has a king bed, as well as a loft with a double bed, and it's furnished with antiques, big windows, TV, VCR, and CD player. The separateness of this one allows guests to bring children. In the bath is an antique tin tub, which was used in one of the Kenny Rogers's *Gambler* movies. Also behind the main house is the new Carriage House. Inside are vaulted timber ceiling, king bed, queen sleeper sofa, TV, CD player, big Jacuzzi tub for two, and a sitting room. The view here takes in gorgeous gardens, as well as the deck's hot tub.

Coppersmith breakfasts are typically French toast or blueberry pancakes with bacon and fresh fruit. Everything's served family style in spacious dining room.

The Mermaid & The Dolphin

1103 Thirty-third Street
Galveston, Texas 77550
Phone: (409) 762-1561; (888) 922-1866

E-MAIL: MERMAIDINN@aol.com

INTERNET SITE: www.Galveston.com/mermaid

INNKEEPERS: Jim and Sally Laney

ROOMS: 6 rooms with private baths, air-conditioning units; 3 with king beds, 3 with queens

ON THE GROUNDS: Rambling gardens with tropical plants and birds, two living rooms, pub, hot tub, front porch; video and book libraries, portable TV/VCR, self-serve soft drink, coffee, and tea areas; bicycles; fax, computer, and copy services

CREDIT CARDS: MasterCard, Visa

RATES: $$-$$$$

HOW TO GET THERE: From U.S. 75, which becomes Broadway, turn south on Thirty-third Street and watch for house on right.

Named for a passage in Shakespeare's *A Midsummer Night's Dream,* this impressive 1866 home exudes Greek Revival opulence—as well as an unusual mix of architectural designs from subsequent additions, which feature Queen Anne and Craftsman styles in a four-floor mansion. Of significant note is the grand ballroom, designed and built in 1889 by prominent Galveston architect, Nicholas Clayton. The formal room has twelve foot ceilings, satin oak floors, the original opulent glass bowl chandeliers, and a fireplace imported from England. No wonder this house was on Galveston's renowned homes tour in 1999.

Behind the period antiques, gleaming wood floors, high ceilings, leaded glass, and twelve ornate fireplaces is a pair of owners who have become renovations experts. Their first work was on a home they bought in 1990, which also wound up on the annual homes tour. Several homes later they bought this one; they wound up living in it while renovating, sleeping on lawn chairs during part of the process. Opened as a B&B in 1997, it's a masterpiece in the attention to detail.

Special room interests include Muirmaid's Rendezvous, with floor-length windows that open onto the rear verandah that overlooks the gardens; Dolphin Dreamtime, with art by John William Waterhouse; Enchanted Nights, a sitting area with fireplace and a comfy daybed for reading; and Island Aires, a three-room suite with a fireplace and large Jacuzzi draped with a lace canopy. All rooms have pillow-topped mattresses and Egyptian cotton sheets, antique claw-foot tubs, and showers.

At the rear of the home are gardens crossed with flagstone pathways, crowded by frangipani transplanted from Key West, as well as orchids, staghorn ferns, night-blooming jasmine, passionflower, hibiscus, and trees bearing coconut, mango, guava, avocado, star fruit, kiwi, and more than a dozen banana varieties. A gazebo holds a hot tub, and a new conservatory features a swim spa, wet sauna, fountains, and areas for aromatherapy massages. A giant verandah across the rear of the home is perfect for sipping coffee or lemonade. In the evenings join the hosts for wine or beer in their cozy pub.

Breakfast is served in the large, formal dining room. Expect a buffet of egg-and-sausage casserole, various pastries and sweet breads, fresh fruits, cold cereal, and fruit juices. And ask about special food events, such as the couple's Caribbean Cooking Weekend.

The Queen Anne Bed and Breakfast

1915 Sealy Avenue
Galveston, TX 77550
Phone: (409) 763-7088; (800) 472-0930

INTERNET SITE: www.welcome.to/queenanne.com

INNKEEPERS: Ron and Jackie Metzger

ROOMS: 6 rooms with private bath; 1 with TV, telephone, dataport

ON THE GROUNDS: Four porches; parlors, antique furnishings

CREDIT CARDS: MasterCard, Visa, American Express

RATES: $$-$$$

HOW TO GET THERE: Drive into Galveston on I-45, which becomes Broadway Avenue. Turn left (north) on Twentieth Street and drive to Sealy Avenue and turn right.

Suitably named for its distinctive Queen Anne style, this 1905 home in the East End Historic District is remarkable for its original stained-glass windows, twelve-foot ceilings, pocket doors, sensational inlaid floor designs, and great porches where you'll find out again what it means to sit still. In every room you'll be amazed by the collection of antiques.

Guest rooms include the Cape Coral, filled with colossal French burl-wood furniture, marble-top dresser, and various chairs; the Suite, with a separate sitting area, refrigerator, coffee bar, cable TV, and phone; and the Cape Cod, with a private porch and a bath with a double sink crafted from an antique buffet piece.

You'll love the Queen Anne's convenience. The Strand Historic District is only 6 blocks away, and bicycles are available to you. In the morning, your breakfast is a big, gourmet affair, served on china and accompanied by soft music and candlelight.

Rose Hall

2314 Avenue M
Galveston, Texas 77550
Phone: (409) 763-1577

INTERNET SITE: www.Galveston.com/rosehall

INNKEEPERS: Tom and Barbara Souza

ROOMS: 8 rooms with private baths, sitting areas

ON THE GROUNDS: Views from roof of gulf and bay; large front porch, porch swings, hammocks; two dining rooms and large living room, tea room; room service; hot tub, big screen TV; fax and e-mail services

CREDIT CARDS: MasterCard, Visa, American Express, Discover, Diners Club

RATES: $$$

HOW TO GET THERE: Drive into Galveston via U.S. 75, which becomes Broadway; turn right or south on Twenty-fourth Street and east on Avenue M.

The spirit of this pre–Civil War home is that of the antebellum South, which is a bit different from the very Victorian spirit of Galveston. Built for a wealthy merchant named Charles Adams, Rose Hall is listed on the National Register of Historic Places and is a survivor of the Great Storm of 1900 that killed some 6,000 Galveston residents. Not so fortunate was Toby Adams, a family member who resided at the home but died in that devastating hurricane.

The home became a B&B in 1997 after Tom and Barbara finished extensive renovations. You can appreciate the magnitude of their efforts by looking through volumes of photos that show before, during, and after stages of restoration. Gorgeous longleaf pine floors were restored, an expansive downstairs lady's parlor became one of two dining rooms, and a 1,500-square-foot bridal suite was created on the third floor. The pair's two-year, seven-state antique hunt turned up such finds as an Austrian hand-carved satin wood half-teaster bed, with ten-karat gold-leaf detailing and matching curtain rods, which are in the Rose Suite.

In addition the Souzas put full bathrooms in each bedroom. Each bedroom also offers ample sitting areas, where you might want to enjoy Barbara's room-service offerings for lunch or dinner. In the large commercial kitchen, Barbara prepares fabulous breakfast spreads, including such specialties as sausage and potato casserole, grilled tomatoes with oregano and leeks, maple nut bread, bagels and cream cheese, omelettes with smoked gouda and Muenster cheeses, and fresh fruits with yogurt. Lunch and dinner offerings—remember to book ahead—include Greek salad, white fish sautéed in lemon, wine, and garlic butter, baked chicken breast Parmesan, and homemade cheesecake.

The Stacia Leigh

Pier 22
Galveston, TX 77550
Phone: (409) 750–8858

E-MAIL: webmaster@stacia-leigh.com

INTERNET SITE: www.stacia-leigh.com

INNKEEPERS: Pat and Bonnie Hicks

ROOMS: 11 shipboard rooms with private baths; 8 with king beds, 3 with queens; 8 with Jacuzzi tubs

ON BOARD: Small TV room on the lower level; common area on upper level; two-story sundeck has a hot tub

CREDIT CARDS: MasterCard, Visa, American Express, Discover

RATES: $$$

HOW TO GET THERE: Once on Galveston Island, stay on U.S. 75, which becomes Broadway; turn left or north on Twenty-fifth Avenue/Rosenberg Avenue until you reach Harborside Drive. Turn right or north on Harborside and drive to Pier 22.

Rare is the chance to even step aboard a yacht laden with colorful history; even less common is the opportunity to sleep aboard such a vessel. But that's what you get in this highly unusual B&B on the island city of Galveston.

The Stacia Leigh Bed & Breakfast is the lodging name given to a boat called the *Chryseis*, which has been owned by such colorful figures as Louis Renault and Benito Mussolini. Renault, known for his French auto manufacturing company, had what was originally a three-masted schooner built in 1906; he raced it until 1937, when he sold it to Count Galeazzo Ciano, Italy's minister of foreign affairs and Mussolini's son-in-law. After Ciano's execution in 1944, Il Duce inherited the yacht, which was later used to smuggle small arms. It appeared in the film *Chitty Chitty Bang Bang*, but later fell into disrepair.

Eventually an investor named Pat Hicks bought the ship, brought it to Galveston, and spent roughly eighteen months renovating the beauty. Hicks and friends installed one-hundred-year-old longleaf pine floors, salvaged from one of the vintage cotton warehouses in the Strand Historic District, and restored and duplicated woodwork in the wheelhouse and the exterior. A steel framework was added to support a new deck, and custom-made mattresses were brought in for the new cabins.

Playing upon the ship's wealth of World War II history, rooms are named not just for owners Renault and Mussolini, but also for period heroes such as Patton, Rommel, MacArthur, Bradley, Roosevelt, and Nimitz. The Truman Suite is a fore cabin, or Visa-berth, usually called the honeymoon suite for its bit of extra space and seclusion below decks; the Churchill Room, furnished with a queen, is especially cheery and light. Some rooms offer a wonderful view of the tall ship *Elissa* moored "next door."

Guests enjoy the sunny common area on the main deck, which is furnished with bright white wicker furniture and decorated with fresh flowers. You won't worry about the heat that descends upon Galveston in summer, because the Stacia Leigh enjoys powerful air-conditioning throughout. Breakfast is a big spread consisting of such pleasures as an egg casserole, fresh fruit, banana nut bread, pastries, and juices, prepared by Bonnie Hicks.

What's Nearby Galveston

The endearing island city near Houston was once the richest city in the Southwest and among the most prestigious in the nation. Days and nights are easily whiled away in the galleries, boutiques, restaurants, bistros, and nightspots spread throughout the restored, revitalized Strand, near the piers, and in the East End Historic District. Favorite diversions include the film, *The Great Storm,* which reports the devastating hurricane of 1900, which claimed 6,000 lives; Moody Gardens, a must for any lover of nature; Ashton Villa and the Bishop's Palace, two architectural masterpieces; and the Texas Seaport Museum, home to the great, Scottish tall ship *Elissa.*

Other Recommended B&Bs Nearby

Carousel Inn, an 1886 home with four rooms and private baths; 712 Tenth Street, Galveston, TX 77550; telephone: (409) 762-2166. *Inn at 1816 Postoffice,* an 1886 beauty in the East End Historic District, with five rooms and private baths; 1816 Postoffice Street, Galveston, TX 77550; telephone: (409) 765-9444. *Harbor House at Pier 21,* a modern inn on the waterfront next to the tall ship *Elissa,* with forty-two rooms and private baths, a three-bedroom suite, nine marina slips, and Continental breakfast; No. 28 at Pier 21, Galveston, TX 77550; telephone: (409) 763-3321. *Out by the Sea B&B,* a new beach house with a gulf-side deck and beach on the Bolivar Peninsula, with two rooms and private baths, phone, TV/VCR; 2134 Vista Drive, Crystal Beach, TX 77650-2046; telephone: (409) 684-1555 or (888) 522-5926; e-mail: info@outbythesea.com; Internet site: www.outbythesea.com.

Angel Arbor Bed and Breakfast Inn

848 Heights Boulevard
Houston, TX 77007
Phone: (713) 868-4654; (800) 722-8788

E-MAIL: b-bhoutx@wt.net

INTERNET SITE: www.angelarbor.com

INNKEEPER: Marguerite Swanson

ROOMS: 3 bedrooms with private bath; suite with adjoining quarters in separate building, each with private bath and Jacuzzi; TV, telephone, dataport

ON THE GROUNDS: Upstairs and downstairs solarium, garden

CREDIT CARDS: MasterCard, Visa, American Express, Discover

RATES: $$-$$$

HOW TO GET THERE: West from downtown on I-10, exit north on Heights Boulevard. Go 5 blocks.

Whether you're in town on business or to see the latest play at The Alley Theater or the current exhibit at the Museum of Fine Arts Houston, this elegant place is worth your consideration. The 1923, three-story, Georgian-style home was built for a couple named John and Katherine McTighe. Today it bears a City of Houston Historic Landmark designation and is found within the Houston Heights neighborhood.

Downstairs you'll find a large parlor shared by all guests. There's also a solarium where you'll have a nice view of the gardens, a pretty backyard pond, and two fountains. Upstairs the three bedrooms are named Raphael, Gabriel, and Angelique; the decor is all about antiques and fine fabrics. In a separate building is a suite with adjoining quarters, each of which has a deluxe bathroom with a Jacuzzi tub for two.

Each morning you'll be served a sizable breakfast. Guests love Marguerite's cooking so much that she's published her own cookbook, *Breakfast with the Angel*. Expect to find a fancy egg dish and breakfast meats, fresh fruit, home-baked breads, juice, coffee, and tea. Ask Marguerite also about her murder mystery dinner parties.

The Lovett Inn

501 Lovett Boulevard
Houston, TX 77006
Phone: (713) 582-5224; (800) 779-5224

E-MAIL: lovettinn@aol.com

INTERNET SITE: www.lovettinn.com

INNKEEPER: Tom Fricke

ROOMS: 10 rooms with TV, telephone, dataport; 8 with private bath

ON THE GROUNDS: Library, sunroom, meeting rooms, garden, hot tub, pool

CREDIT CARDS: MasterCard, Visa, American Express, Discover

RATES: $-$$$

HOW TO GET THERE: From U.S. 59 drive north on Montrose Boulevard, then turn right (east) on Lovett Boulevard.

This 1920s mansion, built by a former Houston mayor, is the ideal location if your stay in Houston has you visiting museums and shopping the eclectic stores in the Montrose neighborhood. A complete updating has put phones and color TV in every guest room, and you'll find that most rooms overlook the meticulously landscaped grounds, pool, and hot tub.

If you can't get the booking date you want, it may be because a wedding party has leased the entire home—that's how romantic its mood is. There's a pretty spread of gardens, complete with a gazebo, and the downstairs common rooms are spacious and elegant. Breakfast is simply Continental, but that makes plenty of sense when you consider the wealth of worthy restaurants in the Montrose neighborhood.

What's Nearby Houston

The nation's fourth-largest city will never leave you wanting for something to do. In the world of arts alone, Houston is mightily impressive: The Houston Grand Opera offers productions at the Cullen Theater in the Wortham Center downtown, and the Houston Symphony performs in Jones Hall, while the Houston Ballet stages productions in the Brown Theater at Wortham Center. The Alley Theatre is a beloved company offering all kinds of stage works, too. Among museums are the Museum of Fine Arts, Houston; the Houston Museum of Natural Sciences; and the Menil Collection. Sports offerings range from the NBA's Houston Rockets and the WNBA's Houston Comets to baseball's Houston Astros at fabulous Erron Field. Don't miss Space Center Houston, a wonderful place for learning more about NASA and the story of space exploration.

Another Recommended B&B Nearby

Captain's Quarters, a newly built, New England-style inn within 3 blocks of twenty-five restaurants and fifty shops, with twelve guest rooms with private baths, TV, telephone; 701 Bay Avenue, Kemah, TX 77565; telephone: (281) 334–4141 or (888) 465–4141; Internet site: www.capts quarters.com.

B Bar B Ranch Inn

325 East County Road 2215
Kingsville, TX 78363
Phone: (361) 296–3331

E-MAIL: bbarb@rivnet.com

INTERNET SITE: www.b-bar-b.com

INNKEEPERS: Luther and Patti Young

ROOMS: 16 rooms with private bath, TV, telephone, dataport; includes 3 suites with Jacuzzi tubs

ON THE GROUNDS: Restaurant and rear patio; seven acres of wetlands, birding along the Great Texas Coastal Birding Trail, dog kennels, pool; wheelchair accessibility in main house

CREDIT CARDS: MasterCard, Visa, Discover

RATES: $–$$$

HOW TO GET THERE: From San Antonio drive Texas 37 south to Corpus Christi, then U.S. 77 south to Kingsville. Drive 8 miles south of Kingsville on County Road 2215.

Found on some of the world's most famous geography, the B Bar B occupies what was once part of the esteemed King Ranch. The main lodge is a renovated old ranch house, made absolutely contemporary and comfortable for travelers looking for something remote and real. Surrounded by eighty acres of working ranch, the lodge is a big destination for *avi-tourists,* the term used to describe birders who come to see the hundreds of species that migrate or live along this stretch of the Great Texas Coastal Birding Trail. Anglers love to see what's biting on a freshwater pond and at nearby Baffin Bay. During certain seasons there is quail, turkey, and antelope hunting, too.

Guest rooms are modern but have Texas touches, such as heavy, hand-carved furniture and animal skin wall hangings. Three suites have Jacuzzi tubs for serious relaxing. Common areas shared by guests range from the hot tub and swimming pool to a picnic area, lodge great room, and dining room. A big country breakfast is included with stays, and you can book a five-course meal—featuring mesquite-grilled steak, rabbit, ostrich, and quail, or fresh fish done with Mexican flair—by advance arrangement.

What's Nearby Kingsville

Thanks to the King Ranch, which was once the world's largest, the town of Kingsville was born in 1904. The ranch, now a National Historic Landmark, was established in 1853 and continues to reign as one of Texas's more famous legends. The Santa Gertrudis cattle breed, the first strain of beef cattle originating in the Western Hemisphere, was developed and is still bred here. You can tour the ranch, and if your timing's right, join in bird-watching events. In town be sure to visit the King Ranch Museum and the King Ranch Saddle Shop. On the Texas A&M University-Kingsville campus, see South Texas history displays at the John E. Conner Museum and plant and animal exhibits at the Kleberg Hall of Natural History.

Inn at Chachalaca Bend

20 Chachalaca Bend Drive
Los Fresnos, TX 78566
Phone: (956) 233-1180; (888) 612-6800
Fax: (956) 233-1932

E-MAIL: inn@chachalaca.com

INTERNET SITE: www.chachalaca.com

INNKEEPERS: Rosemary and Cleve Breedlove

ROOMS: 4 rooms, 2 suites with private baths, Jacuzzi and shower, king-size bed, telephone, individually controlled heating and cooling, TV/VCR; 2 rooms have access for disabled guests

ON THE GROUNDS: Nature preserve with bird-watching blinds, walking trails, observation tower, and herb and tropical gardens; gazebo, verandah, patios with seating

CREDIT CARDS: MasterCard, Visa, American Express, Discover, Diners Club

RATES: $$$–$$$$

HOW TO GET THERE: From Harlingen follow U.S. 77/83 south toward Brownsville; exit South Padre Island/Texas 100 and drive east to Los Fresnos; watch the speed limit drop in Los Fresnos. Turn left (north) at the stoplight on Arroyo Boulevard (Farm Road 1847). Go ¼ mile and turn right (east) on Old Port Road (Farm Road 2480), and go exactly 2 miles. Turn left (north) on Track 43 Road. Go across the resaca (water) and turn right on Chachalaca Bend Drive.

W hen their next-door neighbors decided to move, Rosemary and Cleve thought up a smart way to fill up their empty nest days. Because they live right in the middle of the Rio Grande Valley, now the world's top bird-watching region, the couple decided to create a luxurious bed and breakfast for birders—as well as for travelers who are ultimately headed for a beach vacation at South Padre Island, another twenty miles east—to be open from September through May.

They bought and extensively remodeled their neighbors' 1974 home, putting four bedrooms in the main house and transforming the garage into two more beautiful suites. They spared absolutely no expense, putting in mahogany flooring, installing copper rain gutters, creating paneling salvaged from a large barn in Pennsylvania, crafting headboards from antique doors that had been hand-carved in Mexico, draping beds in Laura Ashley linens and comforters, installing all sorts of hand-painted tiles in bathrooms, and bringing in myriad pieces of wonderful iron and metal furniture pieces. The flagstone porch benefited from perfect engineering: No matter how much it rains, there will never be puddles on the porch.

Even if you aren't sure you're a nature nut, you'll be taken with the forty acres of natural habitat at this retreat, named for the squawking chachalaca bird that's native to this region and northern Mexico, and that you'll see from special blinds the Breedloves built for guests. Fifteen kinds of native brush, such as Brazilian pepper trees, ebony, and palm crowd the grounds, particularly near the resaca, or oxbow, that meanders from a nearby river that runs east into the Gulf of Mexico. Alligator and beaver live in these waters, and owls inhabit the trees. Native plants that Rosemary will point out include the pigeon berry, whose scarlet fruits were used at one time to make rouge, as well as jasmine, which you'll smell on any breeze. Above the butterfly garden are papaya trees that are loved by the chachalaca. Along the walking trail are night-blooming cactus, torchwood, and myriad native grasses that can be colorful during certain seasons.

Rosemary spoils guests with lavish breakfasts, which on a given morning might include half of a giant grapefruit; pineapple juice; an omelette stuffed with feta, Swiss, and cream cheeses; and smoked salmon and Italian parsley; as well as a potato cake, toast with homemade orange marmalade, and a breakfast dessert, which is usually a skillet pie filled with apples and cherries. In the afternoon the Breedloves urge guests to take a glass of wine or beer (complimentary) or a soft drink over to the gazebo and watch the sun drop down into the South Texas horizon.

Another Recommended B&B Nearby

The Kingfisher Inn, with expert fly-fishing and birding guide services, fishing packages, shopping, and dining tours to Mexico, two rooms with private baths and full kitchens on the Arroyo Colorado; 36901 Marshall Hutts Road, Rio Hondo, TX 78583; telephone: (956) 748-4350.

Le Jardin de la Mer, The Garden by the Sea

304 Fifth Street
Palacios, TX 77465
Phone: (361) 972-5983; (800) 895-8934

E-MAIL: dsm@wcnet.net

INTERNET SITE: www.bbhost.lejardindelamer.com

INNKEEPERS: Donnie and Winfrey Horton

ROOMS: 3 rooms with private baths, TV/VCR; 1 with telephone; 1 with wheelchair accessibility

ON THE GROUNDS: Garden/patio; common room with sitting area, TV/VCR, stereo, dining area

CREDIT CARDS: MasterCard, Visa, American Express, Discover

RATES: $–$$

HOW TO GET THERE: From Houston drive U.S. 59 south to Texas 71; go east to Texas 35. Follow Texas 35 south into downtown to Fifth Street. House is at corner of Main (Texas 35) and Fifth Streets.

Originally a commercial building when constructed in 1910, the structure at the corner of Main and Fifth became a post office in the 1940s. Today the brick building is painted a light green and trimmed in ivory; adjacent is a fenced garden with an air perfect for reflection and solitude.

Inside, doors and windows bear a mahogany trim and ceilings soar at thirteen feet. The decor possesses an old New Orleans French Quarter style, found in painted wooden furniture and rooms with wrought-iron canopy beds. No wonder the inn has received awards for its restoration and preservation.

You're only 2 blocks north of Matagorda Bay, so strap on a helmet and climb on a bicycle to do some exploring. If you're a birder, take your guidebook and log with you. You'll want the exercise to burn off the Horton's lavish breakfasts, three- or four-course affairs in which sweet potato pancakes are often the highlight.

Moonlight Bay Bed and Breakfast

506 South Bay Boulevard
Palacios, TX 77465
Phone: (361) 972–2232; (877) 461–7070

E-MAIL: grogers@wcnet.net

INTERNET SITE: www.bbhost.moonlightbaybb.com

INNKEEPERS: Gaye and Earl Hudson

ROOMS: 7 rooms with private bath; 3 with TV; 1 with wheelchair accessibility

ON THE GROUNDS: Library, sunroom, verandah, piano; dinner by reservation

CREDIT CARDS: MasterCard, Visa, American Express, Discover, Diners Club

RATES: $–$$$

HOW TO GET THERE: From Houston drive U.S. 59 south to Texas 71; go east to Texas 35. Follow Texas 35 south into downtown to Fifth Street. Follow Fifth Street south to Bay Boulevard.

ook around this 1910, Craftsman-style home, and you'll find an elegantly comfortable B&B. In the library is a grand piano and places for just sitting quietly and reading; like most guests you'll likely be taken with the original murals inspired by literature found here. The home, which was an unofficial officers' club during World War II, has an upper verandah with another piano.

Gaye and Earl have a habit of pampering guests with such luxuries as afternoon tea, which is accompanied by piano music of the 1940s. Fresh flowers, robes, and slippers are part of the hospitality, too. If you can pull yourself away from the porch views of Matagorda Bay, take a stroll along the lengthy, lighted bayfront walkway.

Breakfast is a formal affair in the dining room, typically pancakes, French toast, and egg dishes. When you call for your reservation, inquire about dinner at the inn.

What's Nearby Palacios

Roughly midway between Galveston and Corpus Christi, this tiny fishing town has a pretty waterfront park area along Matagorda Bay—so plan a picnic or a lovely, quiet walk. A fishing jetty awaits along the town pier, and other piers are found along the bay-front drive. If you've an interest in marine biology, check out the Marine Fisheries Research Station just southwest of town.

Aurora Bed and Breakfast

141 Woodworth Boulevard
Port Arthur, TX 77640
Phone: (409) 983-4205

E-MAIL: wrob670000@aol.com

INTERNET SITE: www.bigtimer.hypermart.net/aurora

INNKEEPER: Wei Robbins

ROOMS: 5 rooms; 2 with private bath; 2 with TV, telephone, dataport

ON THE GROUNDS: Sunroom, fountain

CREDIT CARDS: None accepted

RATES: $

HOW TO GET THERE: From Houston follow I–10 east to Beaumont, then follow U.S. 69 south—it becomes Woodworth—until it dead-ends.

That Port Arthur's first bed and breakfast is found within a marvelous historic home is only a part of the appeal; the rest of the attraction belongs to the story of its owner, Wei Robbins. An immigrant from Tianjin, China, Wei spent her late teens and early twenties living in a mud-hut commune and working in cornfields near Mongolia as part of a government reeducation program forced upon educated city dwellers in the late 1960s. She learned English by listening to the radio and became a teacher before making her way to the United States, where she taught Chinese culture at McNeese State University in Lake Charles, Louisiana.

After meeting her husband in the early 1990s, the two came to the Port Arthur area and wound up buying a noteworthy old, 5,200-square-foot home that needed work. Plenty of hard labor on the couple's part turned this 1915 house—which once belonged to the town's shipping magnate—into a lovely inn; naturally, it's filled with Chinese art.

In addition to the Chinese decor pieces, which guests can buy, are several antique chandeliers. While you're staying here, hang out on the upstairs sunporch to watch the ship traffic on the channel, or take Chinese cooking lessons from Wei. She'll also work with you on Tai Chi.

Mornings bring lovely sunrises over Sabine Lake, as well as an elaborate breakfast, which is enjoyed with your hosts in the sunny breakfast room.

What's Nearby Port Arthur

You've picked the right place if you long for lazy time spent outdoors. At McFaddin Wildlife Refuge, find one of North America's more dense alligator populations, as well as grounds for fishing, crabbing, and birdwatching. At Sea Rim State Park, some 60,000 snow geese use the marshes during their travels, as do Canada geese, twenty-three duck species, and hundreds of other bird species. Music fans will like the Museum of the Gulf Coast's Heritage Room, which honors hometown stars Janis Joplin and J. P. Richardson, Jr., known as the Big Bopper, who died with fellow Texan Buddy Holly. For ethnic interest see the wonderful Oriental Temple in City Park.

The Pelican House Bed and Breakfast

1302 First Street
Seabrook, TX 77586
Phone: (281) 474-5295

E-MAIL: pelicanhouse@usa.net
INTERNET SITE: www.pelicanhouse.com

INNKEEPER: Suzanne Silver

ROOMS: 4 rooms with private bath; 1 with TV, telephone, dataport

ON THE GROUNDS: Hot tub overlooking the Back Bay; porch with rocking chairs; paddleboat

CREDIT CARDS: MasterCard, Visa, American Express, Discover

RATES: $$

HOW TO GET THERE: From Houston drive I–45 south to NASA Road exit. Head east for 8 miles. Cross Highway 146 to Second Street. Go 4 blocks and turn left. B&B is the second house on right.

This seaside retreat is found in a 1906 cottage, amply shaded by aged live oak and pecan trees. You'll be tempted to do nothing but hang out on Suzanne's sweet, gingerbread-encrusted porch, rocking the day away. Should the spirit move you, however, it's an easy walk down to Gazebo Park to watch the fishermen and to shop in the Old Seabrook Art and Antique Colony. Birders will love taking the paddleboat out into the Back Bay to enjoy the water and watch the feathered residents.

Inside the house fresh flowers, feather duvets, and handmade quilts decorate the cozy, sunny rooms. Throughout you'll find nautical adornments and murals of waterbirds, as well. In the morning your breakfast is likely to be Suzanne's specialty, stuffed French toast with apricot glaze. You'll easily find other meals in town.

What's Nearby Seabrook

Immediately southeast of Houston, facing Galveston Bay, is an area called Clear Lake; among its towns are Kemah, Seabrook, Webster, and others. Within the area you'll find several marinas that offer charters for fishing, cruising, and sailing. Places to explore include the shops and restaurants of Kemah Boardwalk, Armand Bayou Nature Center, and the amazing Space Center Houston.

Casa de Siesta

4610 Padre Boulevard
South Padre Island, TX 78597
Phone: (956) 761-5656
Fax: (956) 761-1313

INNKEEPERS: Lynn or Ron Speier

ROOMS: 12 rooms with private bath, phone, cable TV; some are wheelchair accessible

ON THE GROUNDS: Pool, courtyard, fountains, dining room

CREDIT CARDS: MasterCard, Visa, American Express, Discover

RATES: $$–$$$

HOW TO GET THERE: From Harlingen drive south on U.S. 77 /83 toward Brownsville; exit South Padre Island/Texas 100 and drive east, watching for speed limit drops as you go through Los Fresnos. Continue to Port Isabel, where you will cross the Queen Isabella Causeway to the island. Turn left and drive to the inn.

Built in 2000 in a Spanish mission style, this attractive inn seems to have been transported from Southern California or the Arizona desert. What you'll love about it is its tremendous privacy and generous room space, as well as the gorgeous pool in the landscaped courtyard.

Each of the rooms have been designed to incorporate vigas, or carved beams, as well as carved spiral posts, which provide a deep Mexican villa look. The ceilings bear a tongue-and-groove design in ponderosa pine. Rooms and bathrooms feature beautiful craftsmanship, utilizing Saltillo tiles from Mexico. Throughout the rooms and dining room are handmade New Mexican furniture and Texas antiques.

Before your day at the beach or sailing on Laguna Madre Bay—the inn, by the way, is just a block from either—you'll enjoy a large Continental breakfast in the dining area. Look for this to include cereals, pastries, yogurt, juices, fruit, coffee, and tea. For lunch and dinner you'll find dozens of restaurants of all descriptions within a few blocks. For film buffs there's a Cineplex conveniently located next door.

What's Nearby South Padre Island

You'll wind up wishing you were spending at least a week on this skinny strip of sand lining Texas's southernmost point. Long beach walks are wonderful, as are the terrific fishing expeditions in the deep water and in clear, blue Laguna Madre. Dolphin tours in the bay are also loads of fun, as are the boat charters that include bird watching as part of the dolphin tours. There's a good boardwalk near the convention center for bird-watching and sunset viewing, but remember to leave time for horseback riding on the beach. For more birding, check out the massive Laguna Atascosa National Wildlife Refuge. Be sure to set aside a day for shopping and dining just across the Rio Grande in the border town of Matamoros.

Other Recommended B&Bs Nearby

Brown Pelican Inn, a 1995 Nagshead-style house with wraparound porches, a birding area on the Laguna Madre wetlands, and eight rooms with private baths and some wheelchair accessibility; 207 West Aries Street, South Padre Island, TX 78597; telephone: (956) 761-2722. *The Moonraker,* with three rooms and private baths, 107 East Marisol Street, South Padre Island, TX 75897; telephone: (956) 761-2206.

McLachlan Farm Bed and Breakfast

24907 Hardy Road
Spring, TX 77383
Phone: (281) 350-2400; (800) 382-3988

E-MAIL: stay@macfarm.com

INTERNET SITE: www.macfarm.com

INNKEEPERS: Jim and Joycelyn Clairmonte

ROOMS: 3 rooms with phone and on request, TV; 2 with private bath

ON THE GROUNDS: Library, garden, wooded trails, wraparound porch and swings

CREDIT CARDS: MasterCard, Visa, American Express, Discover

RATES: $$

HOW TO GET THERE: From I-45 exit at Cypresswood (exit 68) and drive right to Hardy Road; turn right on Hardy, then turn right on McLachlan Farm's road. Or, from the Hardy Toll Road, exit U.S. 59 and go right briefly to Hardy Road. Turn left on Hardy to McLachlan Farm.

In 1861 Joycelyn's family settled on this land a little north of Houston. Her grandfather built a 600-square-foot homestead here in 1911, which Joyce-lyn and husband Jim remodeled and enlarged in 1988 to a spacious 3,000 square feet. That's lots of room at a countryside house for you to enjoy. Throughout you'll find family treasures.

Outside are thirty-five acres amply shaded by sycamore and pecan trees that reach high into the sky. If you'd like an even greater sense of solitude, take a long walk along the woodsy trails near the house. And when the spirit of shopping moves you, head just a mile away to the village of Old Town Spring. This Victorian whistle-stop area is filled with some 150 merchants.

Meanwhile gently glide on the porch swings and remember what it is to do nothing. Dream, if you like, about the inn's morning meal, which usually includes Swedish oven pancakes, egg and sausage soufflé, mandarin orange pancakes, cinnamon chip scones, and the like.

What's Nearby Spring

Located just north of Houston, this historic town was settled by German immigrants in 1840. The restored railroad village is a testament to a Victorian heyday, thanks to a collection of buildings filled with more than one hundred shops selling antiques and art, as well as museums and restaurants. Spring is also home to a nature center, the Pioneer Homestead Museum, an arboretum and botanical garden, and a water park with slides and wave pools.

Friendly Oaks Bed and Breakfast

210 East Juan Linn Street
Victoria, TX 77901
Phone: (361) 575-0000

E-MAIL: innkprbill@aol.com

INTERNET SITE: www.bbhost.com/friendly/oaks

INNKEEPERS: Bill and CeeBee McLeod

ROOMS: 1 suite, 3 bedrooms with private bath; 3 with TV; 1 with wheelchair accessibility

ON THE GROUNDS: Library, sunroom, verandah, conference room

CREDIT CARDS: MasterCard, Visa, American Express, Discover

RATES: $–$$

HOW TO GET THERE: From San Antonio drive south on U.S. 87 through Cuero. Continue to Victoria, where 87 becomes Main Street. Stay on Main to Juan Linn, where you'll turn left and drive 2 blocks.

Built in 1915 by a rancher named Rob Welder, this expansive, Craftsman-style home stands in the shelter of ancient live oaks in the historic district called Street of Ten Friends, which dates back to 1824. You'll be plenty comfortable in this hardy old homestead, but try to take some time to walk the neighborhood to get a glimpse of the rest of these 200 historic homes that help tell the story of early Texas.

Your lodging choices are the Boudoir, a spacious honeymoon suite with a four-poster bed; the Ranch, with a unique log bed and cowboy decor; the Thrifty Scot, with a wonderful view of the live oaks; and the Preservation Room, done in a Victorian theme. If you need a place to connect your laptop, there's a business area inside the home.

Bill and CeeBee enjoy helping guests see Victoria. They'll work with you with theater tickets and restaurant ideas, and they'll help you figure out golf, birding, hiking, and deep-sea fishing excursions. They'll also fill you each morning with a big breakfast, which begins with either mango "turtles" or another fruit dish, then continues with Scottish pancakes, accompanied by the traditional British bangers. If you have special diet requests, just let them know.

What's Nearby Victoria

Founded by Don Martin de Leon with forty-one Spanish families in 1824, the town was named for Mexico's first president, General Guadalupe Victoria. The town's McNamara Historical Museum offers collections of Texana, as well as documents and artifacts from the state's Spanish, Mexican, and Republic of Texas eras. The Nave Museum houses the works of Royston Nave, a Texas native who distinguished himself as an artist in New York in the 1920s. When you're downtown, see the landmark gristmill, imported from Germany in the 1850s, in Victoria Memorial Square.

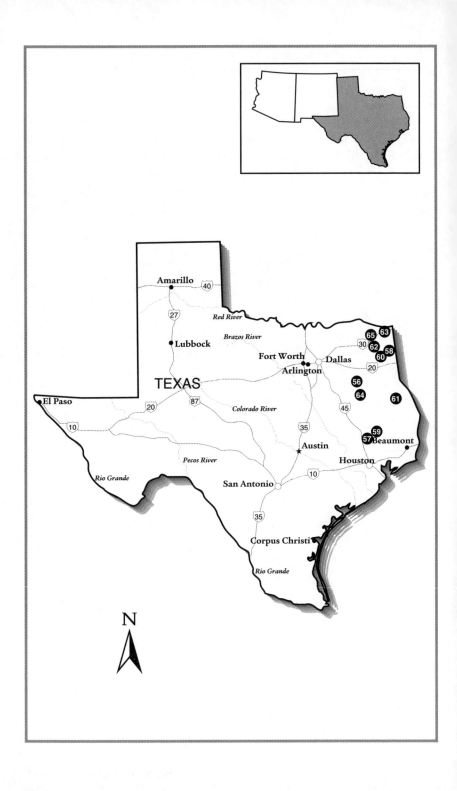

Texas: Piney Woods

Numbers on map refer to towns numbered below.

Oak Meadow Bed & Breakfast

2781 FM 2495
Athens, TX 75751
Phone: (903) 675–3407; (877) 675–3407

E-MAIL: oakmeado@flash.net
INTERNET SITE: www.bbonline.com/tx/oakmeadow
INNKEEPERS: Gwen and Joe Mills
ROOMS: 3 rooms with private baths, 1 with TV
ON THE GROUNDS: Rolling countryside with cutting horses
CREDIT CARDS: None accepted
RATES: $$
HOW TO GET THERE: Drive 70 miles southeast of Dallas on Texas 175 to
Texas 31; ask for specific directions at booking time.

Built in 1983 as a quarter horse breeding ranch, this B&B is well loved by
people who need a true countryside escape. The storybook appeal is
complete with white-rail cross fencing that defines the paddocks and
pastures of the property, where spectacular quarter horses feed and roam.
You'll be swept away by the utter stillness and peaceful setting, shaded by
fifty or so century-old oak trees scattered about the eight and a half acres,
where gentle breezes are felt much of the time.

The home is an especially comfortable place to lounge after a day of
exhausting shopping at nearby Canton, where First Monday Trade Days
offer thousands of great bargains on antiques and collectibles. You can
ponder your purchases and gather your wits for perhaps another day of
spending or just catch up on some reading at the inn's 200-foot great room.
At breakfast time, you'll dig into a full country spread.

What's Nearby Athens

The black-eyed pea capital of the world celebrates that legume with a
big October bash, so play your trip accordingly. Downtown, look for the
historical marker that declares Athens the birthplace of hamburger; it's
just around the corner from a great shopping street called Athens Alley.
Make time also to visit the Texas Freshwater Fisheries Center, an
impressive and informative Texas Parks and Wildlife operation.

Heather's Glen

200 East Phillips
Conroe, TX 77301-2646
Phone: (936) 441-6611; (800) 665-2643

E-MAIL: heathersbb@aol.com

INTERNET SITE: www.heatherglen.com

INNKEEPERS: Ed and Jamie George

ROOMS: 8 rooms with private bath, TV, radio, telephones

ON THE GROUNDS: Sunroom, verandah, garden, lily pond, oversize Jacuzzi tubs for two; private cottage with handicap accessibility, ramps on house, too

CREDIT CARDS: MasterCard, Visa, American Express, Discover

RATES: $-$$$$

HOW TO GET THERE: Enter town on I-45; turn east on Texas 105/Davis Street; turn north on Third Street and west on Phillips.

This grand, century-old mansion features verandahs and porches straight out of the Texas Victorian period. The beautifully restored home is filled with period antiques but has all the updated conveniences that make it a comfortable place to stay. You can't help but be impressed by the twelve-foot ceilings, original pine flooring, and two graceful staircases.

Among rooms are suites that lend themselves well to honeymooners or everyday romantics. Several of the rooms have oversized Jacuzzi tubs, one has an adjoining, enclosed sunroom, and two overlook the lush waterfall in the garden. There is certain luxury in the breakfast of Belgian waffles with whipped cream and strawberries, scrambled eggs, fresh fruit, bacon or sausage, juice, milk, and coffee. If you're staying more than one night, your morning menus will be varied.

What's Nearby Conroe

Perched on the southern edge of the Sam Houston National Forest, the Montgomery County Seat is shadowed by towering pines and offers the four-acre fish pond for anybody feeling lucky. Right in town is the wonderfully restored Crighton Theatre, a landmark venue for opera, ballet, plays, and Texas music performances. In fall take part in the massive Texas Renaissance Festival in nearby Plantersville.

Old Mulberry Inn Bed & Breakfast

209 Jefferson Street
Jefferson, TX 75657
Phone: (903) 665–1945;
(800) 263–5319

E-MAIL: mulberry@
jeffersontx.com

INTERNET SITE: www.
jeffersontx.com/oldmulberryinn

INNKEEPERS: Donald and Gloria Degn

ROOMS: 5 rooms with private bath, cable TV, telephone, dataport

ON THE GROUNDS: Library with fireplace, porch swing

CREDIT CARDS: MasterCard, Visa, American Express, Discover

RATES: $–$$$

HOW TO GET THERE: Three hours east of Dallas; drive into town on U.S. 59 and turn east 2 blocks on Jefferson.

Donald and Gloria became innkeepers on building this Louisiana-style plantation cottage with Greek Revival accents in 1997–1998 in Jefferson's historic district. Gloria, who teaches high school English, and Donald, the former home and garden editor for a California daily newspaper, designed their inn so that it complements the 1850s architectural style found throughout this very Southern town. In keeping with the design of that day, they brought in heart-of-pine flooring from a cotton gin in the Dallas area, other flooring from various period buildings in North Carolina, French doors from the Houston area, and solid doors from Denver and from a landmark hotel in Carmel-by-the-Sea. The result is a lovely new house that's faithful to an important period in East Texas history.

Donald and Gloria had custom bed coverings and window treatments made, and three rooms feature the unique headboards they designed. Each bed has a special handmade mulberry tree pillow; on each is a leaf design copied from an old mulberry tree. And talk about comfort—the rooms each have furniture that actually feels good to sit on, as well as a TV within an armoire, a ceiling fan, and clock radio. Four of the five tiled bathrooms have footed tubs, and all have showers.

How to best pick a room is the trick. The Front Room is the most formal and most Southern, with a king-size rice bed in dark cherry wood, and walls that are painted a color called "pensive sky." Prints in this room by California poster artist David Lance Goines give the room a West Coast spirit. The Star Room honors the Lone Star State, with a handcrafted star quilt and pillow on a very high four-poster queen bed; and Elizabeth's Room has a rose theme and a king-size headboard the innkeepers fashioned from an old door found in a Jefferson store.

Breakfast is an event to remember: Expect juice, yogurt parfait, broiled grapefruit half or fresh fruit, various quiches, meats, side dishes, Texas-shaped biscuits, and coffee cake.

Pride House

409 Broadway Street
Jefferson, TX 75657
Phone: (903) 665-2675; (800) 894-3526

E-MAIL: stay@jeffersontexas.com

INTERNET SITE: www.jeffersontexas.com

INNKEEPER: Sandy Spalding

ROOMS: 11 rooms with private bath, 6 with TV, 1 with VCR; 10 with jacks may have phones on request, 1 room wheelchair accessible; all in 2 homes and cottage

ON THE GROUNDS: Private balcony, porch, wraparound porch on main house with swing, porch swing on Dependency porch

CREDIT CARDS: MasterCard, Visa, Discover

RATES: $-$$$$

HOW TO GET THERE: Enter town on U.S. 50, turn east on Texas 49, which becomes Broadway.

After the state legislature officially recognized this as the first bed and breakfast in Texas, the inn took the registered name of 1st Bed & Breakfast in Texas—Pride House. Because that's a mouthful, we'll just call it Pride House. An 1859 stick Victorian Italianate design, the home was built with stained-glass windows in every room; over thirty remain. Heart-of-pine figures prominently, as do twelve-foot ceilings with original woodwork and hardware on windows and doors.

Certainly one of the state's most beautiful homes, Pride House is also a picture of detail. In each room you'll find lush live plants, a great stock of magazines, huge bath towels and fine bed linens, hair dryers, footed tubs with bubble bath and soaps, original art, antique beds and dressers, and twenty-four-hour access to hot and cold drinks and snacks.

Choose from rooms in the main house and the Dependency, which is an adjacent house on the property. Another option is to book Ruthmary's, which was the home of the founding owner of Pride House. This cottage is all yours, and it has a wonderful, huge porch in the Creole fashion. And be excited about breakfast, which is a legendary buffet of such signature recipes as eggs Galveston, not "eggsactly" Benedict, Texas bluebonnets, strawberry butter, peaches amaretto, banana praline parfait with créme fraiche, and the house coffee.

What's Nearby Jefferson

A town with a distinct southern accent, Jefferson was long ago a riverboat landing and a place thick with the riches of the cotton business. Evidence of this luxurious past is found in the gorgeous old mansions in the historic district and at the wonderful local history museum. Carriage and bayou rides are more than worthwhile, both for the leisure and the historical enlightenment.

Milam Home Bed & Breakfast

412 West Milam Street
Livingston, TX 77351
Phone: (936) 327–1173; (888) 551–1173

E-MAIL: milambb@livingston.net

INTERNET SITE: www.bbhost.com/milamhome

INNKEEPERS: Debra Nelson and Becky Salazar

ROOMS: 4 rooms with private bath

ON THE GROUNDS: Porches, yard with large oaks; double Jacuzzi; wheelchair ramp to porch

CREDIT CARDS: MasterCard, Visa, Discover

RATES: $$–$$$

HOW TO GET THERE: Enter town on U.S. Business 59, which becomes Washington Street. Turn west on Milam Street.

This solid cedar home is thought to have been built around 1890 in the old dog-run style. The earliest history is fuzzy, but it is known that Van Buren "Bunk" Watts bought the house in 1923. Designated a historic landmark by the Polk County Heritage Society, the remarkable house has been completely restored from top to bottom.

You'll find original hardwood floors and wallpapered ceilings, in the period style, as well as exquisite feather-mattress toppers and feather comforters and bedding that were designed and made by your host, Debra. The parlor, where you'll find a TV is a common area for guests. There's the foyer, where a phone is located.

Debra's other specialty is that of hosting spa weekends. During this lavishly planned retreat, you'll get a paraffin wax foot treatment and a round of massages: foot massage, Aveda facial massage, scalp massage, hand massage, a full-body massage, and a therapeutic neck and shoulder massage. To replenish you two three-course candlelight dinners and elaborate breakfast buffets. One of the licensed massage therapists also works as chef, bringing a decade of experience working as both at a Colorado guest ranch.

Breakfasts consist of three meats, eggs, potatoes or grits, muffins or biscuits, with an appetizer of fresh fruits.

What's Nearby Livingston

Just to the southwest is Sam Houston National Forest, containing 27 miles of the 140-mile Lone Star Hiking Trail. East of the forest, Lake Livingston offers 452 miles of woodsy shoreline and every sort of water recreation. Directly east of the lake, find the Alabama and Coushatta Indian Reservation, home to two Native American tribes who have called these woods home for 150 years. You can observe tribal dances and custom craft work and take a miniature train ride through the village before visiting the museum, gift store, and restaurant.

Another Recommended B&B Nearby

Magnolia House, a nuns' residence in the 1930s and 1940s, with five bedrooms and two private baths, verandah, and pool; 602 Milam Street, Liberty, TX 77575; telephone: (936) 334-0188; Internet site: magnoliahouse@yahoo.com.

Heart's Hill B&B & Tour Home

512 East Austin Street
Marshall, TX 75670
Phone: (903) 935-6628; (888) 797-7685

E-MAIL: heartshill@interwork.net
INTERNET SITE: www.heartshill.com
INNKEEPERS: Richard and Linda Spruill
ROOMS: 4 rooms with private bath
ON THE GROUNDS: Verandah, garden, lily pond
CREDIT CARDS: None accepted
RATES: $$ (corporate rates available)
HOW TO GET THERE: Drive into Marshall on U.S. 59; turn left (west) onto Houston Street, then right (north) onto Garrett Street, then left (west) onto Austin Street.

A 1900 home, this pretty Queen Anne was built by a doctor who was a prominent citizen and practicing physician until 1941. There's a lovely wraparound verandah, where you'll be tempted to just sit for hours while the world passes by, and plenty of exterior, gingerbread detail. Inside there are six fireplaces and loads of original woodwork, much of which is cypress.

Your hosts pay particular attention to detail and want to be known for customer service. In fact they liken their home unto a five-star hotel that just happens to be inside a beautiful, century-old home. Bring a good book, your journal, or note paper to catch up on your letter writing. There's an elegance and peacefulness here that make you relaxed and reflective. And in the morning, enjoy a large, elegant breakfast.

What's Nearby Marshall

The Harrison County Seat has a thick Southern heritage, filled with a history of plantations and Civil War events, recalled in some detail on 150 historical markers on homes and buildings. The arts have their place, too, as evidenced by a museum that showcases the work of French impressionist Leo Michelson, and by the artisans at work at Marshall Pottery, the giant workshop and retail center. Take time to examine the ornate old county courthouse, which is covered at Christmas by four million tiny white lights. And when you're ready for a pure sensory treat, head out to Caddo Lake for an otherworldly experience of primeval beauty.

Pine Creek Lodge

Pine Creek Road at Farm Road 2782
Nacogdoches, TX 75961
Phone: (409) 560-6282; (888) 714-1414

INTERNET SITE: www.pinecreeklodge.com

INNKEEPERS: Michael Pitts and family

ROOMS: 17 rooms with private bath, TV/VCR, phone, refrigerators; some in rustic cabins

ON THE GROUNDS: Conference hall; hot tub, decks, hammocks, swings, rockers; nature trails, fishing pond

CREDIT CARDS: MasterCard, Visa

RATES: $$–$$$

HOW TO GET THERE: From U.S. 59 northbound in Nacogdoches, take Loop 224 west to Farm Road 225. Continue on FR 225 west to Farm Road 2782 (watch for Alazan Country Store). Turn left (south) on FR 2782 and watch for Pine Creek Lodge signs about 1.7 miles south.

The Pitts family decided just a few years ago to turn their generations-old family farm into a retreat—and what a retreat it's become. On the wooded and hilly spread of 140 acres a few minutes west of Nacogdoches and near Lake Nacogdoches, this haven is ideal for people who need to commune with nature. The native decor includes dozens of bird species, wild turkey, deer, and raccoon, which you can spot on hikes in the woods or maybe between naps in a hammock.

The rustic cabins scattered around are simple but certainly comfortable. Inside each you'll find king beds of handhewn wood, as well as a couch, chairs, and coffee table in your sitting area. A small refrigerator is in the bath area, and some cabins have private decks, where you'll be tempted to enjoy your leisure reading or writing letters.

Breakfast is served in a large, common dining room in the main building. The buffet typically includes scrambled eggs and bacon, pancakes, cold cereal, yogurt, and fruit. Call ahead if you'd like to book a steak dinner during your stay, and note that the hosts ask guests not to bring alcohol.

What's Nearby Nacogdoches

Known as Texas's oldest town, "Nac" is packed with history. State legends such as Sam Houston, Davy Crockett, and Thomas J. Rusk were a few of the leaders who convened here to chart their fateful quest for Texas's independence from Mexico. Look for details on three attempts to create an independent republic in exhibits at the Old Stone Fort on the Stephen F. Austin State University campus. Other essential history lessons are found at the Sterne-Hoya House, where Sam Houston was baptized; at the beautiful Oak Grove Cemetery, where four signers of the Texas Declaration of Independence are buried; and at Millard's Crossing, a reconstructed pioneer village with authentic structures from this area.

Carson House Inn & Grille and Mrs. B's Cottage

302 Mount Pleasant Street
Pittsburg, TX 75686
Phone: (903) 856–2468;
(888) 302–1878

E-MAIL: carsonig@1starnet.com

INNKEEPERS: Eileen and Clark Jesmore

ROOMS: 6 rooms in main house, plus 2-bedroom cottage, with private bath, TV, telephone, modem capabilities

ON THE GROUNDS: Hot tubs, garden, lily/fish pond; restaurant

CREDIT CARDS: None accepted

RATES: $–$$

HOW TO GET THERE: From Dallas drive I–30 east to exit 160; take Texas 271 south to Loop 238 (Mount Pleasant Street). Drive south 1 mile to inn.

The multigabled inn was built in 1878 and is considered the oldest occupied home in the city. Completely restored in 1991, the interior features a stunning display of curly pine, a rare and exquisitely beautiful wood, that if laid end to end would stretch approximately 1 mile in length. The inn is filled with a combination of antiques and Victorian reproduction pieces appropriate to the period in which it was built.

What makes this inn special is the attention to detail you find in the room decor, as well as that of its the friendly staff. You'll get a lot of privacy, whether you're in one of the queen or king rooms or in the delightful, two-bedroom cottage. You might not find better food in town than the New American Cuisine served at the inn's restaurant, which serves day and night. In the morning you'll be fed a meal cooked to order, which is included with your stay.

What's Nearby Pittsburg

The Camp County Seat is home to a Spring Chick Festival, because the giant poultry producer Pilgrims Pride is based in this town near Lake Daingerfield. Folks like to make a stop in town to eat spicy sausages called Pittsburg hot links at a restaurant called—no surprises here— Pittsburg Hot Links Restaurant. In the sweet little downtown, you'll find antique shops to explore.

Mansion on Main Bed & Breakfast

802 Main Street
Texarkana, TX 75501
Phone: (903) 792-1835

E-MAIL: mansiononmain@aol.com

INTERNET SITE: www.bbonline.com/tx/mansion/

INNKEEPER: Laura Gentry

ROOMS: 5 rooms with private bath, TV, telephone, dataport

ON THE GROUNDS: Enormous verandah, garden; two common rooms, library

CREDIT CARDS: MasterCard, Visa, American Express

RATES: $-$$

HOW TO GET THERE: From Dallas take I-30, turning right (south) onto Stateline Avenue in Texarkana. Follow Stateline to U.S. 67/59 and turn right. Go 3 blocks on U.S. 67/59 to Main Street and turn right.

This house, built in 1895, was a Victorian design that took on neoclassical style when a creative owner added twenty-two-foot-tall columns that were salvaged from the 1904 World's Fair in St. Louis to form an extraordinary 2,500-square-foot verandah. Owned today by Tom and Peggy Taylor, Dallasites who also own the very popular McKay House Bed & Breakfast in nearby Jefferson, the Mansion on Main would be a remarkable B&B in any town.

The Mansion appeals to two kinds of travelers, the romantic escapists who need down time and solitude, and the business traveler who wants something more comfortable and luxurious than a motel. Either way, you'll get a kick out of coming back to the inn after a day of working or shopping to find cookies and coffee waiting for you.

Like its sister inn, the McKay House, the Mansion serves an impressive, filling breakfast of fruit and yogurt, egg-and-meat casserole, pastries and breads, and a selection of coffees, teas, and juices.

What's Nearby Texarkana

The town that dubs itself "Twice as Nice" is distinguished by resting partially in Arkansas and otherwise in Texas; Texarkana has a post office and bistate justice center that serve two cities, two counties, and two states. Downtown also features the Scott Joplin mural, honoring the town son whose storied career counts the writing of music made famous by the film *The Sting* and other musical compositions that earned a Pulitzer Prize; the exquisitely restore, neo-Renaissance Perot Theatre; and the Texarkana Historical Society Museum.

Rosevine Inn Bed & Breakfast

415 South Vine Avenue
Tyler, TX 75702
Phone: (903) 592-2221

E-MAIL: rosevine@iamerica.net

INTERNET SITES:

www.bedandbreakfast.com;
www.rosevine.com

INNKEEPERS: Bert and
Rebecca Powell

ROOMS: 4 guest rooms in
main house; separate
cottage with suite, private
kitchen; all rooms with
private bath, 3 with TV, phone

ON THE GROUNDS: Courtyard, hot tub

CREDIT CARDS: MasterCard, Visa, American Express, Discover

RATES: $–$$$

HOW TO GET THERE: From Dallas take I-20 east to U.S. 69 south; continue until Loop 323, which you will take west to Front Street/Texas 31. Go left (east) past Tyler Rose Gardens and continue to Vine Avenue.

This two-story, redbrick house with a white picket fence seems to be straight out of a modern fairy tale. Built on the site of an old English Tudor home that burned mysteriously in 1969, the Rosevine is an abundantly comfortable getaway. In the main house you'll choose from four guest rooms—such as the Azalea Room, with its double bed and daybed; and the Rose Room, with its antique oak bed and stained-glass window—or you might want the separate cottage, housing the Sherlock Holmes Suite, with a bedroom, living room, dining room, kitchen, and private telephone.

Guests are encourage to enjoy the hot tub, found on the side yard, as well as the fountain in the courtyard and the outdoor fireplace, also found there, which is especially appealing on cooler evenings. A common area shared by guests is the upstairs library, which has a TV, telephone, and a game room. In the mornings you'll be pampered by a breakfast of omelettes, quiche or frittata, as well as fresh breads, fruits, and juices.

What's Nearby Tyler

Pine trees and oil derricks take a back seat in this Smith County Seat to the lovely rose because Tyler's the Rose Capital of America. The world's largest municipal rose garden is the town centerpiece; it produces some 500 varieties of roses on its 38,000 rose bushes. The Rose Museum tells a fragrant agriculture story, while the nearby Caldwell Zoo offers thirty-five pretty acres of animal watching. You can explore Tyler's rich history at the Carnegie History Center and at the Goodman-LeGrand Home or escape to nearby Tyler State Park for fishing, hiking, and swimming.

Another Recommended B&B in Tyler

Charnwood Hill, the grand, former estate of Texas oil giant H. L. Hunt, with seven bedrooms and private baths, gorgeous gardens, and library; 223 East Charnwood Street, Tyler, TX 75701; telephone: (903) 397-3980 or (877) 597-3980.

Oaklea Mansion

407 South Main Street
Winnsboro, TX 75494
Phone: (903) 342-6051

E-MAIL: oaklea@bluebonnet.net

INTERNET SITE: www.bluebonnet.net/oaklea

INNKEEPER: Norma Lea Wilkinson

ROOMS: 12 rooms—including suites—with private bath, 8 with TV, telephone, dataport

ON THE GROUNDS: Spa house with hot tub/Jacuzzi; koi ponds, stone patios, outdoor fireplace, dove cotes, rabbit hutches, miniature pony, miniature beagle, antique rose gardens; some wheelchair accessibility

CREDIT CARDS: MasterCard, Visa, American Express, Discover

RATES: $$-$$$$

HOW TO GET THERE: Drive into town on Texas 37, which becomes Main Street; watch for home in middle of town.

Subtitled "Mansion and Manor House," this bed-and-breakfast inn is the picture of elegance and utter beauty. Built in 1903 by M. D. Carlock, an attorney, the twenty-two-room, Greek Revival home bears a Texas historical marker and contains such prized items as antebellum furnishings brought with the Carlocks to Texas. Dozens of elements are notable, from the fabulous curly pine staircase, 1873 Steinway grand piano, and Waterford crystal to stunning chandeliers, stained-glass windows, antique rugs, and original Dalhart Windberg artwork.

Among third-floor rooms is the O'Hare, with a queen iron bed and handpainted furniture. Second-floor rooms include the Angel Suite, with a balcony, raised Jacuzzi tub, and king brass bed; and the Miss Ima Hogg Suite, with 1820s bedroom furniture and a huge footed tub.

Prepare yourself for a full, formal breakfast that includes a fruit dish, baked omelettes, biscuits, muffins, juice, coffee, and tea. Ask ahead of time about booking a massage, manicure, pedicure, or candlelight dinner, any of which can be enjoyed on the premises.

What's Nearby Winnsboro

Fall is prime time for visiting this pretty hamlet in Wood County. The Autumn Trails Festival, held every weekend in October, offers an antique car show, homes tour, dominoes tournament, rodeo, chili cook-off, parade, queen's coronation, and much more. The town is convenient to both Lake Winnsboro and Lake O' the Pines, both pretty places to visit all year long.

Another Recommended B&B in Winnsboro

Thee Hubbell House Bed & Breakfast, with eleven rooms and private baths, hot tub, and hearty, plantation-style breakfast; 307 West Elm Street, Winnsboro, TX 75494; telephone: (903) 342-5629 or (800) 227-0639; e-mail: hubbellhouse@bluebonnet.net.

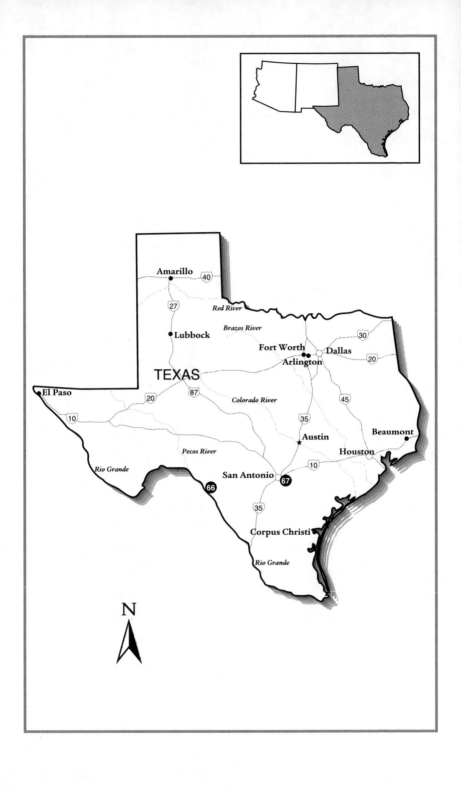

Texas: South Texas Plains

Numbers on map refer to towns numbered below.

The 1890 House Bed and Breakfast Inn

609 Griner Street
Del Rio, TX 78840
Phone: (830) 775-8061; (800) 282-1360

E-MAIL: info@1890house.com
INTERNET SITE: www.1890house.com
INNKEEPERS: Alberto and Laura Galvan
ROOMS: 5 rooms, including 2 suites, with private baths and TV
ON THE GROUNDS: Verandah, garden, courtyard, formal dining room
CREDIT CARDS: MasterCard, Visa, Discover
RATES: $$-$$$
HOW TO GET THERE: Drive into Del Rio via U.S. 90 and turn south on South Avenue F; turn right on Garfield, then right on Griner.

You might feel as though you've arrived in the Old South rather than in South Texas when you see this turn-of-the-century beauty. Built around 1890 by the Price-Woods family, who pioneered the local lumber and banking businesses, the home is a mixture of Victorian, neoclassical, and colonial revival styles, with a strong pull of antebellum plantation. Listed in the local guide to historic Del Rio, the home was thoroughly restored by Alberto and Laura Galvan in 1995 and turned into a bed and breakfast in 1996.

Outside there's a private courtyard and a garden next to a clear stream that will remind you of the definition of serenity. Inside find the foyer, parlor, dining room, and all guest rooms filled with appropriate artwork and period antiques. Beautifully furnished and decorated with original artwork and period antiques. Your guest room choices include the Victorian Suite, with its king-size, four-poster bed, fireplace, love seat, and Jacuzzi tub; the Safari Suite, with a brass queen bed and Jacuzzi; and the Floridian, with twin beds.

In the morning you'll be treated to a big, freshly prepared breakfast, which is served on china, with crystal and silver, and accompanied by candlelight and music in the formal dining room. Laura and Alberto offer a most capable concierge service, too. They'll help you plan trips to the Judge Roy Bean Center in nearby Langtry, as well as to Ciudad Acuna, across the Rio Grande. Even more helpful is their command of Spanish, Italian, and Portuguese.

A Genuine Oasis

Informally called Lake Amistad, the giant, supremely blue body of water just west of Del Rio officially known as Amistad International Reservoir was created jointly by the United States and Mexico. Given a name that means "friendship," the 65,000-acre lake is, of course, an impoundment of the Rio Grande, just below its meeting point with Devil's River. This reservoir extends some 75 miles up the Rio Grande and about 15 miles up the Devil's River. Fishing and boating are extremely popular with folks from both countries—and you'll see why once you view the lake: The shimmering blue-green of its surface can be seen from miles away, glistening like a mammoth aquamarine stone in the midst of the craggy, dusty desert.

Villa del Rio

123 Hudson Drive
Del Rio, TX 78840
Phone: (830) 768-1100; (800) 995-1887

INTERNET SITE: www.villadelrio.com

INNKEEPER: Jay Johnson

ROOMS: 3 rooms, 2 sharing private bath, and 1 suite

ON THE GROUNDS: Living room, dining room, courtyard, yard

CREDIT CARDS: MasterCard, Visa, American Express

RATES: $$-$$$$

HOW TO GET THERE: Drive into Del Rio via U.S. 90 and turn south on South Avenue F; turn right on Garfield, then left on Pecan Street. Continue south on Pecan Street, which becomes Hudson Drive.

Formerly La Mansion del Rio, the spectacular home is framed by twenty-two enormous pecan trees and fifteen stately, century-old palms on two acres of verdant tropical lands within a historic neighborhood. Built around 1887, the home first belonged to a New York businessman named James H. Mason, who also developed a spring on the property for mineral baths and medicinal treatments. James J. Foster bought the home in 1905 and, making major additions to the house, lived there until the early 1960s. Another owner renovated the mansion in 1972, making it ideal for the inn it is today.

Among the eye-popping elements you'll find are hand-painted tiles in the foyer fireplace, a living room that's the size of a ballroom and that's fit-ted with iron gates, and such Mediterranean elements as archways and cypress-beam ceilings. Rooms to consider include the Yellow Rose of Texas, which shares a bath with the Southern Comfort; the Peacock Suite, with has its own sunporch; and the Adobe Cottage, a place of utter privacy.

The Johnsons not only serve a large breakfast, but also offer evening tea, as well. Now that's luxurious.

What's Nearby Del Rio

The seat of Val Verde County lies atop the refreshing babble of San Felipe Springs, which gushes some ninety million gallons of sparkling water daily. Nicknamed "Queen of the Rio Grande," Del Rio's center-piece is an elaborately designed Val Verde County Courthouse, built in 1887, but it's oldest attraction may well be the state's first winery. Named—you guessed it—Val Verde Winery, the wine producer was estab-lished in 1883 by Italian immigrant Frank Qualia, whose descendants continue to offer tours of the vineyards and production facilities, as well as tastings. Just across the Rio Grande from Del Rio, the Mexico town of Ciudad Acuna is a shopper's paradise, thanks to the supply of bas-kets, pottery, leather goods, silver jewelry, glassware, and tile, and the home decor shops lining Avenida Hidalgo.

A Beckmann Inn and Carriage House Bed and Breakfast

222 East Guenther Street
San Antonio, TX 78204
Phone: (210) 229–1449; (800)
945–1449

E-MAIL:
beckinn@swbell.net
INTERNET SITE:www.beck
manninn.com

INNKEEPERS: Betty Jo and
Don Schwartz

ROOMS: 5 rooms in main house and carriage house with private bath, TV, telephone, refrigerator

ON THE GROUNDS: Large wraparound porch, patios, sunporch, carriage house balcony, landscaped gardens

CREDIT CARDS: MasterCard, Visa, American Express, Discover, Diners Club

RATES: $$–$$$

HOW TO GET THERE: Drive into San Antonio via I-10 or I-35, which merge downtown, or via I-37. Exit at Durango and head downtown, turning right (south) on St. Mary's Street. From St. Mary's turn right on King William Street and left on East Guenther.

After a busy day on the River Walk, travelers like to spend some hang time on a lovely sunporch like the one at the lovely Beckmann Inn. One of the stunning homes now functioning as a B&B in the exquisite King William Historic District, the Beckmann is an inn whose hosts are committed to helping guests get the most out of the San Antonio experience by assisting with museum, historic site, shopping, and dining plans.

Albert Beckmann built the home in 1886 for his bride Marie Dorothea of the Guenther flour mill family on the mill grounds. Additions since then have included a 1913 expansion that moved the front porch from Madison to Guenther Streets. This gave the home prestige, as a notorious brothel on Madison cast a shadow on other addresses on that street.

You can't help but be impressed with the home, starting with the rare burl pine front door; a wood mosaic entry floor, which was imported from Paris; fourteen-foot ceilings; arched pocket doors; and tall windows with beveled-glass panels. Guest rooms in the main house and in the carriage house feature queen-size, ornately carved Victorian beds and lavish decor suiting the period.

In the morning Betty Jo and Don will stuff you with a gourmet breakfast that's capped with dessert. Don likes to tell guests, "Our breakfast will take you to nachos and margaritas in the afternoon, and then on to dinner." You've been warned.

Brackenridge House

230 Madison Street
San Antonio, TX 78204
Phone: (210) 271-3442; (800) 221-1412

E-MAIL: benniesueb@aol.com

INTERNET SITE: www.brackenridgehouse.com

INNKEEPERS: Bennie and Sue Blansett

ROOMS: 6 rooms with private bath, TV, telephone, dataport; including the Barn, an adjacent carriage house with kitchen, patio, porch, and private bath

ON THE GROUNDS: Verandah, hot tub

CREDIT CARDS: MasterCard, Visa, Discover, Diners Club

RATES: $$–$$$$

HOW TO GET THERE: Drive into San Antonio via I-10 or I-35, which merge downtown, or via I-37. Exit at Durango and head downtown, turning right (south) on St. Mary's Street. From St. Mary's turn right on Madison. Look for number 203.

Built in 1901 by town leader John Brackenridge, this Greek Revival mansion was being used as "shotgun" apartments until a resident named Carolyn Cole restored the beautiful landmark in 1986. Her work earned a San Antonio Conservation Society Award. Innkeepers Bennie and Sue live on site; they've been in San Antonio since the 1968 World's Fair and have grown deep roots in the community.

The inn is in easy walking distance of the River Walk, but you may be tempted to just hang out on the home's first- or second-story verandah. If you've booked one of the suites, you may never leave the room at all. On the first floor are Monica's Suite, done in shades of peach and jade, with a queen bed, antique pieces, and an adjoining kitchenette and sitting room; and Benet's Room, splashed in blue and mauve with an Eastlake bed and love seat, kitchenette, and sitting room, too. On the second floor find the Bride's Room, with a king bed, Victorian love seat, and private verandah overlooking the gardens. If you're traveling with friends or children, check out the Barn, a carriage house a few doors away. It has a bedroom and a loft, living room, dining area, kitchen, TVs, porch swing, gated arbor, patio, and one bath.

Mornings bring gastronomic pleasures: Earlier risers have coffee and pastries in the parlor at 8:00 A.M., then a large, family-style breakfast is served in courses in the dining room at 9:00. You'll probably want that walk by the river after all.

Seeing Double on the Border

About 150 miles due south of San Antonio, I-35 reaches its southern-most terminus in the city of Laredo. The seat of Webb County, Laredo is home to a surprisingly big, ten-day fiesta in February that celebrates George Washington's birthday. Since 1898 the town of 180,000 has thrown a shindig to honor Washington—the first Western Hemisphere leader to free a New World country from European authority. Celebrating right alongside is the sister city of Nuevo Laredo, whose residents join in the pageantry, rodeos, fireworks, cook-offs, and fun. Downtown Laredo, which sits on the Rio Grande, has a fine little museum that tells the story of the Republic of the Rio Grande, which lasted from 1839 till 1841. In Nuevo Laredo market shopping and great Mexican food are the draws.

Columns on Alamo

1037 South Alamo Street
San Antonio, TX 78210
Phone: (210) 271-3245; (800) 233-3364

INTERNET SITE: www.bbonline.com/tx/columns

INNKEEPERS: Art and Ellenor Link

ROOMS: Main house and guesthouse with 9 rooms with private baths, TV, telephone; adjacent Rock House Cottage with 2 separate units with kitchen, TV, telephone

ON THE GROUNDS: Porches, balconies, libraries

CREDIT CARDS: MasterCard, Visa, American Express

RATES: $$-$$$$

HOW TO GET THERE: Drive into San Antonio via I-10 or I-35, which merge downtown, or via I-37. Exit at Durango and head downtown, turning right (south) on St. Mary's Street. From St. Mary's turn right on South Alamo Street.

This elegant inn consists of two giant homes next door to one another. The main house is an 1892 Greek Revival home; the 1901 home a few feet north is almost a replica. Behind the stately exterior are rooms that have been completely outfitted with period antiques and reproductions without being overdone; in other words, it's not too frilly for men to feel comfortable.

The main house features such choices as a room with a queen Victorian renaissance bed, a shower bath and a walk-through window to a wide verandah. The guesthouse has such pretty selections as a big room with a sitting area, a French king bed, antique armoire and a fainting couch, fireplace, and Jacuzzi tub. Newest to this inn is the very private Rock House Cottage, a limestone house built in 1881. Set in a grove of trees overlooking a garden, this dwelling gets cowboy-style treatment, decorated with pine furniture and old cowboy photos. Inside the cottage are two separate units, each with a queen bed. One has a tub for two, a fully outfitted kitchen, large breakfast area, and TV and telephone; the other has a full bath, enclosed sunporch, minifridge, and coffeemaker.

Guests in the cottage will have a big Continental breakfast basket delivered each morning. Guests in the two large houses eat in formal dining rooms, where big spreads of juices, fruits, yogurts, eggs, meats, and breads are served. Specialties include quiche and poached pears.

Inn on the River

129 Woodward Place
San Antonio, TX 78204
Phone: (210) 225-6333; (800) 730-0019

E-MAIL: adz@swbell.net

INTERNET SITE: www.bbonline/tx/ontheriver/

INNKEEPER: Dr. A. D. Zucht III

ROOMS: 12 rooms with private bath, includes penthouse and cottage

ON THE GROUNDS: Lawns and gardens, wraparound porches, balconies, riverside setting

CREDIT CARDS: MasterCard, Visa, American Express, Discover

RATES: $$-$$$

HOW TO GET THERE: Drive into San Antonio via I–10 or I–35, which merge downtown, or via I–37. Exit at Durango and head east toward downtown; turn left on Dwyer and right on Woodward.

Right on the bank of the San Antonio River, this three-story inn occupies a 1916 home that features plenty of its original appeal. The cupolas and wraparound porches on the outside speak of romantic time, and as soon as you're inside, you can't help but be impressed by the soaring ceilings and original pine floors. Some of the furnishings and decor are far more contemporary, but that shouldn't bother anyone who doesn't have strict aesthetic requirements.

Rooms in the main house include queen beds, private showers, cable TV, phone, and attached sunrooms. The penthouse has a room with a king bed, private bath with a Jacuzzi, a balcony over the River Walk, refrigerator, coffeemaker, cable TV, and phone. Other rooms have a bath with a built-in spa and a balcony overlooking the River Walk, too. Finally, there's a cottage room, with a king bed, bath with Jacuzzi, porch with a River Walk view, TV, and phone.

Wake up to a power breakfast, a full spread that can be enjoyed in the dining room or on your own porch or balcony. Adventure travelers will want to ask your host, Dr. Zucht, for a booking on his hot-air balloon.

Noble Inns

107 Madison Street
San Antonio, TX 78204
Phone: (210) 225-4045; (800) 221-4045

E-MAIL: nobleinns@aol.com

INTERNET SITES: www.nobleinns.com; www.bbonline.com/tx/noble/

INNKEEPERS: Don and Liesl Noble

ROOMS: 9 rooms and suites in two houses with private bath, TV, phone, dataport; Pancoast Carriage House includes 3 suites

ON THE GROUNDS: Fireplaces, pool and heated spa, gardens

CREDIT CARDS: MasterCard, Visa, American Express, Discover

RATES: $$$-$$$$

HOW TO GET THERE: Drive into San Antonio via I-10 or I-35, which merge downtown, or via I-37. Exit at Durango and head east toward downtown, turning right (south) on St. Mary's Street. From St. Mary's turn right on Madison.

Two houses make up this B&B, which explains why the name is plural. First there's the Jackson House, an 1894 home built by Moses Jackson, whose graceful parlor, library, and giant windows offer a beautiful setting. Outside, carefully landscaped gardens with sitting areas will entice you to read a book of poetry or write someone a love letter. There's a conservatory, too, for guests to share, outfitted with a swim-spa and surrounded by stained-glass windows.

Guest rooms in the Jackson House feature queen-size antique beds, two-person Jacuzzi tubs, claw-foot tubs, and lovely views from the second floor.

There's also the Pancoast Carriage House, built in 1886, which offers three beautiful suites for you to consider. The first suite, on the ground floor, opens through French doors onto an enclosed brick patio. Four people can stay in this one, as the living room has a sleeper sofa, in addition to the bedroom.

Owners Don and Liesl are perfect hosts for this area—they represent the fifth and sixth generations of the respective families to live in King William. You can't find more knowledgeable experts on ways to spend your time, nor more thoughtful hosts when it comes to providing luxurious surroundings. Ask ahead if you'd like to be transported to the airport or to appointments in their 1960 Rolls Royce Silver Cloud.

The Ogé Inn Riverwalk

209 Washington Street
San Antonio, TX 78204
Phone: (210) 223-2353; (800) 242-2770

E-MAIL: ogeinn@swbell.net

INTERNET SITE: www.ogeinn.com

INNKEEPERS: Sharrie and Patrick Magatagan

ROOMS: 5 suites and 5 guest rooms with private bath, TV, telephone, dataport

ON THE GROUNDS: Verandahs, library, dining room; one and one-half acres with gazebo of lawns and gardens

CREDIT CARDS: MasterCard, Visa, American Express, Discover, Diners Club

RATES: $$$-$$$$

HOW TO GET THERE: Drive into San Antonio via I-10 or I-35, which merge downtown, or via I-37. Exit at Durango and turn right on Pancoast Street. Watch for intersection of Washington and Pancoast, and find the house at 209 Washington.

Pronounced "Oh-JHAY," the Ogé House is one of the King William District beauties that you'll find listed on both the state and national historic places registers. Widely considered one of the neighborhood's crown jewels, this 1857 Southern antebellum-style plantation house is also one of the city's most luxurious accommodations.

The five suites and five guest rooms are furnished with either a king or queen bed, and most have fireplaces. On each of three flours are lovely verandahs, where you'll want to catch up on reading or journal keeping. Exploration is a worthy option, of course; start with the acre and a half surrounding the house, then wander down to the River Walk, beneath towering cypress and across footbridges to the shopping and dining district.

In eight years of owning and running the Ogé, Sharrie, and Patrick have guided guests to rewarding meals at Rosario's and El Mirador for Mexican fare, La Foccacia for Italian, Blue Star Brew Pub for eclectic meals, and the City Market for gourmet foods and wines to bring back to the inn. In the morning they'll fill you up with an epicurean's feast that starts with fruit and includes a hot entree and breads. If you have special diet needs, just say so. Also in the morning, look for the inn's copies of the *New York Times* and *Wall Street Journal*.

Riverwalk Inn

329 Old Guilbeau Street
San Antonio, TX 78204
Phone: (210) 212-8300; (800) 254-4440

E-MAIL: innkeeper@riverwalkinn.com

INTERNET SITE: www.riverwalkinn.com

INNKEEPERS: Tracy and Jan Hammer

ROOMS: 11 rooms in 5 two-story log buildings with private bath, fireplace, TV, phone with voice mail, refrigerator

ON THE GROUNDS: Balconies, porches, meeting room; business services

CREDIT CARDS: MasterCard, Visa, American Express, Discover

RATES: $$-$$$

HOW TO GET THERE: Drive into San Antonio via I-10 or I-35, which merge downtown, or via I-37. Exit at Durango and head east toward downtown; turn left on Dwyer and right on Old Guilbeau.

If not for Tracy and Jan, these marvelous log cabins would be nothing more than fence posts today. Built in Tennessee around 1840, the five two-story log buildings were rescued from demolition by the Hammers, who relocated and restored them along the River Walk. You can be certain there's nothing else like these lodgings anyplace else in town.

Inside each of the rooms, you'll find braided rugs tossed on the hardwood floors, pencil-post beds graced with quilted canopies, and an assortment of period country pieces. Each of the private baths is a large walk-in shower with a cool flagstone floor.

A breakfast buffet in the main building offers an expanded Continental deal. That means you'll have plenty of cereals, juices, fruit, and breads to choose from, leaving you plenty of room for a Mexican food feast at lunch. Note that some weekends there's a two- or three-night minimum stay.

Royal Swan Bed and Breakfast

236 Madison Street
San Antonio, TX 78204
Phone: (210) 223-3776; (800) 368-3073

E-MAIL: theswan@onr.com

INTERNET SITE: www.royalswan.com

INNKEEPERS: Renee and Sam Martinez

ROOMS: 3 rooms and 1 suite with private bath and TV, telephone, dataport

ON THE GROUNDS: Library, sunroom, verandah

CREDIT CARDS: MasterCard, Visa, American Express, Discover

RATES: $$-$$$

HOW TO GET THERE: Drive into San Antonio via I-10 or I-35, which merge downtown, or via I-37. Exit at Durango and head downtown, turning right (south) on St. Mary's Street. From St. Mary's turn right on Madison.

Look at the carriage stone in front of this graceful home, and you'll see the name of Jabéz Cain, the doctor who built the home in 1892. He couldn't have known how proud he would be of his home's employment over the next century. Converted to apartments during World War II, as many were to accommodate the flood of military wives into San Antonio, the home later slipped into disrepair when families fled to the suburbs in the 1950s and 1960s. After the 1968 World's Fair in San Antonio, development of the River Walk exploded and forward-thinking conservationists began working on restoration of homes in the King William District.

Jabéz Cain's home is one of these. Gradual restoration over twenty-five years returned the home to its grandeur. It became a B&B inn in 1992; Sam and Renee bought it in 1999 and continue its luxurious operation. Striking interior details include crystal chandeliers, a beautiful stained-glass window, original fireplaces, a profusion of loblolly pine in the foyer, and a bridal balcony in front.

Guest rooms include the Crystal, with a carved mahogany bed and crystal chandelier; the Emerald, with a fireplace and claw-foot tub and verandah; the Veranda Suite, with a sitting room; and Garnet, with a fireplace, brass-and-pewter bed, and a private rear deck. When you're ready to explore, the River Walk is just 2 blocks away, and the trolley stop is 1 block away.

Your morning starts with a four-course, homemade breakfast, which Sam and Renee serve either in the sunny morning room or the formal dining room.

A Yellow Rose

229 Madison Street
San Antonio, TX 78204
Phone: (210) 229-9903; (800) 950-9903

E-MAIL: yellowrs@express-news.net

INTERNET SITE: www.ayellowrose.com

INNKEEPERS: Deborah and Justin Walker

ROOMS: 5 rooms in main house and adjacent "Sunday house" with private bath and TV, 2 with Jacuzzi tubs

ON THE GROUNDS: Porches, parlor, gardens

CREDIT CARDS: MasterCard, Visa, American Express

RATES: $$–$$$$

HOW TO GET THERE: Drive into San Antonio via I-10 or I-35, which merge downtown, or via I-37. Exit at Durango and head downtown, turning south on St. Mary's Street. From St. Mary's turn right on Madison.

Another of the magnificent King William Historic District homes, this Queen Anne-style home dates to 1878. Among details inside to note are original pine floors, "bull's-eye" cypress door frames, and a foyer staircase with bird's-eye maple insets. In the adjacent Sunday house, built in 1868, are original maple floors, and beaded walls and ceiling, as well as an original colored-glass window. Perhaps as impressive is the garden work Deborah and Justin have done. In 1998 they won first place in San Antonio Botanical Gardens's Xeriscape Contest and Garden Tour.

You'll love the fabulous front porch on the house, and if you're lucky you've booked one of the two rooms with private entrances and porches. There are cordless phones and a dataport available in the main hallway, and there's a cell phone available for checkout. But why worry about work? Grab one of the conservation society's walking tour brochures and explore this phenomenal neighborhood, or head down to the River Walk or to one of the nearby Mexican restaurants. Deborah and Justin especially like helping guests figure out museum, shopping, and dining adventures. If you're hoping for a good workout, ask for a YMCA guest pass.

Guests help themselves to soft drinks in the refrigerator and sherry in the parlor. Every morning, a lovely, two-course breakfast is served in the dining room. If your business schedule requires such, you can have an early breakfast. Also ask about packages that include massage, flowers, and more.

What's Nearby San Antonio

The Alamo City's as rich in heritage as any place in Texas, thanks to its mixture of Spanish, German, Mexican, and cowboy cultures. Visitors can easily lose a couple of days wandering around downtown historic buildings and exploring the River Walk, which can be romantic or frenzied, depending on the time of day or year. The San Antonio Museum of Art, Hertzberg Circus Museum, and the Buckhorn Saloon & Museum are worthwhile stops, but if you're in a mood to learn more about San Antonio's roots, check out the San Antonio Art & Craft Center, housed within an 1851 Ursuline Academy; the Guenther House, owned by one of the very wealthy flour mill magnates of the nineteenth century; and the exquisite missions, which date from 1720. At the Institute of Texan Cultures, you'll find exhibits focusing on the more than twenty-five ethnic groups comprising Texas. And it's not far from the Alamo, one of the best-known sites on Earth.

Other Recommended B&Bs Nearby

Chabot Reed House Bed and Breakfast, a gorgeous home in the King William Historic District, near Hemisfair Park and the River Walk, with a library, verandahs, beautiful landscaping, five rooms with private baths, TV, and telephone; 403 Madison Street, San Antonio, TX 78204; telephone: (210) 223-8697 or (800) 776-2424; Internet site: www.chabotreedsanantonio.com. *Bonner Garden Bed and Breakfast,* a 1910 two-story copy of an Italian villa, near Brackenridge Park, Alamo Heights, Fort Sam Houston, and San Antonio Country Club, with six rooms and private baths, TV, telephone, library, garden, swimming pool and rooftop patio; 145 East Agarita Avenue, San Antonio, TX 78212; telephone: (210) 733-4222 or (800) 396-4222; Internet site: www.bon nergarden.com.

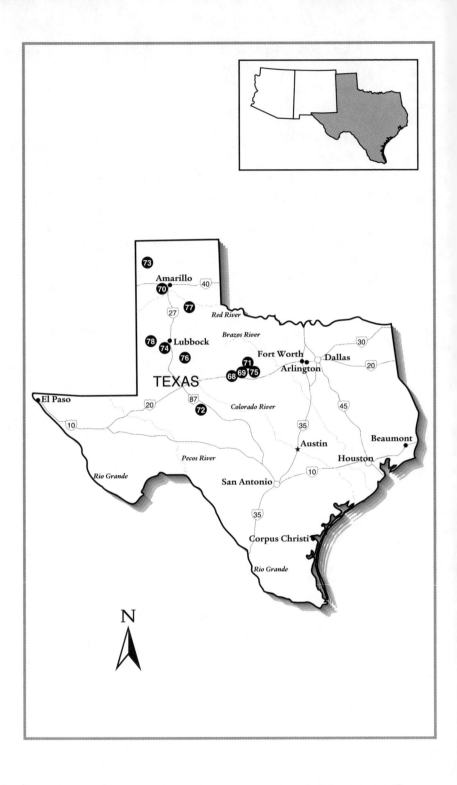

Texas: Panhandle Plains

Numbers on map refer to towns numbered below.

BJ's Prairie House Bed and Breakfast

508 Mulberry Street
Abilene, TX 79601
Phone: (915) 675–5855; (800) 673–5855
E-mail: bfender@earthlink.net

INNKEEPERS: BJ and Bob Fender

ROOMS: 4 rooms with telephone, 2 with private bath, 1 with TV

ON THE GROUNDS: Living room, dining room, large verandah; exercise treadmill

CREDIT CARDS: MasterCard, Visa, American Express, Discover

RATES: $ (weekly and monthly rates also available)

HOW TO GET THERE: From Dallas-Fort Worth drive 150 miles west on I-20. From I–20 turn south on Texas 83, then right on Texas 355, which becomes South First Street. Follow South First Street to Grape Street, then turn left onto North Fifth Street. From there you will make a right onto Mulberry Street.

Built in 1902, this spacious corner house was completely enlarged and remodeled in 1920 in the style of a Frank Lloyd Wright Prairie home. Another renovation took place in 1990. Guests share the comfortable living room, a great place to read or watch movies, as well as the rambling porch. Decor of interest includes antiques and a collection of blue-and-white china.

Rooms to note include Love, the largest, furnished with antique maple pieces and a brass king bed and a private bath; and Peace, with an antique walnut suite and a private bath with a long claw-foot tub. BJ and Bob will let you guess which rooms hosted Clint Eastwood and June Lockhart on their travels to Abilene.

Sit down to breakfast in the dining room, where you'll enjoy a fresh fruit bowl, hot pastries, a choice of five cereals, eggs, yogurt, toast or hot biscuits, coffee, hot tea, and juice.

What's Nearby Abilene

Settlers came around 1876 but the railroad's arrival in 1881 put this town, built on ranching and petroleum, on the map. Downtown you'll find the magnificent museum complex in the renovated Grace Hotel, which faces the elevated train tracks; and a few blocks away, the Paramount Theatre, restored to 1930s glory, is a showplace and arts center, with hand-blown glass chandeliers and a Pueblo-Deco interior. Near downtown are craftspeople who will custom make your saddle and boots, too. You'll find sensational military aircraft displays at Dyess Air Force Base.

Foreman's Cottage

Farm Road 601
Albany, TX 76430
Phone: (915) 762-3576

INNKEEPER: Carolyn Musselman

ROOMS: 3 rooms, 1 with private bath

ON THE GROUNDS: Living room, kitchen, dining area; picnic table, cattle, and horses

CREDIT CARDS: None accepted

RATES: $

HOW TO GET THERE: Drive west from Fort Worth via I-20, north on Texas 6, then east on Farm Road 601.

Surrounded by rugged ranchland about ten minutes from Albany's historic square, this 1950s cottage keeps company with hundreds of ancient, gnarled trees; blooming cactus; and a windmill. There are also the hefty Hereford cattle and gorgeous cutting horses that Carolyn Musselman raises. The little yellow house, trimmed in green on the outside, is cute and cozy inside.

The living area, shared by guests, is hung with fabulous old black-and-white photos that Carolyn shot at a roundup at the Matador Ranch nearly thirty years ago. There's a sleeper sofa in the living room, as well as a TV but no phone. Your cellular phone might work out here, but who would you want to call when you're having such a peaceful escape?

Decor includes an arrowhead collection, quilts, paintings, Indian rugs, and lots of period antiques. A great place to take a small group of friends or family for a long weekend, the cottage has the Pioneer's Room, with a king bed and full bath; and Frenchie's Room, with a double bed and a bath shared with Indian Joe's Room, containing twin beds. Guests share the fully equipped kitchen, which Carolyn stocks with pastries, juices, cereal, coffee, and tea for breakfast.

Galbraith House

1710 South Polk Street
Amarillo, TX 79102
Phone: (806) 374–0237

E-MAIL: reservations@galbraith-house.com

INTERNET SITE: www.galbraith-house.com

INNKEEPER: Dr. Panpit Pansuwana Klug

ROOMS: 4 rooms with private baths

ON THE GROUNDS: Library, living room, TV/sunroom, and outdoor gazebo with hot tub

CREDIT CARDS: MasterCard, Visa

RATES: $$

HOW TO GET THERE: Follow I–40 into Amarillo and exit Washington Street, following it north to 17th Street. Turn right (east) to South Polk Street, which you follow south.

Built in 1912 by George Parr for Kate Galbraith and H. W. Galbraith, an Irish immigrant who founded the Foxworth-Galbraith Lumber Company, this remarkable home was remodeled in 1929 by Guy Carlender to showcase the magnificent interior woodwork. The house changed hands once before it was purchased in 1977 by David and Mary Jane Johnson, who made it into B&B in 1989. Among decor details that mark the Johnson's ownership are opera posters and photographs depicting Mary Jane, an internationally known soprano.

The home became a Registered Texas Historic Landmark on April 21, 1992; it's owned today by Dr. Klug, who is noted for having developed the Bone Marrow Unit at High Plains Baptist Hospital. She has outfitted the library for guests to have use of a computer system, complete with Internet access. The library also contains plenty of books, a fireplace, and soft couches and chairs—a private place to study. You can play chess in the living room, where there's another fireplace and a lovely antique piano. The TV/sunroom is where you can watch movies on video; just outside is the gazebo with its hot tub.

Among guest rooms is the Marie Antoinette, with a queen bed and a garden view; the Puccini, featuring a queen bed, antiques, and a sitting area; and the Emperor, with a king bed and elegant Chinese robes. After a luxurious sleep, you'll be served a full breakfast.

What's Nearby Amarillo

The Old West still lives in Amarillo, a town thick with heritage, colored by explorers such as Coronado and cattle drivers and Texas Rangers like Charles Goodnight. Sitting on the nation's mother road, historic Route 66, it's been the world's leading cattle shipping railhead—some 50,000 head were often here at once—as well as the current home to the world's largest privately owned livestock auction, the American Quarter Horse Association, and the Cadillac Ranch. You can still get a seventy-two-ounce steak free at Big Texan Steak Ranch—provided you eat it and all the trimmings within one hour.

Other Recommended B&Bs Nearby

Parkview House Bed & Breakfast, a 1908 Victorian home with four rooms with private baths; 1311 South Jefferson Street, Amarillo, TX 79101; telephone: (806) 373-9464. *Hudspeth House,* a 1909 home that was once a boarding house where Georgia O'Keeffe took some of her meals while teaching at the local college; eight rooms with private baths; 1905 4th Avenue, Canyon, TX 79015; telephone: (806) 655-9800.

Keeping Room

900 West Walker Street
Breckenridge, TX 76024
Phone: (254) 559-8368

INNKEEPER: LaVerle Tennison

ROOMS: 4 rooms with TV, 2 with private bath; includes suite with private balcony

ON THE GROUNDS: Living room with TV, piano, game table; dining room and breakfast room

CREDIT CARDS: MasterCard, Visa

RATES: $

HOW TO GET THERE: Drive west from Fort Worth via U.S. 180.

uilt in 1929, this roomy home was a wreck when LaVerle bought it in 1996. After eighteen months of utter renovation—which included restoring the original wood floors and rewiring and replumbing the entire home—she opened it as a B&B. She lives in one half of the upstairs, while the other half is the Bluebonnet Suite, with its iron bed, daybed, sitting room with sofa and chair, and a private balcony overlooking the main street through town.

Other rooms include the Goodwin Room, spacious and quiet with its own porch. This room, she says, is popular with business travelers and honeymooners. "Our rates are competitive with the motels', but our place is a lot more comfortable."

LaVerle has a giant kitchen in which to make her hearty breakfasts for guests. You'll dine either in the large, formal dining room or in the cozier breakfast room for two—on eggs, country sausage, biscuits.

What's Nearby Breckenridge

The seat of Stephens County is so laid-back, you can sip a cappuccino at a coffee bar and watch tumbleweeds hopping along the bricked section of U.S. 180 that passes through the middle of town. There's a historical museum inside the old First National Bank building and a 750-piece doll collection at the local fine arts center. Stop and have a look at the wonderful sandstone arch leftover from the 1883 county courthouse, seen on the lawn of the "new" courthouse, built in 1920.

Hummer House

Ranch Road 2084
P.O. Box 555
Christoval, TX 76935
Phone: (915) 255-2254
Fax: (915) 255-2463

INTERNET SITE: www.hummerhouse-texasgems.com

INNKEEPERS: Dan and Joann Brown

ROOMS: 2 rooms in cottage with private bath, kitchen, wheelchair accessibility, TV, telephone

ON THE GROUNDS: Full kitchen, living room, large porch; observation room for viewing hundreds of feeding hummingbirds

CREDIT CARDS: None accepted

RATES: $$

HOW TO GET THERE: From San Angelo drive south on U.S. 277 to Loop 110, which you will follow to Ranch Road 2084. From there it's 1.8 miles to the Brown's ranch.

This private cottage was built in 1996 with an exterior of native stone and an interior that you'll have all to yourselves. The comfortable guest house consists of two bedrooms, two baths, full kitchen, living room with queen-size sleeper sofa and a large porch for kicking back and watching the wildlife.

And what wildlife: This ranch happens to lie in the state's largest feeding and nesting site for black-chinned hummingbirds. In one year the Browns can use 660 pounds of sugar for these little creatures' sugar water. Recognized as a nature tourism site by the Texas Parks and Wildlife Department, the ranch is also a designated Important Birding Area by the Texas Audubon Society. Prime time for viewing is mid-April through mid-August. In fall, winter, and spring, you'll see plenty of deer, as well as wild turkey.

The grounds are wonderful for long, quiet walks, often in the shade of live oak and pecan trees. Bring your own groceries for lunch and dinner, but count on the Browns having your refrigerator fully stocked with breakfast goods.

What's Nearby Christoval

Christoval is just a few miles outside of San Angelo, and you won't find a better example of Texas's frontier heritage than at that city's Fort Concho, widely considered the best-preserved of all nineteenth-century U.S. Army forts, with twenty-three original and restored buildings. From its parade grounds you can gaze across the serene Concho River at a vintage downtown, connected to the fort via an old soldiers' footpath, the El Paseo de Santa Angela. The landscaped walkway takes you past the Concho Pearl Mermaid, a river sculpture, to the contemporary, stunning copper-topped San Angelo Fine Arts Museum, shaped much like a saddle. Downtown destinations include Miss Hattie's Bordello Museum and a wonderful children's museum in the old Cactus Hotel.

Carroll's Bed and Breakfast

1901 South U.S. 87
Dalhart, TX 79022
Phone: (806) 249-6507

INNKEEPERS: John and Paulette Carroll
ROOMS: 2 suites and 6 rooms with private bath, king beds, and TV
ON THE GROUNDS: Great room, parlor, and dining room as common areas
CREDIT CARDS: MasterCard, Visa, American Express
RATES: $–$$$
HOW TO GET THERE: Dalhart is roughly ninety minutes north of Amarillo and two hours from the mountains of New Mexico. Drive into town from Amarillo on U.S. 87. Find the B&B on the main thoroughfare in town.

John and Paulette have surely come up with a first in Texas—the couple transformed a lumberyard, circa 1952, into a luxurious B&B. If anyone else has done something similar, they're keeping it a big secret.

Opened in April 1999, the inn was designed and built by John; Paula served as interior decorator. The result is a charming inn with a honeymoon/anniversary suite, a second suite, and six rooms, each done in a different style. All rooms have TVs and king beds, and the honeymoon suite even has a red, heart-shaped whirlpool tub.

Guests have a chance to visit together in front of the parlor's fireplace. The home's great room includes the dining room, where you'll enjoy John's elaborate breakfasts. The inn is a great stopping place for travelers making the long drives between Texas and New Mexico and Colorado.

What's Nearby Dalhart

Home to the world-famous XIT Ranch, which was once the largest ranch in the world under one fence, Dalhart now offers the XIT Museum. Inside the museum, learn the fascinating story of the ranch, and examine photographs, documents, an antique gun collection, Native American relics, and paintings by Peter Hurd. Over the first weekend in August, Dalhart hosts the XIT Rodeo and Reunion, the world's largest amateur rodeo. Drive about 70 miles east to Lake Meredith National Park, a giant playground with 100 miles of lake shoreline, eight recreation areas, fishing, waterskiing, sailing, golf, and tennis.

Broadway Manor Bed & Breakfast

1811 Broadway Street
Lubbock, TX 79401
Phone: (806) 749-4707

INTERNET SITE: www.broadwaymanor.net

INNKEEPERS: Hank and Lenora Browning

ROOMS: 4 rooms with private bath

ON THE GROUNDS: Sunroom with TV, telephone, music, and games for guests to share; upstairs garden terrace

CREDIT CARDS: MasterCard, Visa

RATES: $–$$

HOW TO GET THERE: From I-27 exit U.S. 62 west and follow it to U.S. 84 north. Drive 7 blocks north to Broadway and turn left.

Built in 1926 for banker and civic leader C. E. Maedgen, the Neoclassical Greek Revival-style manor has been carefully made into a luxury lodging. Found just a few blocks from Texas Tech University, the home sits in the historic, prestigious Overton District.

Guest rooms each have a theme borrowed from the world of Broadway musicals. The Wild West features twin brass beds that can be made up as a king; The Salzburg has an elegant queen bed; The Garden of Siam features a king bed and decor from Asia; and the English Lady is done in Victorian decor and features a private terrace and a whirlpool tub for two.

You can count on a large breakfast, including fresh fruit, an egg entree, meats, and breads. And the afternoon you arrive, you'll be treated to homemade cookies.

What's Nearby Lubbock

Nicknamed the "Hub of the South Plains," Lubbock varied heritage includes that of ranching and music. There's the outstanding National Ranching Heritage Center—a remarkable destination for a fascinating history lesson—at Texas Tech University, as well as a music hall of fame, featuring native sons Buddy Holly, Joe Ely, Mac Davis, and Jimmie Dale Gilmore. Make time to visit the various successful vineyards and wineries in the area, including Llano Estacado, Pheasant Ridge, and Cap Rock.

A Bed & Breakfast on Silk Stocking Row

415 NW Fourth Street
Mineral Wells, TX 76067
Phone: (940) 325-4101

E-MAIL: silkrowbb@aol.com

INTERNET SITE: www.bestinns.net/usa/tx/silkstocking.html

INNKEEPERS: Bob Tyson and Kenn Saxton

ROOMS: 5 rooms, including 1 suite, with private bath, TV, 2 with phone

ON THE GROUNDS: Wraparound verandahs front and back, library, parlor

CREDIT CARDS: MasterCard, Visa, Discover

RATES: $-$$

HOW TO GET THERE: Go west from Fort Worth on I-20. Exit at Mineral Wells-Weatherford exit onto U.S. 180. Turn right onto NW Fourth Street and drive 4 blocks. It's at the corner of Fourth Street and Fourth Avenue.

This delightful inn was originally a boarding house at its 1904 construction. A local physician's wife had it built, capitalizing on the "Crazy Water" boom that brought people in droves to Mineral Wells to partake of the supposed healing properties of the many mineral wells. The three-story Victorian features huge pocket doors, working transoms, limited edition art, a turret, wraparound verandahs, fountains, tree swing, and statuary on its landscaped grounds. It's also in easy walking distance of historic downtown area and shopping.

Bob and Kenn are sticklers for detail: They provide amenities such as soap, shampoo, lotion, sewing kit, shower kit, and shower cap in each bathroom; and they keep the second-floor hospitality area—which has an ice machine and a refrigerator—stocked with goodies. Your coffee is ready here when you wake up.

Guest rooms include the Turret Room, with bay windows and brass twin beds; the Brazos Room, with a king brass bed; and the Tygrette Suite, with its own sitting room and big windows. Be ready for a memorable breakfast feast, as Bob and Kenn feed you by courses. Typically, it's juice, fresh fruit plate, egg entree, meats, and potato or French toast, perhaps cut into the shape of Texas.

What's Nearby Mineral Wells

Ask at the chamber of commerce about the tapes and books you can buy to follow the 173-mile driving tour that details the local history of the legendary cattlemen, Oliver Loving and Charles Goodnight. In town visit the Famous Mineral Water Company, established in 1913 to market the reportedly curative local waters that made the town famous. The visitors area offers cappuccinos, ice cream, and vintage postcards. There's an organic herb garden near town, and a few miles west there are wonderful canoeing opportunities on the Brazos River.

Hotel Garza Bed & Breakfast

302 East Main Street
Post, TX 79356
Phone: (806) 495-3962
Fax: (806) 495-3962

E-MAIL: hotlgrza@gte.net

INTERNET SITE: www.bbhost.com/hotelgarza

INNKEEPERS: Janice and Jim Plummer

ROOMS: 9 rooms, 6 with private bath; Patsy's Guest Cottage nearby with 2 bedrooms, 2 baths, kitchen

ON THE GROUNDS: Library, conference room, fax and modem hookups, laundry facilities, kitchenette access, garden patio

CREDIT CARDS: MasterCard, Visa, American Express

RATES: $

HOW TO GET THERE: Drive 2 blocks east of the intersection of U.S. 84 and U.S. 380, which is Main Street.

The 1915 Hotel Garza historic inn sits in the middle of a town founded in 1907 by cereal magnate C. W. Post. This official Texas Main Street City has several restored period buildings, including an opera house and several boutiques and stores. The inn's 1992 restoration and reopening as a B&B made it an inn with common areas, such as the library, a garden patio with a waterfall—which is mighty refreshing out in the dry Panhandle—and a kitchenette and refreshment area. There are a conference center and party room on site, too.

The updated guest rooms have been made plenty comfortable, too, with air-conditioning, fireplaces, ceiling fans, cable TV, and radio-alarm clocks. At breakfast time bring your appetite for Janice and Jim's special sheepherder's breakfast: a West Texas country spread with eggs, meats, breads, and juices. On weekdays it's an expanded Continental breakfast. Lunch and dinner are available by prior arrangement.

Ask also about Patsy's Guest Cottage, located 10 blocks from the hotel in a residential area. It offers two bedrooms, two baths, and your own kitchen for making meals.

What's Nearby Post

Long before it became famous as a speedtrap, this junction at U.S. 84 and U.S. 380 was the place where cereal manufacturer C. W. Post founded a town to create an independent farmers' community. Sitting at the foot of the magnificent cap rock that characterizes the rugged Panhandle terrain, Post offers a nicely restored Main Street and the O. S. Ranch Museum.

Hotel Turkey

Third and Alexander Streets
Turkey, TX 79261
Phone: (806) 423-1152; (800) 657-7110

E-MAIL: suziej@caprock-spur.com

INTERNET SITE: www.llano.net/turkey/hotel/

INNKEEPERS: Gary and Suzie Johnson

ROOMS: 15 rooms; 7 with private baths

ON THE GROUNDS: Enclosed porch, dining room

CREDIT CARDS: MasterCard, Visa, American Express

RATES: $–$$

HOW TO GET THERE: Take I-27 north from Lubbock or south from Amarillo to Texas 86; turn east on Texas 86 and drive to Turkey. Texas 86 becomes Main Street. Turn left from Main onto Third Street and stop at intersection of Third and Alexander.

Lovers of Western Swing music consider Turkey, Texas, something of a mecca: It was the home of Bob Wills, known as the King of Western Swing, and it's opened a museum named in his honor. When you make the pilgrimage to this rather holy site, it's only right that you should take a load off at one of the outstanding vintage hotels in Texas. The Hotel Turkey was built in 1927 for railroad travelers and has been in continuous operation since. After intermittent restoration work from 1989 through 1996, the quaint old lodging now functions as a B&B and informal history museum.

When you're not visiting the museum or hiking at nearby Caprock Canyons, better just sit a spell in one of fourteen rockers on the hotel's pleasant, glassed-in porch. Or listen to music in the lobby and parlor. Or read a book found on random shelves and tables. Throughout you'll find a profusion of old collectibles, from clocks and antique reading glasses to pictures and records. Rooms come in both small and large sizes.

Suzie is relatively famous for her sweet-potato pancakes, so be sure to wake up hungry. And if you do make it to town for the Bob Wills Days in Turkey, which happens the last weekend in April, make note that the hotel is completely reserved for Bob's family and those of his band, the Playboys.

What's Nearby Turkey

The tiny, quiet town gets a bit crazy in April during the Bob Wills Days. There's a monument honoring the beloved musician at the west end of Main Street, and the Bob Wills Museum tells the story of the King of Western Swing and that of the Texas Playboys. Drive just a short while west to explore Caprock Canyons State Park, a wonderland for hikers, mountain bikers, and nature lovers. At the park, a trailway more than 60 miles long crosses myriad topography and includes a 700-foot, abandoned railroad tunnel.

Country Place Bed & Breakfast

16004 County Road 1600
Wolfforth, TX 79382
Phone: (806) 863-2030

INTERNET SITE: www.members.aol.com/bcon111cp

INNKEEPER: Pat Conover

ROOMS: 5 rooms; 1 with private bath, TV, and dataport

ON THE GROUNDS: Library, sunroom, verandah, gardens, hot tub, large outdoor pool, three patio areas

CREDIT CARDS: MasterCard, Visa

RATES: $–$$

HOW TO GET THERE: From Lubbock drive 82nd Street west to Upland Avenue. Turn left (south) and go 5 miles; it's the last house on right.

This two-story home was built in 1992 and offers true quiet of the Panhandle countryside. Pat has filled her place with souvenirs collected from travels around the world, particularly from Asia. Guests share a living room, where you'll watch movies on the VCR, as well as the swimming pool and its large deck. The outside hot tub is a great place to relax, and it's particularly appealing on snowy days. If you're into hiking, biking, or running, there are plenty of country roads to explore, and some of the neighbors have exotic animals to peek at along the way.

Pat's gourmet breakfasts always include eggs, meat, fruit, and homemade breads. Among her specialties are apricot coffee cake, cheese and spinach pie, and huevos rancheros.

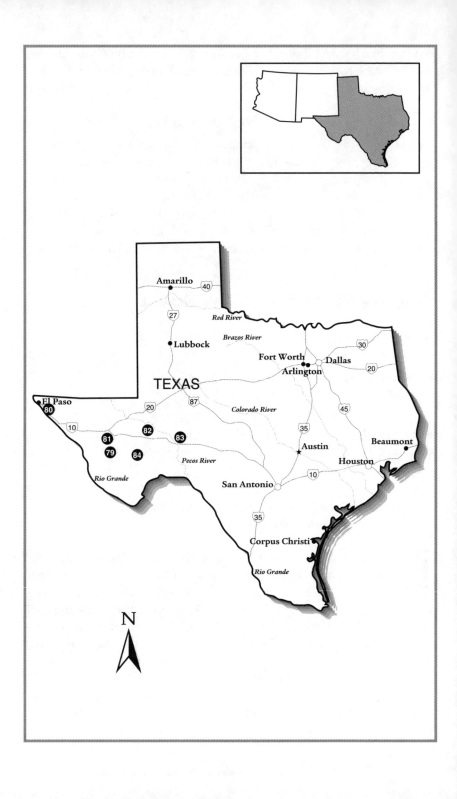

Texas: Big Bend Country

Numbers on map refer to towns numbered below.

The Holland Hotel

209 West Holland Avenue
Alpine, TX 79830
Phone: (915) 837-3844;
(800) 535-8040

INNKEEPER: Carla McFarland

ROOMS: 13 rooms with private
bath, TV, 5 with telephone

ON THE GROUNDS: Beautiful lobby
with wheelchair accessibility; restaurant

CREDIT CARDS: MasterCard, Visa, American Express

RATES: $

HOW TO GET THERE: Enter Alpine via U.S. 90/U.S. 67, which merge in town.
You'll find Holland Avenue in the middle of town. The hotel faces the
Amtrak station.

This graceful old building was constructed in 1912 in the Spanish Colonial style and was expanded in 1928 by the renowned firm of Trost & Trost for a lofty sum of $250,000. One of the landmark railroad hotels of the West, it was considered the finest between Alpine and San Antonio. Today it bears a Texas historical marker and functions both as an inn and an events site.

The lodgings are varied, comfortable, and funky but not what you'd call luxurious. Some rooms are cozy, and some can be made into suites. Lots of the baths feature original fixtures and beautiful tile work, and a few of the rooms have refrigerators and microwaves. From the Penthouse Room, you have a 360-degree, panoramic view of the town, because the Holland is the tallest building in Alpine. This room also has an outdoor deck, which is nice for reading, painting, or watching sunsets.

Carla's Continental breakfast includes very simple pastries, juice, and coffee. The lobby restaurant, which serves lunch on weekdays, is known for serving the only oysters on the half shell in the Big Bend region.

What's Nearby Alpine

The central "city" of the Big Bend area, Alpine offers more retail shopping opportunities than other towns out this way, and it's the town with an Amtrak stop on the Sunset Limited route between San Antonio and Los Angeles. Home to Sul Ross State University and a primary shipping point for the area's big ranching industry, Alpine is a great place to get acclimated for a thorough Big Bend adventure. There's the Museum of the Big Bend at the university, where exhibits detail that history and heritage shaped by the Spanish, Mexicans, Native Americans, and Anglos who have lived here; and there's the Apache Trading Post, a great place to find books, maps, fossils, rocks, minerals, and more. Another good place to stock up on reading is Front Street Books, which is close to several art galleries and shops worth investigating.

Another Recommended B&B in Alpine

White House Inn, a two-story, 1930s home with three guest rooms and private baths, TV, robes, and gourmet breakfast; 2003 Fort Davis Highway, Alpine, TX 79830; telephone: (915) 837–1401.

Cowboys and Indians Board and Bunk

P.O. Box 13752
El Paso, TX 79913
Phone: (505) 589–2653

INTERNET SITE: www.smart.net/~cowboysbb

INNKEEPERS: Don and Irene Newton

ROOMS: 4 rooms with private bath, telephone, patio, coffeemaker; 1 with wheelchair accessibility

ON THE GROUNDS: Desert walking trails, living room, porches, gift shop

CREDIT CARDS: MasterCard, Visa, American Express, Discover

RATES: $–$$

HOW TO GET THERE: Drive west from El Paso on I-10 to ArtCraft Road exit. Travel west on ArtCraft to Doniphan Road. Turn right on Doniphan and then left at Borderland Road. Continue on Borderland Road to New Mexico 273; turn right (north) on 273 and continue to Koogle Road (a dirt road); then turn left on Mountain Vista and continue to top of the hill.

Although you've crossed the state line into New Mexico, this area is considered a suburb of El Paso. You'll swear, however, that you've stepped into a desert movie. This friendly lodging is subtitled "a true west bed & breakfast," and everything and everybody is nicknamed "Bubba," as in "Join Bubba for a cigarette on individual patios or the great outdoors, but not inside."

The three acres surrounding the hacienda give you plenty of space to just collect yourself and enjoy the dry desert climes. Views from the Board and Bunk include sensational vistas of the Franklin Mountains, as well as dramatic sunsets over southern New Mexico. Don and Irene will help you arrange days of golf, horseback riding, shopping, and mission explorations, if you want to leave your digs.

Choices are Bubba's Bunk (natch), a big room with a queen-size covered wagon bed, antiques, and cowboy furnishings; Geronimo's Tree, with a queen bed and couch that converts to a twin, Indian blanket, and corresponding decor; Rumble Seat Room, with a queen antique car bed and car collectibles; and Pocahontas's Palace, a large room with a queen-size bed, sitting room, and lounger that converts to a twin.

Breakfast is served either in the kiva, the large living room, or on the back porch, offering views of the Franklins. Expect a spread of hearty, flavorful grub that combines the best of Mexican, chuck wagon, and Dutch oven cooking—all straight from the Wild West. Ask about dinner arrangements for parties of six or more, and do accept a nightcap before you bunk down at night.

What's Nearby El Paso

Spend a four-day weekend in El Paso and you can really see it all, or if you have less time, break it down to the stuff that interests you most. There are lovely missions that predate some of those in Southern California, and there is the marvelous Tigua Indian Reservation, where the music, traditions, art, and food of a 320-year-old settlement of people from New Mexico are exhibited daily at its cultural center. At Fort Bliss, museums tell the story of the original adobe fort and frontier military period and of the more recent U.S. Army Air Defense history. But for shopping and dining pleasures and treasures, hop the Border Jumper, a trolley that will take you across the Rio Grande to Juarez and its fabulous stores, markets, and restaurants. Places to find include the City Market, a giant store called El Patio, and a terrific, old-fashioned bar called the Kentucky Club, where the margarita is said to have originated.

Boynton House Guest Lodge & Conference Center

5 Dolores Mountain Trail
Fort Davis, TX 79734
Phone: (915) 426-3123; (877) 358-5929

E-MAIL: info@boynton-lodge.com

INTERNET SITE: www.boynton-lodge.com

INNKEEPER: Elizabeth (Betty) J. Boynton

ROOMS: 5 rooms with private bath, TV, VCR, telephone, and wheelchair accessibility

ON THE GROUNDS: Two library areas, solarium, music room, three porches, garden; basketball goal, volleyball equipment, picnic/barbecue areas, bicycle rack; gift shop; game room, exercise room

CREDIT CARDS: MasterCard, Visa, American Express

RATES: $–$$

HOW TO GET THERE: Drive south from Fort Davis via Texas 118 continuing a half mile south of the highway department offices. Watch for the brown rock gate and turn to Delores Mountain; drive 0.7 mile on this road to the lodge at the mountaintop.

Betty designed her dream hacienda after those in the Mexican colonial towns of Taxco and San Miguel de Allende. At her lavish hacienda you'll find a 28-by-28-foot solarium with a Mexican canterra stone fountain and bistro tables in the company of banana trees, poinsettias, and bougainvillea. Interiors are adorned with antiques, hand-carved doors and hand-painted tile work, and Oriental rugs.

Guest rooms are furnished with king, queen, double, or twin trundle beds, and some sleep as many as five people. There's an apartment that sleeps four and offers access to a kitchen. Among the numerous common areas are meeting rooms, game and exercise rooms, and a music room; some or all are used when Betty hosts health and fitness workshops and Christian seminars. Weddings and reunions are welcome here, but the lodge's brochure is clear about rules against "smoking, drinking, fornicating, cussing, fighting."

The setting is truly hard to beat. Set about 350 feet above the historic, rejuvenating town of Fort Davis, the lodge offers panoramic views of lava cliffs and the Big Bend countryside. Breakfast is a huge buffet, so bring an appetite.

Veranda Country Inn Bed & Breakfast

210 Court Avenue

Fort Davis, TX 79734

Phone: (915) 426-2233; (888) 383-2847

E-MAIL: info@theveranda.com

INTERNET SITE: www.theveranda.com

INNKEEPERS: Kathie and Paul Woods

ROOMS: 11 rooms inside inn, 2 rooms in Carriage House, 1 in Garden Cottage; all with private bath

ON THE GROUNDS: Large reading room; two walled courtyards with covered verandahs and rocking chairs, walled grounds and gardens

CREDIT CARDS: MasterCard, Visa, Discover

RATES: $$

HOW TO GET THERE: Drive into town on either Texas 118 or Texas 17. Court Avenue intersects the two, as they become the main road through town.

Built in 1883, this unique adobe Territorial-style inn features walls measuring two feet thick and rooms with ceilings twelve feet high. The mellow, mountain mood that is Fort Davis's trademark is felt in every inch of this country escape, where eleven rooms and suites are inside the inn, two rooms are in the Carriage House, and one is in the Garden Cottage. This is a place where you simply have no choice but to relax: There are no phones or TVs in rooms, and the place contains courtyards, verandahs, and gardens, which invite you to sit and rest a spell.

Antiques and period collectibles are found throughout this lovely inn. If you can pull yourself away from the spacious reading room or the comfort of your own room, you can wander into the nearby downtown to look through shops, or you can drive to the nearby national historic park.

In the morning prepare to be spoiled. Kathie and Paul serve a massive spread of juices, seasonal fruits, coffee cake, sausage, biscuits, Scotch eggs, soufflés, or crepes. It varies, but it's always stylish and fresh from the oven.

Wayside Inn Bed & Breakfast

400 West Fourth Street

Fort Davis, TX 79734

Phone: (915) 426-3535; (800) 582-7510

Fax: (915) 426-3574

E-MAIL: wayside@overland.net

The Wild, Wild West

If you're looking for a town loaded with old west history, you're in luck. Founded and fostered under the U.S. Army, the military post known as Fort Davis was established in 1854 at the crossing point of the Chihuahua Trail and the Butterfield Overland Mail Route. Offering safe travel routes for pioneers and prospectors heading west on the 600-mile-wide wilderness between San Antonio and El Paso, the fort emptied during the Civil War years and was frequently and easily raided by Indians during the military's absence. Subsequent building finally produced the rock and adobe buildings you see today; these housed twelve companies of cavalry and infantry, including the renowned "buffalo soldiers," many of whom were former slaves on southern plantations. Explore the fort, now a national historic site, and visit the fine little museum there.

INTERNET SITE: www.texasguides.com/waysideinn.html

INNKEEPERS: J. W. and Anna Beth Ward

ROOMS: 7 rooms with private bath, cable TV

ON THE GROUNDS: Sunporch

CREDIT CARDS: MasterCard, Visa, American Express, Discover

RATES: $–$$$

HOW TO GET THERE: Drive into Fort Davis via Texas 118 or Texas 17; Fourth Street intersects these as they join together in town. (Stone Village Grocery is your landmark.) Turn west and go to end of Fourth Street to the inn.

Built in 1947 as a private home, the inn sits on an 1855 land grant deeded to Pedro Guano of Bexar County for his service during the Texas Republic period. The pine frame house has been expanded numerous times in the past half century, growing from 1,850 square feet to more than 4,000.

J. W. and Anna Beth are retired schoolteachers who offer plenty of homey touches in their comfortable, unpretentious lodge. Lots of country accents are found in the decor, particularly in Anna Beth's collection of old hats, quilts, and clothing. Each of the guest rooms has either a king or a queen bed.

Views from the inn take in colossal volcanic boulders and cliffs, and your hiking paths—if you can handle them—will lead you to the mountain called Sleeping Lion. The inn's property abuts that of the Fort Davis National Historic Site, worth at least a full morning or afternoon of touring. One block away from the inn is the Overland Trail Museum, which details much of the area's pioneer history.

The sunporch is where guests play parlor games and have breakfast, a giant buffet prepared by J. W. He and Anna Beth say that he acquired valuable cooking skills while she and their four daughters got ready for school every day. It wouldn't have done for Anna Beth to be late, as J. W. was her principal.

What's Nearby Fort Davis

It's all about the outdoors at Fort Davis. At Davis Mountains State Park, set in a basin surrounding by the hulking mountains of the same name, hiking trails and nature study beg interruption only for a picnic with the best scenic views in Texas. And one of the finest scenic drives in West Texas will take you to McDonald Observatory, atop 6,791-foot Mount Locke. A University of Texas installation, the observatory offers you the chance to look at the magnificent, cloudless night sky at its twice-weekly Star Parties. The delightful staff there takes the geeky science out of the equation so that laypeople can actually understand more about stars, planets, and the solar system.

Other Recommended B&Bs Nearby

Neill House, an 1898 Queen Anne-style home furnished with antiques, with four rooms and two private baths; P.O. Box 1034, Fort Davis, TX 79734; telephone: (915) 426–3838. *Cibolo Creek Ranch,* a 25,000-acre ranch with a trio of meticulously restored private fort buildings (circa 1857), sensational Mexican decor, bird-watching and nature study, horseback riding, skeet shooting, three lavish meals daily, and luxurious bedding, furnishings, and toiletries; twelve private rooms with baths and two private cottages; P.O. Box 44, Shafter, TX 79850; telephone: (915) 229–3737. *Prude Ranch,* a century-old working cattle ranch with guest lodges, bunkhouses, horseback riding, swimming, and volleyball; with meal plans; Texas 118, Fort Davis, TX 79734; telephone: (915) 426–3202 or (800) 458–6232; Internet site: www.pruderanch.com.

Glass Mountain Manor

U.S. 385
P.O. Box 426
Fort Stockton, TX 79735
Phone: (915) 395-2435; (800) 695-8249

E-MAIL:
furman@brooks-
data.net

INNKEEP-ERS: Scott
and Kendra
Furman

ROOMS: 3 rooms, 1 with private bath

ON THE GROUNDS: Ranchlands for hiking, nature watching, mountain biking

CREDIT CARDS: MasterCard, Visa, American Express

RATES: $

HOW TO GET THERE: Drive into Fort Stockton via I-10 or U.S. 285. Go south from town on U.S. 385, traveling 26 miles to a sign that reads, MONTGOMERY-FULK WALKER RANCH. Turn in here and drive 0.2 mile to another gate, through the gate and left at the Y in the road. Drive another 0.8 mile to a dirt road, where you'll turn right. The B&B is just ahead on the left.

This working ranch—open to guests from January 1 to November 19—was a homestead circa 1900 and continues to function as a commercial cattle, horse, and goat ranch. B&B guests have the original ranch house, built in 1906, to themselves. It's not fancy by any means—it was last decorated in the 1970s—but this place is precisely what you want if you're looking for utter privacy and solitude.

Lounge about in your jammies all day if you like—or take a hike to see what kinds of rocks and fossils are around or look at the Boer and Spanish goats raised on this family ranch. Bring your mountain bikes if you're into rugged rides; bring your binoculars for superior bird-watching in late fall, winter, and early spring.

Scott and Kendra live in the ranch's main house, which isn't too far away. They'll stock your refrigerator with items for breakfast, which you'll make yourself. Bring groceries for your other meals or take a late-afternoon drive into town to eat homestyle Tex-Mex at one of the vintage cafes.

Fort Stockton

Another town that grew up around a military post, Fort Stockton is a frequent stopping point for today's travelers heading down to Big Bend National Park. But that doesn't mean you just gas up and go; take a little time to appreciate how well the Pecos County Seat has restored its historic sites. The Annie Riggs Hotel Museum, an 1899 stagecoach stop, is an excellent small museum housing period collections of clothing, photography, cowboy artifacts, housewares, and geology. It's close to the Courthouse Square, which offers an 1883 courthouse, 1875 Catholic church, 1883 schoolhouse, and the 1872 St. Stephen's Episcopal Church, the first Protestant church west of the Pecos, built in 1972. Look also for a spot called Zero Stone, positioned by a survey party in 1859 to mark as the originating point for all land surveys done in this part of West Texas.

Parker Ranch Bed and Breakfast

U.S. 190 at Crockett County Road 310
Iraan, TX 79744
Phone: (915) 639–2850; (877) 639–2850

E-MAIL: parker.ranch.b.b@apex2000.net

INTERNET SITE: www.bedandbreakfast.com

INNKEEPER: Dickie Dell Ferro

ROOMS: 4 rooms, 2 with private bath

ON THE GROUNDS: Library, sunroom, verandah, garden, front porch, pecan orchard, stock tank with deck

CREDIT CARDS: None accepted

RATES: $

HOW TO GET THERE: From I-10 drive either east on Texas 190 or north on Texas 349 to Iraan. Map and directions will be provided at booking.

Out in middle West Texas along the banks of the legendary Pecos River is a town called Iraan, pronounced "IRA-Ann." Those who know such things know it's halfway on a long stretch of highway between El Paso and San Antonio.

Travelers headed to Big Bend National Park are advised to slow down and enjoy the trip, because it takes so darned long to get there. A great place to get acclimated to the region and to get adjusted to the languid pace in this part of the world is at the Parker Ranch. Founded in the late 1920s oil boom by a rancher named O. W. Parker, it's run today by his granddaughter, a charming lady who seems to have stepped from the pages of a Larry McMurtry novel.

The home looks like it might have come from an old Hollywood movie set: A Spanish Colonial house, it sits beneath three giant palms and next to plenty of cactus in the middle of the 3,700-acre ranch. That's plenty of land on which to hike, look for rocks and fossils, or ride your mountain bike (if you brought one). In the morning and early evening, hang out on the porch and watch for wild turkey and mule deer; when night falls, watch for the Milky Way to emerge as it almost always does. You've never seen stars so bright as in this part of the state.

The home's interior is just as pleasant: Stucco walls and original hardwood floors are part of the long-ago beauty. Guests can watch TV in the living room, or ask Dickie Dell to point you to the nearby nine-hole golf course and city park, with its swimming pool. In the morning she'll be up early making biscuits or muffins, eggs, sausage, fruit, and coffee.

What's Nearby Iraan

Everyone wants to call this town of just over 2,000 West Texans "Iran," like the country, but the correct pronunciation is "IRA-Ann." Decided in a contest, it was named for the townsite owners Ira and Ann Yates after the community erupted into existence with the 1928 discovery of oil. In the forty-acre City Park, you'll see a historical marker that gives details about Discovery Well A No. 1, the astounding gusher that remains one of the largest producing wells in North America. Its initial blow was so powerful, it sprayed a tent city pitched 4 miles away. Adjacent to City Park, see Fantasyland's colossal figures of Ally Oop, the comic strip caveman created by one-time Iraan resident V. T. Hamlin.

Captain Shepherd's House

Avenue D and Second Street
Marathon, TX 79842
Phone: (915) 386–4205; (800) 884–4243

INNKEEPER: Brock Waldon

ROOMS: 5 rooms with private bath

ON THE GROUNDS: Living room, parlor, kitchen, balconies, porch, restaurant, bar; pool, courtyards

CREDIT CARDS: MasterCard, Visa, American Express

RATES: $$

HOW TO GET THERE: Drive into Marathon via U.S. 90 or U.S. 385; find the managing property, the Gage Hotel, on U.S. 90. Register there, then find the house directly behind the hotel.

This old home takes you back to an utterly different place and time. The original resident was Captain Albion Shepherd, the town founder, who built this two-story adobe home in 1889. The rooms aren't especially fancy, but they're comfortable and stylish with Mexican blankets, hides, and period pieces. One bedroom has its own little balcony and a large bath, while the two smaller bedrooms have private baths that aren't in the rooms but are on the hallway.

Downstairs two common rooms have telephones and TVs that guests share. There's a kitchen and a dining room in the rambling old house, but you'll have breakfast over at Cafe Cenizo. The restaurant is part of the venerable Gage Hotel, a wonderful 1927 railroad hotel that also owns the house. At check-in, you'll get a $5.00 voucher for breakfast, which is a simple selection of bacon and eggs, biscuits, pastries, cereals, and yogurt.

The Gage also has a large lobby with an inviting fireplace, which you're welcome to enjoy. On one side of the hotel is a newer spread of rooms, where a marvelous swimming pool offers sensational relief from the warm afternoons.

What's Nearby Marathon

Sitting on U.S. 90 at its intersection with U.S. 385, Marathon is the gateway to Big Bend National Park. Some folks breeze through, stopping long enough to wander around the lovely old Gage Hotel, but the town's worth a close look. Spend a lazy afternoon browsing the handful of art galleries, boutiques, and casual cafes that line the tiny boardwalk facing U.S. 90. You'll find yourself melting into that relaxed mood and mindset you'll need for the unfettered place that is Big Bend. And as you turn south on U.S. 385 to head for the national park, leave yourself time to detour east on Farm Road 2627, about 40 miles south of Marathon. You'll find a place called Hallie Stillwell's Hall of Fame, a tiny regional museum of sorts, dedicated to one of the most remarkable modern pioneer women to grace West Texas.

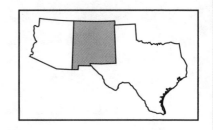

New Mexico: Northern

Numbers on map refer to towns numbered below.

Casa del Rio

P.O. Box 702
Abiquiu, NM
87510
Phone: (505)

920–1495

753–2035; (800)

E-MAIL: casadelrio@newmexico.com

INTERNET SITE: www.bbonline.com/nm/casadelrio

INNKEEPERS: Eileen Sopanen and Mel Vigil

ROOMS: 2 rooms with private bath

ON THE GROUNDS: Meditation room, water garden, private patios, river front, spectacular view, twelve acres

CREDIT CARDS: MasterCard, Visa

RATES: $$–$$$

HOW TO GET THERE: Drive north out of Santa Fe on New Mexico 84/285 through Española; continue on 84 for approximately 10 miles. At mile marker 199, go precisely another 0.5 mile. Find a closed gate with a small sign suspended above it saying CASA DEL RIO. Drive down the dirt road to the main house, which is on the right, where Eileen or Mel will greet you.

A native New Mexican, Mel Vigil built this traditional adobe hacienda completely by hand, using vigas and latillas made from wood he carried himself from the area's mountains. Choosing to build in the land north of Santa Fe known as Georgia O'Keeffe country, Mel and Eileen created a retreat in an authentic northern New Mexico design, filled with hand-carved Spanish Colonial-style furnishings crafted by a local furniture maker.

Guests have at their disposal two people intimately familiar with this corner of the world. Between Mel's lifelong understanding of the region and Eileen's experiences gathered over her three-decade residency, the two can map out terrific tours customized to your interests. Looking for hiking quests, mountain picnic sites, forest drives, or pueblo explorations? They'll tailor something special for you. Mornings are made brighter with a thoughtfully prepared meal, such as quesadillas or eggs Florentine, home-made muffins, biscuits with local honey, juice, coffee, or tea.

What's Nearby Abiquiu

The mystical landscape that so inspired Georgia O'Keeffe offers plentiful diversions. Go fishing, swimming, boating, windsurfing, and picnicking at Abiquiu, and visit the naturally hollowed sandstone Echo Amphitheater. Learn more about the native fauna and flora of the Southwest at Ghost Ranch Living Museum and examine fossil displays at Ruth Hall Museum of Paleontology. And at the Ghost Ranch Conference Center at Presbyterian Church, find Indian anthropology and Indian and Spanish history exhibits at Florence Hawley Ellis Museum of Anthropology.

Brittania & W. E. Mauger Estate B&B

701 Roma Avenue NW
Albuquerque, NM 87102
Phone: (505) 242-8755; (800) 719-9189

E-MAIL: maugerbb@aol.com
INTERNET SITE: www.maugerbb.com
INNKEEPERS: Mark Brown and Keith Lewis
ROOMS: 9 rooms with private bath, TV, telephone, dataport
ON THE GROUNDS: Parlor, breakfast room, huge front porch
CREDIT CARDS: MasterCard, Visa, American Express
RATES: $$-$$$$
HOW TO GET THERE: From the airport drive north on I-25; exit Martin Luther King Boulevard. Turn west, drive through downtown to 7th Street. Turn right 1 block to Roma. The B&B is located on the corner of 7th Street and Roma.

This circa 1897 home was built by Maude Talbot, daughter of a local tavern owner. She returned to her native New York and sold the home to William E. Mauger (pronounced "major") and his wife Brittania. The restored Victorian, listed on the National Register of Historic Places, has been a charming B&B for over twelve years, hosting such esteemed guests as Linda Ronstadt and Martin Sheen.

Comfort is a high priority, as you'll see: Each room has not only TV and phone with voice mail, but also a small fridge, down comforter, coffeemaker, and snack basket. Guests unwind by reading or writing letters in the parlor and watching the sun set from the 30-foot-long front porch. Business and leisure travelers both like the Mauger Estate for its convenience; downtown is just a 4-block walk, and Old Town is just 1 mile away. In the morning you'll be spoiled by the full breakfast buffet.

The W. J. Marsh House Victorian B&B

301 Edith SE
Albuquerque, NM 87102-3532
Phone: (505) 247–1001; (505) WJ–MARSH
Internet site: www.marshhouse.com
Innkeeper: West Burke
Rooms: 6 rooms, 2 with private bath

ON THE GROUNDS: Private phone line for guests to share; high Victorian decor, lovely garden, porch swing

CREDIT CARDS: MasterCard, Visa

RATES: $–$$$

HOW TO GET THERE: In Albuquerque take I–25 to the Martin Luther King exit; turn left (west) on Martin Luther King, then turn right (south) on Edith and drive 4 blocks.

Look in Albuquerque's storied Huning's Highland Historic District, also called Railroad Town, to find the exquisite March house, built in 1892. One of 500 Victorian structures in a 46-block section of town, the home belonged to the town's first Congregational minister, the Reverend W. J. Marsh, who lived here until 1910. Ironically it's rumored to have become a popular bordello the following decade.

Among the lovely, six lavishly outfitted rooms—each of which is done in a different color combination—are appealing choices such as the Rose and Peach Rooms, which have queen-size beds. Others have doubles or twins. Each room has deep carpeting, an old-fashioned alarm clock, reading material relevant to the Southwest, writing paper and pens, and 100 percent cotton linens. For those rooms without private baths, there are crisp cotton bathrobes for guests to use.

When you're not touring Albuquerque's Old Town or museums, you're welcome to hang around the house. The beautiful parlor is outfitted with a completely restored 1904 Baldwin Cabinet grand piano and antique and modern games, fine for enjoying in front of the hard-carved fireplace. On pretty days—and there are plenty of these in Albuquerque—you'll be tempted to squander time on the porch swing, gazing at the flower gardens.

In the morning you can plan your day over breakfast, which is always a gourmet affair. Adding to the luxury is the meal's setting, a formal dining room with French lace curtains and a table spread featuring antique china and gleaming crystal upon white damask tablecloths.

What's Nearby Albuquerque

Historic Route 66 cuts through the middle of town, known to have a stunning sky in October when the annual hot-air balloon festival brings thousands of celebrants for one of the most photographed events in the world. History is on display in Old Town, where the nearly 300-year-old San Felipe de Neri Church overlooks the fabled plaza. Within Old Town you'll find hundreds of shopping, art, dining, and sightseeing opportunities. Other great places to visit include the Rio Grande Zoological Park, San Felipe Winery, Albuquerque Museum, and the Sandia Peak Tramway, which zips you to the top of the Sandia mountains.

Other Recommended B&Bs Nearby

Devonshire Adobe Inn, with spectacular views of the Rio Grande and Sandia Mountains, lavish breakfast dishes, afternoon tea, and seven guest rooms with private baths, telephone, dataports, and one wheelchair accessible room; 4801 All Saints Road NW; Albuquerque, NM 87120; telephone: (505) 898-3366 or (800) 240-1149; e-mail: devon@nmia. com; Internet site: www.devonshireadobeinn.com. *Casa del Granjero,* with a great room, library, artifacts, big-screen TV, hot tub, fireplaces, handmade Mexican furnishings, three guest rooms with private baths, separate guesthouse with three suites and kitchen; 411-C de Baca Lane NW, Albuquerque, NM 87114; telephone: (505) 897-4144 or (800) 701-4144; e-mail: granjero@cwix.com.

Hacienda Rancho De Chimayo

297 County Road 98
Chimayo, NM 87522
Phone: (505) 351-2222

INNKEEPER: Viola Martinez

ROOMS: 7 rooms with private bath and telephone

ON THE GROUNDS: Courtyard, parlors, living rooms; restaurant, art gallery, and shop

CREDIT CARDS: MasterCard, Visa, American Express

RATES: $–$$

HOW TO GET THERE: Drive north from Santa Fe via U.S. 84/285 and turn right onto NM 503. Drive approximately 8 miles; turn left onto County Road 98. Watch for the Rancho de Chimayo driveway 3 miles ahead on the left.

Tucked within the ruggedly beautiful Chimayo Valley, which stretches from the foothills of the breathtaking Sangre de Cristo Mountains toward the Rio Grande Valley, is a charming town built on a prehistoric settlement named by the Tewa Indians for the red flaking stone characteristic of the area.

Settled by the Spanish in 1693, Chimayo has been known in recent years—since 1965, that is—for a ranch home owned by the Jaramillo family, a place where travelers could count on a sensational meal within a romantic setting warmed by firelight. As has been the case for nearly forty years, diners can also count on a lovely meal on the terraced patio when the weather permits. As the result of a 1984 restoration, seven guest rooms were added, and in 1991 a family art and jewelry gallery was added.

Room choices, all of which include a private bath, fireplace, and door to the courtyard, include the Uno, with an antique mahogany king bed, sitting area with twin hide-a-bed, and a private balcony; and the Siete, with an antique cherry king bed and double hide-a-bed. Breakfast is Continental, including pastry and fruit, but a full breakfast in the restaurant is discounted 50 percent for inn guests.

In the late afternoon enjoy a Chimayo cocktail, a mixture of gold tequila, crème de cassis, and apple juice. Then savor a fabulous dinner of native New Mexican fare.

What's Nearby Chimayo

Pilgrims from everywhere make important journeys for healing at the Santuario de Chimayo Church, said to be built on magical grounds. Among the wonderful shops in town is Ortega's de Chimayo, where eighth-generation weavers offer beautiful works in handwoven 100 percent wool. In addition to blankets, rugs, purses, pillows, vests, and coats, the Ortega family has a shop selling folk art, books, gifts, music, and native food items. At Chimayo Trading and Mercantile, you'll find artwork, basketry, pottery, and other works.

Yours Truly Bed & Breakfast

160 Paseo de Corrales
P.O. Box 2263
Corrales, NM 87048
Phone: (505) 898-7027, (800) 942-7890

E-MAIL: yourstrulybb@aol.com
INTERNET SITE: www.yourstrulybb.com
INNKEEPERS: Pat and James Montgomery
ROOMS: 4 rooms with private bath, king bed, TV and phone; 2 with dataport
ON THE GROUNDS: Sunroom, verandah, garden, lily pond, hot tub, nice patios, great views; hot-air balloon
CREDIT CARDS: MasterCard, Visa, American Express, Discover, Diners Club
RATES: $$-$$$

HOW TO GET THERE: From the Albuquerque Airport, drive north on I-25 to Alameda Boulevard. Go west 4.3 miles on Alameda to Corrales Road. Turn right (north) on Corrales Road. Go 1.7 miles to Meadowlark. Turn left (west) on Meadowlark to Loma Larga (1 mile). Turn right, go to second road (Paseo de Corrales), and turn left up the hill.

Inside this contemporary adobe home, you'll warm up instantly to brick floors, daytime views of the mountains, and nighttime views of city lights in the distance. Nearby are hiking trails and the ski mountain at Sandia Peak, as well as llama treks, canoeing, river rafting, kayaking, fishing, and horseback rides—but chances are, you won't want to leave the hot tub, garden, and patio at this welcoming place. Unless, that is, to take flight in the inn's hot-air balloon.

Each of the four guest rooms has a king-size bed, fireplace, private bath, cable TV, and air-conditioning. The Kachina Room has an oversized shower and reading lights, the Spirit Room has dramatic windows, the Sandia Room has a mountain view, and the Sundance Room has a beamed ceiling. Guests especially like the coffee trays that Pat and James leave outside their doors in the morning. They are laden with a small loaf of fruit bread, a carafe of coffee, personalized napkins, and fresh flowers. Breakfast in the dining room always includes a fresh fruit platter; an entree such as breakfast enchiladas or sausage, biscuits, and green-chile cream gravy; and something sweet for dessert.

Just a short drive north of Albuquerque, Corrales is a great place for outdoorsy types. Hiking, bird-watching, and nature walks along the Rio Grande are great at the Corrales Bosque Nature Preserve, and there are marked bicycle paths throughout the village. Animal lovers can't resist the riding lessons at Acheval Stables, nor the pretty creatures at Vista Hermosa Llama Farm. Historic sites include Casa San Ysidro, a nineteenth-century ranch house collection of Colonial and Territorial period artifacts, and the San Ysidro Church, built in the 1860s.

Alta Mae's Heritage Inn

1950 Old Route 66
Edgewood, NM 87015
Phone: (505) 281–5000

INTERNET SITE:
www.altamae-
nm.com

INNKEEPERS: Kathy
Schuit and David
Aigner

ROOMS: 5 rooms with private baths, TV, telephone, dataport; 4 with whirlpool tubs, fireplaces, and private entrances; 1 with wheelchair accessibility

ON THE GROUNDS: Large enclosed courtyard, hot tub, pool table, horseshoes, antique juke box, carved fireplace in common area, front portal with views

CREDIT CARDS: MasterCard, Visa, Discover

RATES: $$–$$$

HOW TO GET THERE: From Albuquerque take I–40 east to the Edgewood exit (187). Turn right at the end of the off ramp. Turn left at first stop sign. Go 0.2 mile to a street on your right called Pioneer Park. Turn right. Alta Mae's is the large building with red roof directly in front of you.

Built in 1995, the home was a collaborative effort between Alta Mae and her children. Interestingly, it sits on the site of a "bean house," a place where pinto bean farmers in the area brought their beans to be cleaned, weighed, bagged, and shipped to Albuquerque via Route 66. One of the support or outbuildings, which was occupied until 1963, still stands outside Alta Mae's courtyard. Kathy and David call it their "ruin."

Constructed in the Territorial New Mexico style with dormers, portals, corbels, and posts, the inn is filled with an elegant and entertaining mix of antiques from different eras and fine art depicting themes from nature. This is particularly fitting for a place that delights guests with the beautiful, enclosed courtyard. A large, green area with utter quiet, it offers a place to truly unwind and soak in desert peace and sunshine.

Before setting out for a day of hiking, skiing, or pueblo visits, you'll stock up on a full breakfast. Kathy and David always offer a hot entree, as well as fresh fruit, cereal, juice, and homemade sweet breads.

What's Nearby Edgewood

This village just east of Albuquerque is most convenient for adventurers wishing to explore the Turquoise Trail. To reach it drive on I-40 west toward Albuquerque, then turn north on New Mexico Highway 14, an official Scenic and Historic Byway. Along this 52-mile route north, you'll have dozens of photo opps of the mountains, ruined farmhouses, and ghost town relics. Be sure to stop in wonderful Madrid to eat and to buy wonderful artwork and home furnishings.

The Galisteo Inn

9 La Vega
Galisteo, NM 87540
Phone: (505) 466-4000

E-MAIL: galisteoin@aol.com

INTERNET SITE: www.galisteoinn.com

INNKEEPERS: Joanna and Wayne Aarniokoski

ROOMS: 12 rooms, 9 with private bath, 4 with TV

ON THE GROUNDS: Library, verandah, garden, hot tub, pool, duck pond, pastures with horses and llamas

CREDIT CARDS: MasterCard, Visa, Discover

RATES: $$-$$$$

HOW TO GET THERE: From Santa Fe drive I-25 north to U.S. 285; follow 285 south to NM 41 south to Galisteo. Turn left when you get to La Vega.

Well removed from any bustle and hustle, this 250-year-old Spanish hacienda is the ideal retreat, just 25 miles from Santa Fe. Built by one of the area's original settlers when New Mexico was a Spanish territory, the estate remained in one family for more than 200 years. Galisteo today is an enclave of artists, writers, and healers, and this inn is certainly a place to absorb the prevailing energy.

The Galisteo is open from February through December. Set on eight acres, the inn is a Territorial-style Southwestern adobe, with pine floors and ceilings, kiva fireplaces, and Mexican-tiled baths. Just inside the front door, you feel welcomed by the simple and beautiful look of the wide hall, where creamy walls and rough-hewn ceiling woods provide an authentic impression of the era's architecture.

Room choices range from those with either king or queen beds or fold-out double beds, and those with fireplaces and private baths. You may be tempted to hole up in your room, with its lovely rugs and furnishings and corners for meditation and reading, but there's much more to enjoy: hikes and mountain bike excursions, as well as soaks in hot tub and swimming pool leisure. Ask about arranging for horseback riding, massage, and picnic lunches.

In the morning enjoy a full breakfast buffet, where features might include a chile-packed frittata, fresh fruit bowl, yogurt, sweet bakery breads, and smoothies. For an additional charge you can take advantage of the inn's fixed-price dinners, which may include sweet potato-green chile chowder, smoked venison sausage strudel, braised Chilean sea bass, roasted guinea hen, coriander-crusted pork tenderloin, and black pepper fettucine with grilled fennel and roasted squash.

Inn at Santa Cruz

Route 1
P.O. Box 331
Santa Cruz, NM 87567
Phone: (505) 753–1142; (505) 753–2227

E-MAIL: capilla@innatsantacruz.com

INTERNET SITE: www.innatsantacruz.com

INNKEEPERS: Justin and Sari Jobe

ROOMS: 3 rooms with private bath, TV, telephone, dataport; 1 with wheelchair accessibility

ON THE GROUNDS: Sunroom, courtyard, gardens, lily pond, lawn, porches

CREDIT CARDS: MasterCard, Visa

RATES: $–$$

HOW TO GET THERE: Drive north of Santa Fe on New Mexico 84/285 for approximately 18 miles. Turn right on NM 106 for 1 mile; at the T and stoplight, turn right on NM 76. The Inn at Santa Cruz is 0.4 mile on the right.

This historic hacienda dates back to 1810 and was a horse-change and stagecoach stop on the route between Santa Fe and Taos. Believe it or not, the large guest room was the original stable for the horses, and the interior's *postes* (hand-carved lateral and vertical beams) are original to the period. Throughout the house, you'll note adobe walls that are of double thickness, or thirty-one inches, which was traditional for the area during this time. Also typical are the profuse old beautiful vigas throughout the home—with many extraordinary *latillas* (wooden slats) between them—and the softwood floors and antique furnishings.

As is traditional to this design, the hacienda is built around a central courtyard, where *portales* (columned porches) open onto a sun-filled space with a fountain and a 300-year old tamarisk tree. Spread over the inn's spectacular shaded grounds are a lawn, double French lilacs, and roses. There's even a pond with goldfish and lilies, topped only by the stunning views of the Sangre de Cristo Mountains. Need more? There's a walking track and a swimming pool. One guest called it "the quintessence of haciendas."

Justin and Sari serve a full breakfast every morning, with offerings from traditional Spanish and American cuisines. All breakfasts, which include fresh fruit, orange juice, and coffee or tea, are served in the sunroom.

What's Nearby Santa Cruz

Santa Cruz is close to Chimayo but it's closest to the town of Española. There your diversions include tours of the Black Mesa Winery and Los Luceros Winery. The latter is adjacent to Hacienda de los Luceros, with its seventeenth-century fort, a 1710 chapel, and one of the first jail-houses in northern New Mexico. Española is home, also, to Onate Monument, with art and cultural exhibits pertaining to Hispanic and Pueblo farming communities and to the town's mission and convent replicas. For a relaxing day take a winding drive up U.S. 285 to Ojo Caliente, where you'll spend several hours at the old-fashioned spa getting soaked and massaged.

Blueberry Hill Bed & Breakfast

P.O. Box 881

Taos, NM 87571

Phone: (505) 758-8553

E-MAIL: info@taosbbhill.com

INTERNET SITE: www.taosbbhill.com

INNKEEPERS: Ed and Victoria Truijillo Ramsey

ROOMS: 6 rooms with private bath; includes casita with kitchen

ON THE GROUNDS: Large sunken kiva-style living room, family room, second-story deck overlooking Taos Valley, hot tub

CREDIT CARDS: None accepted

RATES: $$–$$$

HOW TO GET THERE: From the Taos Plaza, drive 3.4 miles west on New Mexico 240/Ranchitos Road, turn north (uphill) on Blueberry Hill Road and continue for 1.4 miles.

The oldest house on Blueberry Hill, which was known as Taos's historic "Lover's Lane," this charming inn overlooks Taos Valley. Everyone is impressed with the adobe-and-frame construction that incorporates solar energy and with the large and sunken, semicircular kiva-style living room, offering still more lovely mountain and sunset views.

You'll really like the large and numerous common areas in this B&B, as well as the beautiful antiques, artwork, custom tile work, and Mexican-Southwestern details, such as vigas, latillas, and Saltillo tiles. Victoria, a native Taosena, has utilized various architectural elements from her grandmother's 1862 home, which stood next door to Hacienda Martinez, which was Taos's oldest Spanish Colonial hacienda.

Rooms are in the main house as well as in the casita, which offers its own kitchen. The grounds also offer greenhouses, garden, courtyards, patios, and sensational views. TV, phone, and Internet access is available in guest rooms, and wheelchair accessibility has been provided.

Do look forward each morning to memorable gourmet breakfasts from Ed and Victoria. You'll enjoy fresh fruits, as well as local, homegrown ingredients in specialty dishes.

Casa de las Chimeneas

405 Cordoba-5303
NDCBU
Taos, NM 87577
Phone: (505) 758-4777;
(877) 758-4777

E-MAIL: casa@newmex.com

INTERNET SITE:
www.visittaos.com

INNKEEPER:
Susan Vernon

ROOMS: 8 rooms, including 1 suite, with private bath, TV, phone, data-port; 1 with wheelchair accessibility

ON THE GROUNDS: Outdoor hot tub, extensive gardens; fitness facility with workout room and sauna, on-site staffed massage room

CREDIT CARDS: MasterCard, Visa, American Express, Discover, Diners Club

RATES: $$$–$$$$

HOW TO GET THERE: Located 2 1/2 blocks from Taos Plaza. Drive east on Kit Carson Road and turn right (south) on Montoya, continuing to Cordoba.

Built as a private home in the traditional Territorial style in the 1930s, the property became an inn in 1988. This was two years after Susan Vernon moved from California to Taos to take over publicist duties for the Taos Ski Valley. Soon she became the publicity chief for Taos County, and it wasn't long before she opened her own inn.

Susan's attention to valuable if small details is seen in such amenities as oversized bath towels, hair dryers, and Mexican tins filled with cotton balls and Q-tips in the bathrooms. On the beds you'll find sheep-wool mattress covers, and rooms have tiled bars stocked with complimentary soft drinks, juices, mineral water, and more. You'll also see a leather-bound book with information on area dining, complete with Susan's personal experiences with restaurants.

Considered a destination unto itself, the inn stands out for—among many reasons—its well-loved and extensive spa facilities, as well as lofty standards for service and hospitality. Susan prides herself also on her flower, herb, and vegetable gardens, and she's won prizes at the county fair for her bouquets. The food will have you swooning, too, as Susan's breakfasts include such joys as iced fruit frappe, breakfast burritos, oven-browned potatoes, baked apples stuffed with granola, omelettes with artichoke hearts, and fancy French toast with whole wheat orange-date-nut bread.

And, oh yes, the rooms. There's the Willow Room, with a king or two twin beds, carved yellow-pine furniture from Mexico, and an antique writing table; the Library Suite, with a kiva-style fireplace, queen-size bed and a queen-size sofa sleeper, game table with chess and backgammon, and white-pine antiques; and La Sala de Patron, with a king bed, fireplace, vaulted skylight, antique cherry desk, sensational bath with jetted tub under a skylight, and a separate sitting room with huge windows.

What's Nearby

A photographers' favorite stop on the High Road to Taos, Truchas is a hamlet of less than 1,000 hardy souls, which got busy in 1987 when Robert Redford brought a film crew in to shoot *The Milagro Beanfield War*. Originally named Neustra Señora de Rosario de las Truchas (Our Lady of the Rosary of the Trout), the town sits on a hillside high in the Sangre de Cristos and offers extraordinary views. Shopping and dining are in easy reach at Chimayo and Taos.

Casa Europa Inn & Gallery

840 Upper Ranchitos Road-HC68
P.O. Box 3F
Taos, NM 87571
Phone: (505) 758–9798; (888) 758–9798

E-MAIL: casa-europa@travelbase.com

INTERNET SITE: www.travel-base.com/destinations/taos/casa-europa/

INNKEEPERS: Rudi and Marcia Zwicker

ROOMS: 7 rooms, including 1 suite, with private bath and telephone; 5 with cable TV; 1 with wheelchair accessibility

ON THE GROUNDS: Two large sitting rooms first and second floors, water fountain in front courtyard, pretty gardens, outside hot tub and sauna

CREDIT CARDS: MasterCard, Visa, American Express

RATES: $$–$$$$

HOW TO GET THERE: From Taos Plaza drive 1.3 miles west on Ranchitos Road/New Mexico 240 and turn right on Upper Ranchitos Road. Drive 0.3 mile.

The sprawling pueblo-style adobe was begun over 200 years ago and underwent six years of restoration in the 1980s. What you'll find inside are the centuries-old Spanish influence combined with modern conveniences, resulting in a comforting elegance. Large rooms feature whitewashed walls sparkling with sunlight and a blend of European antiques and Southwestern accent pieces. The courtyards offer the best of New Mexico's foliage and tempting extras, such as a hot tub.

Rooms to consider include the Taos Mountain, a second-story corner room with a kiva fireplace, black marble bathroom, and stunning views at sunrise and sunset; the three-room Southwest Suite, with a central sitting room, porcelain wood stove, white-marble bathroom and whirlpool tub, and king bed; and the Spa Room, with a two-person hot tub, sitting area with sofa, fireplace, TV, steam shower, and king bed.

Afternoon treats include European-style pastries made in-house, followed by fireside hors d'oeuvres to be enjoyed before you head out to dinner. Breakfast always includes fresh fruit, juice, coffee, and tea, as well such specialties as vegetarian eggs Benedict, whole wheat–oatmeal waffles, or pecan French toast with dried fruit and sausage or ham.

Inn on the Rio

910 Kit Carson Road
Taos, NM 87571
Phone: (505) 758-7199; (800) 859-6752

E-MAIL: innonrio@plaza.org

INTERNET SITE: www.innontherio.com

INNKEEPERS: Robert and Julie Cahalane

ROOMS: 12 rooms with private bath, TV, telephone, dataport

ON THE GROUNDS: Farmer's porches, heated outdoor pool, outdoor hot tub, many gardens; gathering room with kiva fireplace

CREDIT CARDS: MasterCard, Visa, Discover

RATES: $$–$$$

HOW TO GET THERE: From Taos just 1.5 miles east of historic Taos Plaza in a quiet residential neighborhood. *Not* on the "strip."

Clinging to the banks of the Rio Fernando, under the shade of centuries-old silver cottonwoods, the Inn on the Rio offers twelve rooms decorated in the rich Southwestern style typical of northern New Mexico. You'll be pampered in every corner of this 200-year-old adobe home by such touches as fluffy towels, handmade organic bath amenities, cable TV, and artful decor that includes furniture, murals, and sculpture hand-painted by local folk artists.

Julie, an author and gourmet cook, outdoes herself each morning with a fabulous homemade breakfast that's lighter on weekdays and heartier on weekends and holidays. Robert is the consummate outdoorsman who can fill your time with hiking, biking, skiing, white-water rafting, and such.

Touchstone Inn Spa & Gallery

110 Mabel Dodge
Lane
Taos, NM 87571
Phone: (505)
758-0192; (800) 758-0192

E-MAIL: touchstone@taosnet.com

INTERNET SITE: www.touchstoneinn.com

INNKEEPER: Bren Price

ROOMS: 7 rooms with private bath, TV, telephone

ON THE GROUNDS: Hot tub, sunroom, sauna, massage room; river, huge trees, unobstructed mountain views, labyrinth, gardens, patios, two acres of wildflowers, fountains indoors and out

CREDIT CARDS: None accepted

RATES: $$–$$$$

HOW TO GET THERE: From Taos Plaza drive north on New Mexico 68/64, veering left onto 64 at split in road (after about 1 mile). Follow the highway to Mabel Dodge Lane and turn right.

On this quiet, peaceful adobe estate, shadowed by tall trees at the edge of the Taos Pueblo land, is a home whose center dates to about 1800. People who come to the hacienda find generous portions of serenity throughout the house and on its grounds.

Rooms have fireplaces, luxurious textiles, intimate patios, beautifully tiled baths, and plenty of cozy corners. Guests enjoy an outdoor hot tub, which just happens to afford lovely vistas of the Taos Mountains, and the double hammock is a prime napping spot on the patio. Art aficionados will appreciate artist-owner Bren Price's studio and gallery, where she writes and creates watercolor glories.

An on-site day spa offers professional therapeutic massage, and skin and body treatments by licensed therapists. To further your sense of well-being, Touchstone offers gourmet and vegetarian breakfasts each morning.

What's Nearby Taos

Simpler than Santa Fe, but just as rich in culture and history, Taos can be explored on your own driving and walking tours or aboard the Historic Taos Trolley Tours. Wander around Taos Plaza, a hub for shops, galleries, and dining, then make your way over to the Kit Carson Museum, the Governor Ben House and Museum, Martinez Hacienda, Millicent Rogers Museum, and the Van Vechten-Lineberry Taos Art Museum. Spend at least a morning or afternoon exploring the incomparable Taos Pueblo, then take an Enchanted Loop drive up to Red River, stopping along the way to examine the D. H. Lawrence Shrine and the Vietnam Memorial. Feeling energetic? Try some of the nation's toughest skiing at Taos Ski Valley and exciting rafting along the Rio Grande.

Other Recommended B&Bs Nearby

Casa Escondida, a fifty-year-old adobe with antiques and American Mission-style furnishings, six acres of countryside with exceptional landscaping and views of clouds and mountains, close proximity to the Santuario de Chimayo, full breakfast, and eight rooms with private baths; P.O. Box 142, Chimayo, NM 87522; telephone: (505) 351-4805 or (800) 643-7201; e-mail: casqes@newmexico.com. *Little Tree B&B,* a 1990s adobe home built in traditional style with a garden courtyard in the countryside, with four guest rooms with private baths, three with TV and VCR; 226 Hondo-Seco Road, P.O. Drawer II, Taos, NM 87571; telephone: (505) 776-8467 or (800) 334-8467; e-mail: little@newmex.com; Internet site: www.littletreebandb.com. *Rancho del Llano,* with a library, garden, lily pond, hiking trails, cookout areas, gardens, three guest rooms with private baths, a separate guesthouse with three bedrooms and a full bath; 371 County Road 0078, Truchas, NM 87578; telephone: (505) 689-2347 or (800) 378-4942; e-mail: vmarkley@la-tierra.com; Internet site: www.la-tierra.com/vmarkley. *Rancho Arriba Bed & Breakfast,* a Spanish-Colonial design in the Southwestern style, with three rooms and a porch; P.O. Box 338, Truchas, NM 87578; telephone: (505) 689-2374. *The Willows Inn Bed & Breakfast,* built in 1926 by the Taos Pueblo Indians and owned for many years by E. Martin Hennings, a member of the Taos Society of Artists; five guest rooms with private bath, huge music library, flagstone courtyard with fountain, gourmet breakfast; 412 Kit Carson Road, Taos, NM 87571; telephone: (505) 758-2558 or (800) 525-TAOS (8267); e-mail: willows@ newmex.com. *The Inn & Mercantile at Ojo,* within an 1800s local store and post office, remodeled in 1995 to offer six rooms with private bath and one room with wheelchair accessibility, Ping-Pong room, fresh breakfast goods, access to old-fashioned spa and pool; P.O. Box 215, Ojo Caliente, NM 87549; telephone: (505) 583-9131; e-mail: innojo@ojocaliente.com; Internet site: www.ojocaliente.com. *Hacienda Del Sol,* the first Taos home of the celebrated, late Mabel Dodge, who entertained Georgia O'Keeffe, Ansel Adams, D. H. Lawrence, and others within; eleven guest rooms with private baths, living room with TV and telephone, garden, hot tub, patio, century-old cottonwood trees; 109 Mable Dodge Lane, Taos, NM 87571; telephone: (505) 758-0287; e-mail: sunhouse@newmex.com; Internet site: www.taoshaciendadelsol.com. *La Posada de Taos,* a 1904 home and town's first B&B features adobe architecture, kiva fireplaces, antiques and local art, courtyard, sunroom, hot tub, six guest rooms with private baths and full, hot breakfast; 309 Juanita Lane, Taos, NM 87571; telephone: (505) 758-8164; e-mail: laposada@newmex.com; Internet site: www.newmex. com/laposada.

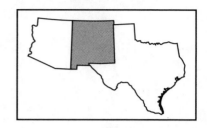

Rio Grande
River

Gallup

Santa Fe

25

Canadian
River

10

40

40

Albuquerque

NEW MEXICO

Gila
River

25

Pecos River

10

Las Cruces

Carlsbad

N

New Mexico: Santa Fe

Numbers on map refer to towns numbered below.

Adobe Abode Bed & Breakfast Inn

202 Chapelle Street
Santa Fe, NM 87501
Phone: (505) 983-3133

E-MAIL:
adobebnb@sprynet.com

INTERNET SITE:
www.adobeabode.com

INNKEEPER: Pat Harbour

ROOMS: 6 rooms—3 casitas—with private bath, cable TV, telephones, answering machines; 1 with wheelchair accessibility

ON THE GROUNDS: Garden, courtyard

CREDIT CARDS: MasterCard, Visa, Discover

RATES: $$$-$$$$

HOW TO GET THERE: Take I-25 north from Albuquerque, get off at St. Francis exit. Go 3 miles to Cerrillos Road, turn right to Guadalupe. Turn left on Guadalupe and continue to Johnson Street. Turn right on Johnson, then left on Chapelle. Go 1 block to corner of Chapelle and McKenzie.

After enjoying intriguing careers in journalism, fashion promotion and advertising, and real estate, Pat made a dream come true by opening her own B&B in 1989. She did so by overhauling a 1907 Pueblo-style Fort Marcy officers' quarters and creating three casitas in the courtyard compound. Historic details are intact, of course, and there are lovely private patios, a garden, and intimate Santa Fe spirit to show for her diligent work.

Among favorite rooms are the Cactus, with a fireplace, queen bed, and oversized shower; the Bronco, with fireplace, western scheme, private covered porch and brick patio; and the Provence Suite, with a living room, separate bedrooms, and beautifully tiled bathroom.

Adobe Abode is the perfect balance of the authentic and sophisticated. Throughout the guest rooms are such touches as French and English antiques, a mahogany planter's chair from the Philippines, Spanish-Colonial furniture, handmade Aspen pole beds, puppets from Java, and folk art animal creations from Oaxaca. Luxury elements include custom-made soaps and shampoos, designer linens, thick terry robes, and complimentary sherry and cookies on hand at all times.

Each morning you'll greet the day with a gourmet breakfast with fresh juice, fresh fruit, homemade muffins, and a different Southwestern entree for every day of the week. Some of the specialties have included spinach-sausage egg scramble with fiesta baked tomatoes, caramelized French toast with fresh fruit, blue-corn waffles with banana-pecan syrup, and green chile soufflé.

Alexander's Inn

529 East Palace Avenue
Santa Fe, NM 87501
Phone: (505) 986–1431; (888) 321–5123

E-MAIL: alexandinn@aol.com
INTERNET SITE: www.collectors guide.com/alexandinn
INNKEEPERS: Carolyn Lee and Keith Spencer-Gore
ROOMS: 10 rooms with phones, 8 with private bath, TV/cable; including the Cottage with kitchen and double Jacuzzi tub
ON THE GROUNDS: Beautiful gardens, hot tub
CREDIT CARDS: MasterCard, Visa, Discover
RATES: $$–$$$$
HOW TO GET THERE: From Albuquerque drive north on I–25. In Santa Fe exit at St. Francis and follow St. Francis to Cerillos Road. Turn right on Cerillos and continue to Paseo de Peralta; then turn right and follow Paseo de Peralta to Palace Avenue, and turn right again.

For twelve years this 1903 Craftsman-style home has been one of Santa Fe's more charming, old-fashioned B&Bs. Unlike the overwhelming supply of Southwest-style architecture found in neighboring inns, Alexander's is something more like an elegant version of Grandma's house. Stained glass, stenciling, and antiques are common throughout the main house, as are gleaming hardwood floors, lace curtains, and fresh flowers. Behind the house are private casitas built in a Southwestern style.

The hosts go out of their way to make guests feel at home at the inn and in Santa Fe. There are soft, fluffy bathrobes to wear, perfect for snuggling in after a soak under the stars in the inn's backyard garden hot tub. Breakfast each morning is a pleasant spread of gourmet coffee, delightful homemade muffins and granola, whole grain breads, cheeses, fresh fruits, and yogurt. In winter you enjoy this near the roaring wood-burning stove in the cozy kitchen; in spring and summer breakfast is a verandah event, beneath the shade of apricot trees, in the company of singing birds. A sweet end to the day is found in a basket of chocolates left at your door.

Each guest room features comforts such as down pillows and comforters. Room choices include the Peony, with an iron-and-brass queen bed and shared bath; the Wildflower, with twin beds and shared bath; the Lilac, with a four-poster king bed, stained glass, and private bath with claw-foot tub; and the Cottage, with a queen bed upstairs, a living room with queen sofa sleeper and kiva fireplace, kitchen, private bath, and double Jacuzzi tub.

Alexander's has an ideal location, within walking distance of both the plaza and Canyon Road shopping and gallery districts. The hosts are great at helping with itinerary planning, restaurant choices, and ideas for outstanding hiking, biking, skiing, and rafting excursions. They'll also provide guest privileges at the full-service El Gancho Health Club.

El Farolito Bed & Breakfast

514 Galisteo Street
Santa Fe, NM 87501
Phone: (505) 988-1631; (888) 634-8782

E-MAIL: innkeeper@farolito.com

INTERNET SITE: www.farolito.com

INNKEEPERS: Walt Wyss and Wayne Mainus

ROOMS: 8 rooms in 5-building grouping with private bath, TV, telephone; 7 with fireplaces

ON THE GROUNDS: Semiprivate or private patios

CREDIT CARDS: MasterCard, Visa, American Express, Discover

RATES: $$-$$$$

HOW TO GET THERE: From I-25 take exit 282 and drive north on St. Francis Drive. Turn right onto Cerillos Road. Turn right onto Paseo de Peralta, then left on Galisteo.

This appealing compound that was wholly transformed to an inn in 1991 and fully renovated, redecorated, and landscaped in 1997 and 1998 is within easy striking distance of the Santa Fe Plaza. Four of the five buildings in the grouping are adobe structures that were in place before 1910. Naturally, adobe is the primary construction here, with lovely Saltillo tile floors and brick floors, plaster walls, skylights, kiva fireplaces, French doors, viga and wood ceilings, corbels, and hand-forged gate and trellises providing the distinctive detail.

Walt and Wayne—who also own Four Kachinas—have put a wealth of thought and planning into the atmosphere of this B&B. Inside the casitas you'll be taken with the quality furnishings, particularly the original Southwest paintings and handcrafted furniture by local artists and craftspeople, as well as Navajo weavings, collection of Pueblo pottery, Kachinas, hand-carved doors, and hand-forged tables. You can curl up in front of the fireplace in your room or linger over tea or a bottle of wine on your patio, while contemplating your next museum visit or gallery purchase.

In the morning enjoy an expanded Continental breakfast of fresh fruit plates, homemade baked goods, yogurts, granolas, coffees, teas, juices, cereals, granolas, and bagels.

El Paradero en Santa Fe

220 West Manhattan Avenue
Santa Fe, NM 87501
Phone: (505) 988-1177

E-MAIL: elpara@trail.com

INTERNET SITE: www.elparadero.com

INNKEEPERS: Thom Allen and Ouida MacGregor

ROOMS: 14 rooms with TV, phone; 12 with private bath; 1 with wheelchair accessibility; including 2 suites in adjacent coachman's house

ON THE GROUNDS: Coffee room, living room, parlor courtyards

CREDIT CARDS: MasterCard, Visa, American Express

RATES: $-$$$

HOW TO GET THERE: Drive north on I-25 from Albuquerque to Santa Fe. Take the Old Pecos Trail exit and head north. At third light veer to right and stay on Old Pecos Trail. Turn left on Paseo de Peralta and continue to Manhattan Avenue.

Here's one of the wonderful lodgings that reflects the deep character for which Santa Fe is famous. Originally a Spanish farmhouse, this building was constructed between 1800 and 1820 and given Territorial detailing in the 1880s. In 1912 the main house was remodeled, and the Victorian doors and windows were added. During the time they've owned it, Thom and Ouida have done some remodeling, but they've been careful about keeping the eccentric, hodgepodge personality intact.

There are nine rooms on the ground level, facing the courtyard. Three are upstairs, while two suites sit in an adjacent, 1912 double-brick coachman's house. Some of the quarters have skylights, and others have porches, fireplaces, and/or balconies with mountain views. Decor includes handwoven textiles, tiles, folk art, and Southwestern furniture.

Thom and Ouida say that guests comment most on how much they enjoy the inn's breakfast—which typically includes a gourmet entree, homebaked breads, fruit, and juice—and staff. The hospitality includes attention to detail in terms of the art and architectural elements, as well as the homey qualities that make everyone feel like staying a while. The piano in the living room is often used by guests for impromptu concerts, and guests enjoy talking to Ouida, who has Ph.D. in mythology, and share stories and observations about Spanish and Native American cultures that provide such depth to the area's cultural heritage.

Four Kachinas Inn Bed & Breakfast

512 Webber Street
Santa Fe, NM 87501
Phone: (505) 982-2550; (800) 397-2564

E-MAIL: info@fourkachinas.com

INTERNET SITE: fourkachinas.com

INNKEEPERS: Walt Wyss and Wayne Mainus

ROOMS: 5 rooms in 2 buildings with private bath, TV, telephone; 1 with wheelchair accessibility

ON THE GROUNDS: Quiet residential location, garden courtyard with fountain

CREDIT CARDS: MasterCard, Visa, American Express, Discover

RATES: $$–$$$

HOW TO GET THERE: From I–25 take exit 282 and drive north on St. Francis Drive. Turn right onto Cerillos Road. Turn right onto Paseo de Peralta, then turn right onto Webber Street.

Walt and Wayne have learned a thing or two about running a fabulous Santa Fe B&B, as they have two in town—this one and El Farolito. You'll see immediately on a glance around Four Kachinas that these hosts put quality furnishings and certain eye appeal into every corner of their lodgings. Throughout there is a collection of original regional art, regionally themed guest rooms, Spanish and Navajo weavings, Hopi Kachinas, Native American pottery, and wonderful handcrafted furniture by regional artisans.

The main cottage at Four Kachinas was built by in 1910 by Carlo Digneo, one of the masons who built the exquisite St. Francis Cathedral just off the Santa Fe Plaza. The cottage has wood floors, ten-foot ceilings, stucco exterior, and a red-metal pitched roof. In contrast the Kachina Building was erected in 1991 and exhibits a northern New Mexico Territorial architectural style, as well as small patios and Saltillo tile floors.

Mornings, you'll join other guests in the breakfast room lounge area, which is an adobe Southwestern pueblo setting. There you can fortify yourself for a day of shopping, hiking, horseback riding, or museum browsing with an expanded Continental breakfast of fresh fruit, home-baked breads, yogurt, cereal, granola, coffees, teas, and juices.

Grant Corner Inn

122 Grant Avenue
Santa Fe, NM 87501
Phone: (505) 983-6678; (800) 964-9003

E-MAIL: gcinn@aol.com

INTERNET SITE:
www.grantcornerinn.com

INNKEEPER: Louise S. Stewart

ROOMS: 10 rooms, including suite, with private bath,

TV, and telephone; 3 with dataport; 1 with wheelchair accessibility

ON THE GROUNDS: Verandah, garden; upstairs guest lounge, gift shop, comfortable living room

CREDIT CARDS: MasterCard, Visa, American Express

RATES: $$–$$$$

HOW TO GET THERE: From Albuquerque drive north on I-25, exit St. Francis and drive north 4.5 miles. Turn right on Alameda, then turn left to Guadalupe and go north 2 blocks. Turn right on Johnson and continue to Grant.

For years this has been one of the best-known B&Bs in town—and for several good reasons. It's memorable in that it isn't of adobe construction, as is much of Santa Fe. This 1905 Colonial home with wraparound porch is also one of the more gracious lodgings anyplace in the Southwest. Built for a wealthy New Mexico ranching family named Winsor, the home has been owned by a Presbyterian minister and his family, one of whom married an eccentric justice of the peace who did business—marriages and collecting traffic fines—in the home's parlor. It's been a boarding house and an office building; eventually it was converted to an inn in 1981.

Owner Louise Stewart came by her innkeeping talents honestly: Her parents founded the legendary Camelback Inn in Scottsdale, where Louise learned about elegant hospitality. With a thirteen-person staff, she runs a well-loved place, where you'll undoubtedly meet guests who have stayed here time and time again. One of the reasons is surely Louise's breakfasts, which are so impressive that she was compelled to write and publish the *Grant Corner Inn Breakfast and Brunch Cookbook*. The morning meal varies, but you can expect things like apricot blintzes, fruit frappes, blue-corn waffles, and raisin rice griddle cakes. And don't be surprised to find tables in the dining room occupied by diners not staying at the inn; Louise welcomes the public by reservation.

Rooms range from a first-floor suite with a queen bed and a twin daybed to the third-floor room with twin studio beds. What you'll love, beyond the exquisite antiques and fabrics, is the convenience to the plaza and to the Georgia O'Keeffe Museum.

In addition, Louise has the Grant Corner Inn Hacienda at 604 Griffin Street, which is a Southwestern-style condo with two guest rooms on the upper level, along with living room, dining room, kitchen, and half-bath downstairs. This is ideal for a family or friends traveling in a group.

Hacienda Nicholas

320 East Marcy Street
Santa Fe, NM 87501
Phone: (505) 992-8385; (888) 321-5123

E-MAIL: alexandinn@aol.com

INTERNET SITE: www.collectorsguide.com/alexandinn

INNKEEPERS: Carolyn Lee and Glennon Grusch

ROOMS: 7 rooms with private bath, TV/cable, phone; 1 with wheelchair accessibility

ON THE GROUNDS: Lovely garden, courtyard, huge great room with big fireplace

CREDIT CARDS: MasterCard, Visa, Discover

RATES: $$-$$$$

HOW TO GET THERE: From Albuquerque drive north on I-25. In Santa Fe exit at St. Francis and follow St. Francis to Cerillos Road. Turn right on Cerillos and continue to Paseo de Peralta; turn right on Paseo de Peralta and follow it to Marcy Street. Turn right on Marcy.

Originally a 1950s-era adobe hacienda, this decade-old B&B is built around a garden courtyard filled with roses, wisteria, iris, daisies, pansies, and geraniums and is within quick striking distance of the plaza and Canyon Road. You'll feel immediately at home in this hospitable setting, and particularly in the wonderful great room, with its twenty-foot ceilings, fat wooden vigas, faintly colored and hand-troweled plaster walls, and a gigantic fireplace. The overstuffed couches are just right for curling up with a good book or a favorite companion, especially in front of a roaring fire.

Like her other two inns, Carolyn Lee has named this one for one of her adored children. And as with the others, she and her large staff—who are known to work long hours in providing all the many comforts for guests—are wonderful at helping you figure out which museums, galleries, restaurants, stores, and outdoor pursuits will best complete your stay.

Deciding which room is your favorite could be a trick, however. The Nicholas has a wrought-iron king bed, as well as a living room with a fireplace; and the Sunflower has a four-poster king with a fireplace, as does the Chamisa. Each room is decorated in simple but exquisite taste.

Mornings are made merry with a hot dish, such as French toast, pancakes, quiche, or frittatas, as well as fresh fruit salad, homemade muffins, fresh granola, whole grain breads, cheeses, and yogurt. Afternoons are cozy times when you're welcome to homemade cookies, brownies, pies, and cakes, accompanied by coffee, cocoa, cider, and hot teas.

Hacienda Vargas Bed and Breakfast Inn

1431 Highway 313
Algodones, NM 87001
Phone: (505) 867-9115; (800) 261-0006

E-MAIL: hacvar@swcp.com

INTERNET SITE: www.swcp.com/hacvar

INNKEEPERS: Cynthia and Richard Spence

ROOMS: 8 rooms with private bath, including 3 suites

ON THE GROUNDS: Library, pond, gardens, rooms with fireplaces and private Jacuzzis

CREDIT CARDS: MasterCard, Visa, American Express

RATES: $-$$$

HOW TO GET THERE: From Albuquerque drive north on I-25 to exit 248, Algodones; go left on exit to end of New Mexico 313, left again on U.S. 66 to Hacienda Vargas sign.

Tucked away on old Route 66, also El Camino Real, this appealing B&B is a good choice for travelers wanting to be between Santa Fe and Albuquerque. Resting on the primary road between Mexico City and Santa Fe, which itself has roots in the sixteenth century, this site is one where Spanish conquistadors rode in search of the fabled Seven Cities of Gold. Located here have been a stagecoach stop, train depot, and an Indian post. There remains an adobe chapel—unchanged and in use—that ties together the spirit of the Spanish settlers and the Christian conversion of the Pueblo Indian culture.

Hacienda Vargas is noted for having preserved authenticity when the historic structures were renovated in 1991. The resulting inn offers a lovely blend of comfort and traditional New Mexican styling. The Santa Ana Suite is a large, two-room area with a private entrance, Jacuzzi, and fireplace; the Santa Fe Suite is distinguished by the century-old bricks on the bathroom floor; the Kiva Suite has a fireplace, Jacuzzi, and French doors that open onto a courtyard, with a 200-year-old tree; and the Pueblo Room has a private entrance on an inner courtyard.

Before a day of skiing, golf, casino gambling, or horseback riding, load up on the inn's full Southwestern-style breakfast spread.

La Tienda Inn

445-447 West San Francisco Street

Duran House

511 West San Francisco Street
Santa Fe, NM 87501
Phone: (505) 989-8259; (800) 889-7611

E-MAIL: info@latiendabb.com

INTERNET SITE: www.latiendabb.com

INNKEEPERS: Leighton and Barbara Watson, James Meyer

ROOMS: 11 rooms, in 2 houses, with private bath, TV, telephone; 2 with wheelchair accessibility

ON THE GROUNDS: Garden and fountain, private courtyards

CREDIT CARDS: MasterCard, Visa

RATES: $$-$$$$

HOW TO GET THERE: Drive north from Albuquerque on I-25 and exit St. Francis Drive. Turn right onto Cerillos Road, left onto Guadalupe Street, and right onto San Francisco.

Found just 4 blocks west of the Santa Fe Plaza, this pair of old homes turned into B&Bs are just what you want if you are looking for fast access to the town's action but plenty of luxury and quiet when it's time to rest and regroup.

Only sixty years ago, La Tienda's common room was a small neighborhood market. Your hosts have taken it and the Territorial-style house next door and turned them into a lovely inn. The effort warranted an award from the City of Santa Fe, and the Territorial house—nearly a century old—is listed on the State Historical Register. The extension of this intriguing inn is called Duran House, circa 1900, a red-roofed house, located just a few doors down from La Tienda. A formidable restoration resulted in four sensational new rooms.

Among your choices for lodging at the complex are the Territorial house's Montoya-Mascarell Suite, which offers two bedrooms, a common hallway, and a view of the front garden and fountain; the Trujillo Room, with wheelchair access, fireplace, and king or two twin beds; and the Ortiz

Room, with a courtyard view, fireplace, and queen bed. In the Duran House, consider Maria's Room, with a kiva fireplace, breakfast nook with portal, and garden; Rosa's Room, also with a kiva fireplace and wheelchair accessibility; and Aurora's Room, a second-floor choice with a wonderful view of the Sangre de Cristo Mountains.

Your mornings will begin with La Tienda's own warm breads, cereal, fresh fruit salad, juice, yogurt, coffee, and tea. Enjoy the meal in your room or in the garden during warmer months.

The Madeleine

106 Faithway Street
Santa Fe, NM 87501
Phone: (505) 982-3465;
(888) 877-7622

INTERNET SITE:
www.madeleineinn.com

INNKEEPERS: Carolyn Lee and Susan Norton

ROOMS: 8 rooms with TV/cable, phone; 6 with private baths; including garden cottage with fireplace, private bath

ON THE GROUNDS: English garden, hot tub

CREDIT CARDS: MasterCard, Visa, Discover

RATES: $–$$$$

HOW TO GET THERE: From Albuquerque drive north on I-25. In Santa Fe exit at St. Francis and follow St. Francis to Cerillos Road. Turn right on Cerillos and continue to Paseo de Peralta; turn right and follow Paseo de Peralta to Palace Avenue, and turn right again.

Formerly known as the Preston House, innkeeper Carolyn Lee renamed this B&B after her daughter, Madeleine, just as she named her other inns, Hacienda Nicholas and Alexander's Inn, after her sons. Carolyn said that in doing so, she married the two passions in her life, that the family connection carries over into the inns. It's not just a promotional line, either; the inns do offer a warm and welcoming spirit.

The Madeleine, built in 1886 by railroad tycoon George Cutter Preston, is one of two Queen Anne Victorian homes in all New Mexico. Ornate with intricate detail both inside and out, the home features stained-glass windows, window seats, dark wood molding, brick-and-tile fireplaces, and a large front porch on which to rock the day away. Throughout you'll find Carolyn's sensational knack for placing antiques. The gardens burst in summer with scents and colors from a mix of roses, pansies, iris, snapdragons, and mint.

Guests share common rooms with couches, chairs, tables, and fireplaces, as well as a dining room. Guest rooms include the gorgeous Columbine, with an iron-and-brass king bed, fireplace, stained-glass bay windows, private bath; the similar Morning Glory; and the Violet, a Queen-Anne-style garden cottage with a fireplace, king bed, single window-seat bed, and private bath.

In the mornings you'll be pampered with homemade muffins and granola; a hot dish such as quiche, pancakes, or frittata; whole grain breads; and fresh fruit. In the afternoon you'll end a day of shopping and gallery browsing with a tea time, complete with homemade cookies, cake, cheesecake, or torte.

Pueblo Bonito Bed & Breakfast Inn

138 West Manhattan Avenue
Santa Fe, NM 87501
Phone: (505) 984-8001; (800) 461-4599

E-MAIL: pueblo@cybermesa.com

INNKEEPERS: Herb and Amy Behm

ROOMS: 18 rooms with private bath, TV, telephone, dataport

ON THE GROUNDS: Hot tub, courtyards, fireplaces, garden

CREDIT CARDS: MasterCard, Visa, American Express, Discover

RATES: $-$$$

HOW TO GET THERE: Drive north on I-25 from Albuquerque to Santa Fe. Take the Old Pecos Trail exit and head north. At third light veer to right and stay on Old Pecos Trail. Turn left on Paseo de Peralta and continue to Manhattan.

Tucked with thick adobe walls, Pueblo Bonito is a century-old adobe estate right in the middle of Santa Fe's historic center and a five-minute walk from the famed plaza. Aesthetics are key at this lodging, as each of the eighteen rooms has hand-crafted furniture within the foot-thick walls, as well as works by local artisans. All have queen beds, and oak, maple, brick, or flagstone floors; others have fireplaces, pull-out sofa beds, kitchens, sitting rooms, and private yards.

Newly renovated, the inn occupies quiet grounds with courtyards, narrow brick pathways, adobe archways to the street, and a garden shaded by enormous, old trees. Guests enjoy afternoon margaritas, a glass of wine with meat and cheese platters, or tea specialties, as well as nighttime hot tub dips to assure sweet dreams. In the morning there's a breakfast buffet of fresh fruits, juices, pastries, muffins, yogurt, cereal, coffee, and tea.

The Spencer House Bed & Breakfast

222 McKenzie Street
Santa Fe, NM 87501
Phone: (505) 988-3024; (800) 647-0530

E-MAIL: jan@spencerhse-santafe.com
INTERNET SITE: www.spencerhse-santafe.com
INNKEEPERS: Jan McConnell and John Pitlak
ROOMS: 6 rooms with private bath, 3 rooms with TV, telephone, dataport; including the Casita, a private cottage with kitchen and patio
ON THE GROUNDS: Garden, dining room
CREDIT CARDS: MasterCard, Visa, American Express
RATES: $$-$$$$
HOW TO GET THERE: Drive north from Albuquerque on I-25 and exit St. Francis Drive. Go 3-4 miles, turning right on Cerillos Road, left on Guadalupe Street, and right on McKenzie.

Built in 1923 and restored in 1994, this subtly elegant house has won architectural awards and a place on the National Register of Historic Places. Although clad with sand-colored adobe and topped with red tile, the home has an unusual Mediterranean styling that fits perfectly with the mix of cultural influences for which Santa Fe is revered. Creature comforts have been added, including cable TV and central air-conditioning—which was unheard of in this area until recent years.

Days at Spencer House begin with a bountiful breakfast, which stars the hosts' homemade breakfast cakes, rolls, and breads. Hot entrees are made from scratch, and Jan and John are glad to accommodate special dietary needs with a little notice. A wonderful way to top off breakfast is with an espresso or cappuccino, which certainly gets you revved for the museum-and-gallery journey ahead.

At the end of the day, you can curl up in front of the living room fireplace to review all you've seen, plan the next day, and consider dinner options. Or you can hide out in your room, with the luxuries of a fireplace, Sealy Posturepedic mattress, and Ralph Lauren linens. Rooms to note are the Irish Room, with a bay window and an antique brass bed; the English Room, with plenty of sunlight and steps leading to the high queen four-poster bed; and the Casita, a particularly private cottage with living room, kitchen, and private patio.

Water Street Inn

427 Water Street
Phone: (505) 984-1193; (800) 646-6752

E-MAIL: info@waterstreetinn.com

INNKEEPER: Mindy Mills

ROOMS: 12 rooms with private bath, telephone, dataport, TV

ON THE GROUNDS: Three sunrooms, sundeck, hot tub, courtyard

CREDIT CARDS: MasterCard, Visa, Discover, American Express

RATES: $$–$$$$

HOW TO GET THERE: Drive north from Albuquerque on I-25 and exit St. Francis Drive. Turn right on Cerillos Road, left on Guadalupe Street, and left on Water Street.

What guests love about this restored historic adobe is its quiet convenience to the famous Santa Fe Plaza. It's certainly close enough for an easy walk, but not so close that you'll be trampled by the legions of shoppers when you walk out the front door.

Rooms at this seductive inn are filled with handmade wood furniture, colorful rugs and wall hangings, warm light, and the ambience you expect—down to brick floors, stucco walls and wood viga ceilings—in a finer Santa Fe lodging. Mindy aims to spoil you, offering cable TV/VCRs, phones with voice mail, and air-conditioning and ceiling fans in the guest rooms. There is a video library for you to share with other guests, as well as sunrooms, sundeck, and courtyard—with a fabulous hot tub.

Among room choices is the one with a king-size antique pine bed, sitting area with daybed, fireplace, and patio access; another with private deck and a spiral staircase leading to a second floor; and another with a wraparound balcony.

At breakfast time you'll be treated to a buffet of fresh pastries, fruit bowl, cereals, juices, and coffee. In the evening the inn hosts a happy hour, offering New Mexican wines and hot hors d'oeuvres.

What's Nearby Santa Fe

The 7,000-foot-high capital city offers incomparable shopping on Canyon Road, a wonderland of galleries, and around the historic plaza downtown. Take cooking lessons at Santa Fe School of Cooking or study the myriad facets of the Native American people by visiting such museums as the Institute of American Indian Arts, Museums of Indian Arts and Culture, Museum of International Folk Art, and the Wheelwright Museum of the American Indian. Go on a tour of the Indian pueblos that are near Santa Fe or take part in outdoorsy pursuits—snow skiing, hiking, mountain biking, horseback riding, rafting, and mountain climbing. When you need pampering, go for a massage, wrap, scrub, and soak at Ten Thousand Waves.

Other Recommended B&Bs Nearby

Dancing Ground of the Sun, 2 blocks from the plaza, with decor of varying ceremonial Indian dancers in eleven rooms with private baths, TV, telephone, and many with private patios; 711 Paseo de Peralta, Santa Fe, NM 87501; telephone: (505) 986-9797 or (800) 645-5673. *Casa de la Cuma*, a 1940s adobe-style house on a historic hill near the plaza, with Mexican furniture, Native American rugs, terrific sunset and sunrise views, outdoor Jacuzzi, patio with fire pit, and four rooms with TV, 2 private baths; 105 Paseo de la Cuma, Santa Fe, NM 87501; telephone: (505) 983-1717 or (888) 366-1717; Internet site: www.casacuma.com/bb.

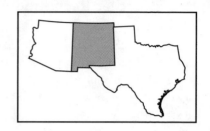

Gallup

Santa Fe

Rio Grande
River

25

Canadian
River

40

Albuquerque

40

NEW MEXICO

13

Pecos River

11

14

Gila
River

25

15

Carlsbad

12

10

Las Cruces

N

New Mexico: Southern

Numbers on map refer to towns numbered below.

Monjeau Shadows

New Mexico Highway 37
Alto, NM 88341
Phone: (505) 336-4191; (800) 463-1934

E-MAIL: shadows@zianet.com

INTERNET SITE: www.Ruidoso.net/shadows

INNKEEPERS: Dale and Brenda Travis

ROOMS: 5 rooms with private baths; including a 2-bedroom suite

ON THE GROUNDS: Large covered deck, big dining room and kitchen, satellite TV, two roomy common areas, eight wooded acres for hiking and mountain biking

CREDIT CARDS: MasterCard and Visa

RATES: $$-$$$

HOW TO GET THERE: From Albuquerque drive south on I-25 to Socorro, then travel east on U.S. 380 to New Mexico 37, past Nogal. Watch for the inn on your right. From El Paso go north on U.S. 54 to Tularosa, then take U.S. 70 east to Ruidoso, turning north on New Mexico 48, through Alto. Turn left on New Mexico 37 and watch for inn on left.

This pleasantly remote B&B provides a sense of seclusion, but it's really a quick drive from Capitán, home of the Smokey Bear Museum, and to the Lincoln County museums, as well as to Spencer Theater. The road to Ski Apache ski area is just 6 miles away.

A comfortable family home that's been converted to a country inn, Monjeau Shadows is named for a nearby mountain peak. If you've come in hope of hiding out, take the downstairs bedroom; it's tucked behind the big common room, where couches, pool table, jigsaw puzzles, videos, books, and games are available to all guests. The other rooms are found on the third floor, where a two-bedroom suite with an adjoining bathroom is available to families or a small group of friends traveling together. If the house isn't full and you have one of the bedrooms, the other won't be rented so that you're not sharing a bath with strangers. Other guest rooms on this floor have queen beds or two double beds.

On the home's main floor, big dining and living rooms with soaring ceilings are tastefully furnished with pretty couches, polished tables, and flowers. There's also a big, sunny kitchen with a breakfast area, where guests like to hang out and visit with Brenda while she whips up bountiful breakfasts. Her typical spread includes bacon and biscuits with gravy, omelettes stuffed with cream cheese and jalapeño, bread pudding, and homemade breads. And in the afternoon she'll bake her famous oatmeal cookies for you.

Happy Trails B&B

1857 Paisano Road
Las Cruces, NM 88005
Phone: (505) 527–8471
Fax: (505) 532–1937

E-MAIL: htrails@zianet.com

INTERNET SITE:
www.las-cruces-new-mexico.com

INNKEEPER: Sylvia Byrnes

ROOMS: 2 rooms sharing bath, 1 suite with private bath

ON THE GROUNDS: Courtyard, swimming pool, Jacuzzi; pecan orchards

CREDIT CARDS: MasterCard, Visa, American Express, Discover

RATES: $$

HOW TO GET THERE: Drive west on I-10 from El Paso and take the Old Mesilla exit 140; follow NM 28 south to Onate Plaza. Turn right at the plaza onto Calle Del Norte, after about 0.2 mile turn right onto Paisano. Happy Trails will be on your right, just 0.4 mile down the road.

This fabulous 1950 home, built by architect Horace Porter, a ranch house of genuine Mexican adobe brick construction, begs you to stay awhile on its blue portales (verandahs), beneath a blue, Territorial-style roof. You'll love kicking back with some of Sylvia's cowboy coffee and gazing across the home's five acres toward the beautiful Organ Mountains. Swim in the pool and have a drink on the patio, but leave yourself time to wander down the road and explore Old Mesilla or visit the seven-stall stable and corrals with boarding horses.

A B&B since 1995, the home offers rooms with queen-size beds and creamy adobe walls, painted from designs by a local artist. One room is a suite, and two others share a bath. There are tile floors throughout, and plenty of healthy green plants about. Two rooms open onto a sunroom that leads to the courtyard, complete with its gorgeous pool and outdoor Jacuzzi. You can't help but be taken by the artist's poolside mural of a pecan orchard. The common area is a great room, decorated in Mexican folk art, and there's a cheery hallway that offers guests a wet bar, teas, and fruits.

Breakfasts are inspired and far from skimpy. Sylvia and her husband,

Barry, usually serve chile breakfast burritos, omelettes, pancakes, fresh fruits, homemade breads, juices, teas, and good strong piñon cowboy coffee. A trademark dish is Sylvia's stuffed French toast, filled with jams and yogurt. When it's time for lunch or dinner, Sylvia can point you to the best eats in Old Mesilla.

Hilltop Hacienda Bed & Breakfast

2600 Westmoreland Street
Las Cruces, NM 88012
Phone: (505) 382–3556

E-MAIL: hilltop@zianet.com

INTERNET SITE: www.zianet.com/hilltop

INNKEEPERS: Bob and Teddi Peters

ROOMS: 3 rooms with private bath, TV, telephone, dataport, wheelchair accessibility

ON THE GROUNDS: Library, verandah, garden, tennis court nearby

CREDIT CARDS: MasterCard, Visa, American Express, Discover

RATES: $–$$

HOW TO GET THERE: From El Paso drive I-10 west to Las Cruces, then follow I-25 north to exit 6A. Next follow U.S. 70 to Del Rey Boulevard. Turn left on Del Rey and right on Westmoreland

If your heart is set on a B&B with romance and seclusion built in, don't hesitate to run to this retreat. Stunning sunrises and sunsets are yours from the perch with a 360-degree view of the surrounding mountains, and the Mesilla Valley. Crowning twenty spectacular acres, this majestic mansion has a design style of adobe brick with arches that suggests Spanish Moors.

Inside the hacienda find lovely rooms decorated with antiques, artwork, crafts, and family heirlooms. Just a couple of steps outside your guest room, and you're surrounding by rose and desert gardens. Those who feel inspired can take a hike or run on trails into the adjacent desert. The exercise isn't a bad idea, considering the breakfast spread offered by Teddi in the mornings: Served on the patio with views on the side are her Dutch babies, eggs Benedict, green-chile quiche, and Bob's special granola mix.

T. R. H. Smith Mansion B&B

909 North Alameda Boulevard
Las Cruces, NM 88005
Phone: (505) 525-2525; (800) 526-1914

E-MAIL: smithmansion@zianet.com

INTERNET SITE: www.smithmansion.com

INNKEEPERS: Marlene and Jay Tebo

ROOMS: 4 rooms with private bath, telephone, dataport; a suite combining 2 rooms available

ON THE GROUNDS: Library, sunroom, verandah, garden

CREDIT CARDS: MasterCard, Visa, American Express, Discover

RATES: $-$$$

HOW TO GET THERE: From El Paso drive west on I-10 to exit 140 (NM 28) and turn right (east), then turn right (north) on Main Street/U.S. 70 and take Alameda right (north) to the mansion.

In the heart of the historic Alameda Depot District is the largest residence in Las Cruces, which now operates as a B&B inn. Built in 1914 by Henry Trost, a contemporary of Frank Lloyd Wright, the home's architectural style is called Hip Box, a type of Prairie School design. The original owner and namesake was T. R. H. Smith, a banker and reputed pillar of the community—until he declared bankruptcy and went to prison. While the mansion was in receivership, so the rumor mill maintained, it was used as a high-class brothel.

It's changed hands seven times and now belongs to Marlene and Jay, who turned the 5,700-square-foot masterpiece into a gracious B&B. Guests share spaces, the living room with a green marble-fronted fireplace, plant-filled sun parlor, and stained-glass-adorned dining room. In the inn's pool hall, you can shoot a game, play a board game, or watch a movie on TV.

Upstairs, guest rooms include the Americas, the largest, with a fireplace, love seat, walk-in closets, king bed, Latin American carved furniture, and a spacious bathroom; the European, with a king bed, vintage pink-tiled bath, writing desk, sitting area, and view of the Organ Mountains; the Southwest, with a queen bed and Indian drums; the Polynesian, with queen bed, dressing area, and tropical touches; and a suite, a combination of the Southwest and Polynesian Rooms. Each room has an air purifier, air-conditioner, phone with modem port, clock radio, and fir wood floors.

Breakfast is a very big deal at the Smith Mansion. Typically Marlene makes fluffy French toast with real maple syrup, fresh fruit, homemade breads, a platter of German meats and cheeses, and pine nut coffee.

What's Nearby Las Cruces-Mesilla

More than a weekend is needed to take in the pleasures of this historic area. On Wednesday and Saturday mornings, buy arts and crafts, baked goodies, and Southwestern products at the Las Cruces Farmers and Crafts Market. Hiking and picnicking are fine at Dripping Springs, just east of town, and at Leasburg Dam State Park. Set a day aside to visit White Sands National Monument and the nearby Missile Range Museum. Old Mesilla, a historic Spanish village built atop an Indian community, is packed with shops, galleries, museums, and restaurants, as well as the lovely 1851 mission church and the 1905 vaudeville house called Fountain Theater. Do visit the town's wineries and try to time your visit with the plaza market, which happens on Thursday morning and Sunday afternoon.

Other Recommended B&Bs Nearby

Meson de Mesilla, with swimming pool, gourmet restaurant, balcony, patio, and 15 rooms with private baths; 1803 Avenida de Mesilla, Mesilla, NM 88046; telephone: (505) 525–9212 or (800) 732–6025. *Lundeen Inn of the Arts,* a century-old Mexican Territorial inn and extraordinary Southwestern fine arts gallery, with twenty rooms named for a famous New Mexican or Indian artist; 618 South Alameda Boulevard, Las Cruces, NM 88005; telephone: (505) 526–3326 or (888) 526–3326.

Casa de Patron

U.S. Highway 380
Lincoln, NM 88338
Phone: (505) 653–4676; (800) 524–5202

E-MAIL: patron@pvtnetworks.net
INTERNET SITE: www.casapatron.com
INNKEEPERS: Cleis and Jeremy Jordan

ROOMS: Main house with 3 rooms with private bath; Trail House duplex with 2 rooms, 1 with Jacuzzi, 1 wheelchair accessible; 2 casitas, 1 with two-bedroom suite

ON THE GROUNDS: Tree-shaded courtyards, gardens, large porches, horseshoes, five acres frequently roamed by deer

CREDIT CARDS: MasterCard, Visa

RATES: $$

HOW TO GET THERE: From Albuquerque drive south on I-25 to Socorro; east on U.S. 380 about 90 miles to Lincoln. From El Paso drive north on U.S. 54 to Tularosa, then take U.S. 70 east through Ruidoso to Hondo, then U.S. 380 west to Lincoln.

The casa, or main house—listed on the National Register of Historic Places—is an adobe that was built in the mid-1860s in the traditional Territorial flat-roofed style. Noteworthy in the interior are high ceilings and original viga wood beams, placed by builder and owner Juan Patron, who was the elected county clerk during territorial days. The home owes its infamy to the Lincoln County sheriff, who ordered Billy the Kid kept within its confines for twenty-seven days in 1879.

Throughout the house you'll see Cleis's own additions, such as a massive collection of old washboards, as well as a pipe organ and a grand piano. A professional musician, Cleis entertains guests at breakfast on the organ.

Like the town of Lincoln, Casa de Patron is quiet, well-preserved, and terribly authentic. Staying in the main house, which has three rooms with private baths, gives you a chance to appreciate the period's solid simplicity. If you prefer quarters that are more modern, yet still in a Western vein, consider the duplex out back called the Trail House. One room is the Eastburn Room, with a two-person Jacuzzi tub, and the other is the Vaquero Room, with wheelchair accessibility and an ADA shower. Both have wet bar and refrigerator, plenty of space, kiva fireplaces, Saltillo tiles, and wonderful western decor and furniture.

Next door are more remote casitas, include a honeymooners' cottage with a queen bed in a loft, nicely tiled bath, and a living area with a futon, as well as a small, complete kitchen and a great view of the grounds and hills. The second is a two-bedroom suite with a full bath, small living area, and a nice porch with a great view of the hills. Here, you can sit on the porch and look at the mountains from the shade of various evergreens.

Guests staying the main house and the Trail House enjoy a huge, hot country breakfast, served in dining room; typical offerings are citrus-pecan waffles with sausage or ham, four kinds of fresh fruit, Dutch babies (pancakes), baked egg dishes or French toast stuffed with cream cheese, apples, and pecans. Guests staying in the slightly more remote casitas are provided a supply of Continental breakfast fixings.

Casa de Patron is open March through December.

Ellis Store & Company

U.S. Highway 380
Lincoln, NM 88338
Phone: (800) 653-6460
Fax: (505) 653-4610

E-MAIL: ellistore@pvtnetworks.net

INTERNET SITE: www.ellisstore.com

INNKEEPERS: Jinny and David Vigil

ROOMS: 3 bedrooms with private baths and wood-burning stoves in main house; 4 bedrooms, 1 loft room, 1 private and 2 shared baths, as well as a large great room with couches, easy chairs, and kitchenette in Mill House; 1 suite with private bath, living and dining rooms and kitchen; and 1 suite with private bath and sitting room with futon in Casa Nueva

ON THE GROUNDS: Long porch on main house with garden views; grounds for hiking and mountain biking; horseback riding is nearby

CREDIT CARDS: MasterCard, Visa, American Express

RATES: $$–$$$

HOW TO GET THERE: From Albuquerque drive south on I-25 to Socorro, east on U.S. 380 about 90 miles to Lincoln. From El Paso drive north on U.S. 54 to Tularosa, then take U.S. 70 east through Ruidoso to Hondo, then U.S. 380 west to Lincoln.

Tucked into the lovely, rocky Rio Bonito Valley in the Lincoln National Forest, the Ellis Store occupies an 1850s adobe building. It became a store and inn in 1876. Like Casa de Patron, Ellis Store can rightfully hang the sign that reads, BILLY THE KID SLEPT HERE, as the young outlaw did so under house arrest just after the bloody Lincoln County Wars.

The wild times are long gone from this charming place; Jinny and David Vigil have run it as a gourmet restaurant and inn since the early 1990s. After living in Virginia and Texas, the couple decided this would be the place to spend time in utter seclusion and comfort—and they're right. It's an especially inviting place, right down to the terrifically friendly Maine coon cat named Spook.

Inside the main house find a large living room with big, overstuffed white couches on either side of a giant fireplace, surrounded by lots of antique furnishings, period table lamps, and carved tables and chairs placed atop beautiful wood floors and Oriental rugs. Choose from a CD collection that includes everything from Roy Orbison to classical music, and books, such as *Ghost Towns of the West,* and plenty of novels. Guest rooms in this building are charming, even if the carpet has tended toward shabby, but the antique beds, quilts, and furnishings do a lot for the overall integrity of the place. One of the rooms has a king-size bed with lots of lace, perfect for honeymooners. Two of the three rooms have private entrances.

Next door is the Mill House, which was built in the 1880s and has served as a nurses' quarters, bunkhouse, and a lodge hall. Today it's perfect for families traveling together, and for groups, as there's a great hall meeting area with couches, chairs, coffee tables, microwave, refrigerator, and coffeepot. Bedrooms have double beds, twin beds, and queen beds. And finally there's Casa Nueva, a house with two suites, also of period construction.

Guests enjoy breakfast either in the parlor and dining room, or, in late spring, summer, and early fall, on the beautiful verandah, which in New Mexico is called a portal. At breakfast Jinny does a cinnamon bread French toast with sautéed apples, alongside fresh fruit and freshly ground coffee. She also makes a wonderful omelette with asparagus, red bell pepper, and green onion. Sometimes David makes blue cornmeal buckwheat pancakes, served with maple syrup; homemade raspberry, plum, or peach jams; pear compote, or blackberry jam with sour cream. Ingredients are usually fresh from their vegetable and herb gardens.

Jinny does a gorgeous six-course dinner Wednesday through Saturday by reservation only. It's $50 per person, plus gratuity and wine. Appetizers include oysters Rockefeller, clams casino, roasted garlic soup, and baby greens with walnut pieces, Gorgonzola cheese, and fresh raspberry vinaigrette. Entrees typically include grilled New Mexico lamb chops dusted in herbs, halibut in a fennel white wine sauce, and grilled salmon in a ginger glaze.

Packed with history of Billy the Kid, Lincoln sits on the State Scenic Byway connecting Hondo and Capitán. Within the town is a museum detailing the bloody Lincoln County War, as well as the sensational last escape of Billy the Kid. A few miles away at Fort Stanton, see the endless view of white crosses at the unique Merchant Marine Cemetery. At San Patricio see the magnificent works of artists Peter Hurd and Henriette Wyeth at Hurd La Rinconada Gallery; and at Capitán visit the birthplace and museum of Smokey Bear.

Apple Tree Bed Breakfast & Spa

100 Lower Terrace
Ruidoso, NM 88345
Phone: (877) 277–5322
Fax: (505) 257–1718

E-MAIL: flyer@appletreebb-spa.com

INTERNET SITE: www.appletreebb-spa.com

INNKEEPER: Sandra Davis

ROOMS: 11 rooms with private baths, private entrances, TV, telephone, and dataports

ON THE GROUNDS: Treadmill, rowing machine, steam room, large hot tubs in spa pavilion

CREDIT CARDS: MasterCard, Visa, Discover

RATES: $$–$$$$

HOW TO GET THERE: From Albuquerque drive south on I–25 to Socorro, then travel east on United States 380 to Capitán and take New Mexico 48 south to Ruidoso. From El Paso drive north on U.S. 54 to Tularosa, then take U.S. 70 east to Ruidoso. Follow Sudderth Drive to Mecham Drive, turning north on Mecham for a short distance. Watch on right for Lower Terrace.

Here's a great place to stay for several days, whether you're in Ruidoso to ski in winter or bet on the horses in summer. Formerly a small apartment complex, the inn has several large rooms with small living areas, complete kitchen and small dining areas, and gas-log fireplaces. The occasional room has its own bathroom, which isn't entirely separate from the bedroom but is partitioned off by a room divider.

All rooms have contemporary furniture and plantation shutters, and some have marble-top tables and vanities. All have plenty of elbowroom and space to lounge, read, watch TV, and take those all-important cat naps. Rooms with names such as El Paso, Salt Lake City, Santa Fe, Fort Worth, and Del Rio are hung with framed posters or other prints that refer to the destination name. And adjacent to the main building, find the new spa pavilion, with its own TV and music system. Here you can work out on the treadmill or take a long hot tub soak. Sandra can arrange for you to have a massage from a licensed masseuse in the pavilion or in your room.

Also on the property is a rock house, built in 1943 and recently, extensively, renovated. Most impressive is the living room's original large rock fireplace done in a mosaic of lava rock, petrified wood, clam shells, quartz, and striated sandstone. This is a great place for families or a small group of friends staying together, thanks to a full kitchen—but be aware that the bedrooms are tiny and share a bath. Whether or not you stay in the rock house, do take time to take a good look at the exterior of the chimney. The architect crafted a tree design from petrified wood that extends the height of the rock structure.

All guests are served a big breakfast of bacon, sausage, eggs made to order, hash browns, four kinds of fruit, bagels, waffles, and yogurt. Sandra is happy to accommodate special diet requests with notice, and she frequently uses organic vegetables and farm-fresh eggs in preparations. In addition Sandra and her crew offer concierge services, such as making reservations at restaurants in town or obtaining tickets to musical performances at the very grand Spencer Theater.

Black Bear Lodge

428 Main Road
Ruidoso, NM 88345
Phone: (505) 257–1459 or (877)
257–1459

E-MAIL:
blackbear@Ruidoso.net

INTERNET SITE:
www.Ruidoso.net/blackbear

INNKEEPERS: Carol and Steve
Olson

ROOMS: 4 rooms with king bed,
cable TV, Jacuzzi tubs; 1 with
wheelchair accessibility

ON THE GROUNDS: Front porch; telephone and fax machine in lobby/parlor
area; dining area with self-serve kitchen

CREDIT CARDS: MasterCard, Visa, American Express

RATES: $$–$$$

HOW TO GET THERE: From Albuquerque drive south on I–25 to Socorro,
then travel east on U.S. 380 to Capitán and take New Mexico 48 south to
Ruidoso. From El Paso drive north on U.S. 54 to Tularosa, then take U.S.
70 east to Ruidoso. In town follow the main drag, Sudderth Drive, west
until you see signs to the Upper Canyon. Follow Main Road until you see
Black Bear Lodge.

Rustic but terribly comfortable and attractive, this small mountain lodge
in the historic Upper Canyon of Ruidoso has been a B&B since 1998.
Regular visitors to Ruidoso will recall that this building was the very
popular Whispering Pines Lodge Cafe for thirty years.

You'll adore the Upper Canyon, an especially scenic place in September
and October, when the aspen trees paint a deeply gold swath across the
robin's egg blue skies of southern New Mexico. The lodge's rooms are spacious enough, with comfortable king-size beds covered in velour spreads
and made cozy with down comforters. Each of the guest rooms have gas-log
stoves, king-size log beds, armoires, cable TV, hair dryers, spa robes, and
large bathrooms with skylights, Jacuzzi tubs, and separate showers. A nice

touch is that each bathroom has its own water heater, so there are no worries about running out of hot water on cold afternoons after a day of skiing, wind-chapped faces, and chilled toes.

The lodge's large common room has a picture-perfect stone fireplace, leather couches, knotty pine wall and ceiling panels, TV, CD player, games, and a big dining table; over the fireplace is an old painting of black bears dancing in the forest. Adjacent to the living/dining area is a self-serve kitchen big enough for two to cook in. A full complement of cooking wares, including pots and pans and utensils, oven, stove top, refrigerator, toaster, and blender are there for your use. Carol says she's had guests make an entire Thanksgiving dinner there. At breakfast time you're provided muffins, sweet rolls, oatmeal, cereals, fresh fruit, and juices, but there's room in the refrigerator for you to stash anything from sandwich makings to beer and wine. Fresh, homemade cookies are on hand for that sweet tooth, too.

What's Nearby Ruidoso

Outdoors enthusiasts can't resist Ruidoso's snow skiing high atop Sierra Blanca at Ski Apache or the fishing at Bonito Lake. Horseback riding opportunities abound, as do golf courses. If you're feeling lucky, bet on the horses at Ruidoso Downs, but if your cultural needs cry out, head to a concert or musical production of Spencer Theater. The Hubbard Museum of the American West offers more than 10,000 items pertaining to the horse and the Wild West. Nearby Roswell has its intriguing International UFO Museum and Research Center.

Another Recommended B&B in Ruidoso

Park Place, a house on three shaded acres along the Rio Ruidoso with a large hot tub, tennis courts, barbecue grill area, picnic table, fishing, video library, living room with fireplace, dining room, three guest rooms with private baths, TV/VCR, and coffee pots, 137 Reese Drive, Ruidoso, NM 88345; telephone: (800) 687-9050 or (505) 257-4638; fax: (505) 630-0127.

The Carter House Bed & Breakfast Inn

101 North Cooper Street
Silver City, NM 88061
Phone: (505) 388-5485

INTERNET SITE: www.gilanet.com/carterhouse/

INNKEEPER: Lucy Dilworth

ROOMS: 4 rooms, 1 suite with private bath

ON THE GROUNDS: Library, garden, porch

CREDIT CARDS: MasterCard, Visa

RATES: $-$$

HOW TO GET THERE: 156 miles west from El Paso via I–10 and U.S. 180. From U.S. 180 turn south on U.S. 90, which becomes Hudson Street. Turn right (west) on Market Street. Continue to the corner of Market and Cooper.

Built in 1906 by Theodore W. Carter, who made his fortune at the nearby Burro Mountain Copper Mine, the Carter House became a clinic in the 1930s and 1940s, serving the town's medical needs. It was renovated in 1990 as an inn and a hostel.

Set overlooking the Silver City Historic District, the Carter House is a grand old home full of ornate oak woodwork, rooms with high ceilings, and plenty of areas—such as the parlor and library—for reflection, conversation, and reading. You may well find yourself content simply to sit on the wrap-around porch and gaze at the mountains.

Inn guests can choose among four rooms and a two-room suite, each with a private bath. The Antelope Creek Room has a full-size bed, the Black Hawk Canyon and Crow Canyon Rooms each have a queen-size bed, the Deer Springs Room has twin beds, and the Eagle Peak Suite has a queen bed and a sleeper sofa. If you're traveling with a group, the Carter House's downstairs has a twenty-two-bed dorm-style hostel with a full kitchen, washer, dryer, and TV/VCR. Inn guests are offered a full breakfast, served buffet style in the dining room, with their stay.

What's Nearby Silver City

The Grant County town in southwest New Mexico grew up with the silver mining boom that erupted in 1870. Today's fortune hunters will find collections of black-on-white pottery developed 1,000 years ago by the Mimbres Indians and the wonders of the Gila National Forest and Wilderness Area. About 20 miles east of town, see the monolith called the Kneeling Nun, and about 45 miles north of town, find the thirteenth-century Gila Cliff Dwellings National Monument. A scenic byway, clothing-optional hot springs, old U.S. infantry fort, historic churches, and museums will fill your days, as well.

Another Recommended B&B in Silver City

Bear Mountain Lodge, a Nature Conservancy of New Mexico facility with fireplaces, library, decks, verandahs, hot tub, garden, pond, seminar room, ten rooms with private baths; Bear Mountain Road, Silver City, NM 88061; telephone: (505) 988-3867.

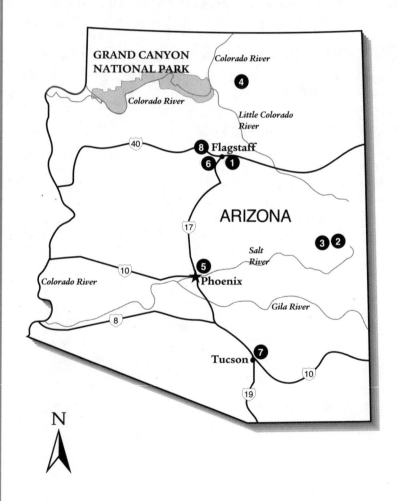

GRAND CANYON
NATIONAL PARK

Colorado River

④

Colorado River

Little Colorado
River

40 ⑧ Flagstaff
⑥ ①

ARIZONA

17

③ ②

Salt
River

10 ⑤
Colorado River Phoenix

8

Gila River

Tucson ⑦

10

19

N

Arizona

Numbers on map refer to towns numbered below.

The Inn at 410 Bed & Breakfast

410 North Leroux Street
Flagstaff, AZ 86001
Phone: (520) 774-0088; (800) 774-2008

E-MAIL: info@inn410.com

INTERNET SITE: www.inn410.com

INNKEEPERS: Howard and Sally Krueger

ROOMS: 9 rooms with private bath, 8 with fireplace, 3 with Jacuzzi; including suites

ON THE GROUNDS: Quiet garden gazebo, perennial gardens, library, sitting room

CREDIT CARDS: MasterCard, Visa

RATES: $$$-$$$$

HOW TO GET THERE: From I-40 take exit 195 B north onto Milton. Follow Milton under the railroad bridge and curve to the right. Turn left at the first light onto Humphreys Street. At Dale, turn right. Turn left off Dale onto North Leroux and right into the parking lot.

Built in 1894, this home was purchased in 1907 by a wealthy banker, rancher, and businessman named Tom Pollock, who enlarged and remodeled the place in the Craftsman style for his new bride. In the 1940s the home was expanded again and converted to apartments; in the 1970s it became a fraternity house. Its life as a bed-and-breakfast inn began in 1991, and it became Sally and Howard's place in 1993. They've remodeled and redecorated periodically since buying the property.

The result is a destination they call "the place with the personal touch." Each guest room has its own theme and individual decor: The Southwest Room, for instance, is a tranquil Santa Fe Jacuzzi suite with Native American crafts; and the Tea Room is a romantic Jacuzzi suite with Victorian roses and teapots. In the Dakota Suite, with Old West decor, you'll find a queen-size log bed and a separate sitting room with a fireplace and a sofa bed that's perfect for two children.

The inn appeals especially to two kinds of travelers—those who want an adventurous vacation, and those who just want to chill. Sally and Howard are good consultants for hiking, biking, and skiing day-trip plans, as well as for Grand Canyon touring ideas. But if you're seeking nothing more than a respite from faxes, cellular phones, and e-mails, this is the place to kick back and read in a sunny sitting room.

Sally and Howard's breakfasts have been featured on PBS-TV's *Country*

Inn Cooking with Gail Greco. Expect such pleasures as a Mexican cactus cooler (juice drink), fresh melon and kiwi, hominy piñon bread, and Southwestern egg puffs with salsa or whole wheat carrot pancakes with spiced orange sauce.

The Sled Dog Inn

10155 Mountainaire Road
Flagstaff, AZ 86001
Phone: (520) 525–6212, (800) 754–0664

E-MAIL: info@sleddoginn.com

INTERNET SITE: www.sleddoginn.com

INNKEEPERS: Wendy White and Jaime Ballesteros

ROOMS: 10 rooms with private bath, 1 with wheelchair accessibility

ON THE GROUNDS: Hot tub, sauna, guided outdoor adventures, mountain bikes, rock climbing wall

CREDIT CARDS: MasterCard, Visa, American Express, Discover

RATES: $$–$$$ (double occupancy)

HOW TO GET THERE: From Flagstaff take I–17 south to exit 333 (approximately 6 miles). Go east on Mountainaire Road approximately 1.3 miles then turn right on driveway.

Wendy and Jaime built their dream place in 1997 in a north woods executive cabin style. And talk about great accommodations—you'll want for nothing. Each of the rooms has a private bath, as well as down comforters. There's an outdoor Jacuzzi and an indoor sauna, plus lots of decks for lounging, reading, and sunbathing. There's a rock fireplace in the great room, workout equipment in the upstairs living room, a library of guidebooks and maps for you to borrow, and a load of outdoor and indoor games. Big breakfasts are served in the family-style dining room.

The hosts are geared for adventure. From the inn you'll find plenty of convenient biking and hiking trails, and there are mountain bikes for you to use. Wendy and Jaime will take you to visit their Siberian husky kennel, and they'll accompany you on guided outdoor adventures, such as rock climbing, dog sledding, cross-country skiing, and snowshoeing. Ask about packages that include various instructions, including lessons using their on-site rock-climbing wall.

Among the rooms are Northern Lights, a two-room suite on the first floor with one bath and three double beds, all decorated with images of huskies and dog sledding; Rock Rabbit, a corner room with a queen bed and a mountain-biking theme; and the Wolf Den, with one king or two extra-long twin beds and a window looking at the ponderosa pines. Honeymooners like the Bear's Lair, a second-floor perch looking at the tree tops and furnished with a wrought iron and lodgepole bed.

What's Nearby Flagstaff

A ski destination in winter, Flagstaff draws lots of folks from around Arizona who crave cooler climes in summer. If you like geology and archaeology, waste no time in exploring the ruins of Walnut Canyon, Wupatki National Monument, Oak Creek Canyon, Sunset Crater, and Meteor Crater. Of course the Grand Canyon is just 80 miles north of town, too. Other good stops include the Museum of Northern Arizona and the Lowell Observatory. In summer get tickets to the Flagstaff Festival of the Arts.

Red Setter Inn & Cottage

8 Main Street
P.O. Box 133
Greer, AZ 85927
Phone: (520) 735-7441;
(888) 99-GREER

E-MAIL:
jsankey@redsetterinn.com

INTERNET SITE:
www.redsetterinn.com

INNKEEPERS: Jim Sankey and Ken Conant

ROOMS: 12 rooms with private bath, 3 with TV and wheelchair accessibility; including the Cottage with king bed, fireplace, TV/VCR

ON THE GROUNDS: Library, verandah, fishing on property, game room, video collection

CREDIT CARDS: MasterCard, Visa, American Express

RATES: $$$–$$$$

HOW TO GET THERE: From Flagstaff drive I–40 to Holbrook and then pick up Arizona 77 to Show Low. Next follow Arizona 260 east to Greer at junction with Arizona 373.

Designed and built by Jim and Ken in 1995, it's easy to see how this inn was named the state's best bed & breakfast by the *Arizona Republic* and how *Real Money* magazine was prompted to call it one of the best in the nation. The handhewn natural Colorado and Montana log home lies in the Greer Valley, next to a million acres of national forest on the West Fork of the Colorado River. It is an all-seasons vacation paradise, offering everything from stunning scenery, birding, hiking, and picnicking to cross-country and downhill skiing.

Little has changed in this area since the first settler, a Norwegian transplant named Amerion Englevalson, built a one-room cabin in the late 1870s near what is now the Red Setter Inn property. Even today the year-round population of Greer is only about 150 people. If there's a crowd, it consists of wildlife: Animal populations here include elk, deer, black bear, mountain lion, bald eagle, and wild turkey, as well as raccoon, skunk, and squirrel. Anglers can catch brown and rainbow trout, and birders can just sit in the Adirondack chairs on the redwood decks and spot a wealth of feathered friends.

Inn rooms include Number One, with outside access, forest views, a queen bed with a feather comforter, and a large walk-in shower; Number Four, with a queen sleigh bed and feather comforter, twin skylights, private balcony with views of the river, a rock gas fireplace, and a jetted spa tub; and Room Eight, with a private deck right by the river, a queen hickory bed, and a rock gas fireplace. In the Cottage, Room Ten is the most private, with a king sleigh bed, freestanding gas fireplace atop a large rock heath, windows overlooking the forest, a TV/VCR with videos, and a coffee service area.

Stays include a full, hot breakfast. If you're staying two or more nights, sack picnic lunches are included, too.

What's Nearby Greer

This hamlet in eastern Arizona's White Mountains is a dream escape for anybody who finds joy in skiing, horseback riding, hiking, fishing, bicycling, curling up in front of a fire, or sitting beside the crystal waters of the Little Colorado River. Situated at an altitude of 8,500 feet next to the Apache-Sitgreaves National Forest, which is the largest stand of ponderosa pine in the world, Greer is home to the Butterfly Lodge Museum. Built in 1914, it sits on the site of a pioneer-artist family's mountain home and hunting lodge.

Canyon Colors Bed & Breakfast

225 South Navajo Drive
Page, AZ 86040
Phone: (520) 645–5979; (800) 536–2530

E-MAIL: canyoncolors@webtv.net

INTERNET SITE: www.canyon-country.com/lakepowell/colors.htm

INNKEEPERS: Bev and Rich Jones

ROOMS: 3 rooms with private bath, TV, VCR, telephone; 1 with whirlpool bath and fireplace

ON THE GROUNDS: Lovely large patios, pool, gas grill; extensive video library and Christian reading library

CREDIT CARDS: MasterCard, Visa, American Express, Discover, Diners Club

RATES: $ (for two, tax included) November 16 through April 14; $–$$ (for two, tax included) April 15 through November 15

HOW TO GET THERE: From Flagstaff follow Route 89 north to Page. Take first Page exit onto Lake Powell Boulevard. Follow Lake Powell Boulevard to second traffic light and turn left at South Navajo Drive and proceed to number 225, approximately 0.25 mile on left.

The rambling ranch-style house is spacious at more than 3,000 square feet, and Bev and Rich say that guests are particularly impressed with the roomy guest quarters and quiet, residential neighborhood. Guests may also appreciative of the Jones's strong Christian values, that they have no minimum-stay requirements, and that they accommodate pets and kids.

Each of the rooms features queen-size beds and queen-size futons. If you're visiting in summer, Bev and Rich will welcome you with iced tea and chips and salsa; if it's cooler weather, you'll be treated to hot chocolate and cookies. The hosts are also great at helping you plan visits to Lake Powell, 6 miles away, as well as to a nearby national golf course, Antelope Canyon, Water Holes Canyon, Lee's Ferry, Marble Canyon, and the Paria Wilderness Area. Within a few hours' drive, you'll find the Grand Canyon, Zion and Bryce Canyons, Monument Valley, and Kodachrome Basin.

At breakfast time, you'll enjoy cold cereals, muffins, yogurt, melon, juice, coffee, tea, and an entree, such as French toast, waffles, pancakes, or omelettes with bacon or sausage. Ask ahead about special dietary plans.

What's Nearby Page

Northeast of Grand Canyon National Park, Page lies close to the Utah state line, next to the Colorado River and very close to Glen Canyon National Recreation Area and Lake Powell. Here, you have easy access to houseboating and other fabulous water fun on Lake Powell, as well as extraordinary hiking opportunities in Paria Canyon. It's also a good place to find information on guided trail hikes, rafting trips, and helicopter or airplane tours into Grand Canyon.

Maricopa Manor

15 West Pasadena Avenue
Phoenix, AZ 85013
Phone: (602) 274–6302; (800) 292–6403

FAX: (602) 266-3904

INTERNET SITE: www.maricopamanor.com

INNKEEPERS: Mary Ellen and Paul Kelley

ROOMS: 6 rooms, including suites with king bed, refrigerator, private entrance

ON THE GROUNDS: Pool, gazebo spa, patio with waterfalls, library

CREDIT CARDS: MasterCard, Visa, American Express, Discover

RATES: $$$

HOW TO GET THERE: Follow Squaw Peak Parkway past Indian School Road to Highland Avenue. Turn left on Highland Avenue to Sixteenth Street, right to Camelback, then left to Central. Continue 1 block to Pasadena and go left.

The name Maricopa is most appropriate for the Manor, as it's the name of a Native American tribe that inhabited these lands together with the Pima (River People) long before the Apache, the Spanish, the Mexican, or the Anglos settled here. For hundreds of years the Maricopa and the Pima offered hospitality and ample food supplies to travelers making journeys through the Sonoran Desert along the Gila and Salt Rivers.

The manor house, built in 1928 by B. J. and Naomi Showers, was purchased with the adjoining house in 1970 by the Kelley family. Within this compound Mary Ellen and Paul have raised their children and provided a home for an extended family of close relatives, foster children, and exchange students. In 1989 the old homestead and adjoining guesthouses were converted into the first bed-and-breakfast inn to be approved and licensed by the City of Phoenix.

The Manor is a small resort in the heart of the nation's sixth-largest city, characterized by an enclosed acre with mature landscaping, along with a pool with waterfalls, a gazebo spa, patios with fountains, and gardens bursting with bougainvillea, palm, shade, and citrus trees. Guests can easily walk to Uptown Plaza's boutique shops, antique malls, restaurants, and fine food stores.

Breakfast in a basket is a Manor trademark: Delivered each morning to each guest suite, the breakfast can be enjoyed by the pool or in one of several common areas, if not in bed. And you'll be tempted to just spend most of your time in your suite, thanks to a king bed, sitting room with desk, cable TV and VCR, CD player, phone and modem jack, individual heat/AC, refrigerator and microwave, coffeepot, iron and ironing board, and private entrance. Three of the luxury suites have gas fireplaces and double whirlpool tubs.

What's Nearby Phoenix

Now a major metropolitan force to be reckoned with, Phoenix sprawls over a section of Sonoran Desert with its incongruent abundance of green—that of dozens and dozens of golf courses. Chief among a cluster of cities and towns that make up the Valley of the Sun, Phoenix offers such diversions as the Desert Botanical Garden, Phoenix Art Museum, the Phoenix Zoo, and a collection of Victorian homes and buildings at Heritage Square. Downtown Scottsdale has galleries galore, and the Fleischer Museum in Scottsdale offers more than 200 paintings from the California Impressionist School, while Taliesin West is Frank Lloyd Wright's desert masterpiece.

Rawhide and Roses Bed & Breakfast

P.O. Box 1153
Lakeside, AZ 85929
Phone: (520) 537-0216; (888) 418-5963

E-MAIL: rawhideroses@wmonline.com
INTERNET SITE: www.rawhide-roses.com
INNKEEPERS: Patti and Ron Ayers
ROOMS: 3 rooms, including suite, with private bath
ON THE GROUNDS: Ponderosa pines, hot tub
CREDIT CARDS: MasterCard, Visa, Discover

RATES: $$-$$$

HOW TO GET THERE: From Phoenix drive east on U.S. 60 to the town of Show Low. In town take Cub Lake Road south to Flores Drive; turn left on Flores and drive to South Flores Road. Turn left again, and you will see the B&B.

Tucked into the woods between Pinetop-Lakeside and Show Low, Rawhide and Roses Bed & Breakfast is an understatement in seclusion and restorative qualities. Hidden within the White Mountains, the retreat is perfect if you require a getaway with fishing, hiking, mountain biking, and skiing—or nothing at all. You might be happy just reading a good book under the tall ponderosa pines on an acre and a half, backing the Apache-Sitgreaves National Forest.

Pleasantly outfitted in a rustic but tasteful western style, this B&B offers rugged log construction, wonderful antiques, cozy fireplaces, picture windows, large covered decks, and a secluded hot tub under the pine canopy. Among room choices is the Belle Starr Suite, furnished with an antique bed brought from Boston. There's a fireplace, claw-foot tub with shower, and extraordinary views from the second-story windows.

Patti, a teacher on the White Mountain Apache Reservation, and Ron, an employee of Navajo County and an avid bow hunter and fisherman, can help you find diversions from golf and tennis to horseback riding, casino play, and visiting archaeological sites. Patti and Ron will also spoil you with coffee brought to your door each morning, a full, gourmet breakfast, dessert each evening, and—on request—backpack lunches and massage therapy appointments.

What's Nearby Pinetop-Lakeside

Northeast of Phoenix in the White Mountains, this community of less than 3,000 does a great job of serving vacationers who come to fish for rainbow and brown trout in the twenty-five lakes dappling the mountains, and the skiers attacking the trails at Sunrise Ski Resort, owned and operated by the White Mountain Apaches. The town has community theater, as well as ski touring on nights when the moon is full, golf tournaments, and access to some of the state's best scenic drives.

Casa Sedona Bed & Breakfast

55 Hozoni Drive
Sedona, AZ 86336
Phone: (520) 282-2938; (800) 525-3756

E-MAIL: casa@sedona.net
INTERNET SITE:
www.casasedona.com

INNKEEPERS: John and Nancy True

ROOMS: 16 rooms with private bath, fireplace, refrigerator, TV, telephone; 1 with wheelchair accessibility

ON THE GROUNDS: Hot tub, beautiful garden, and wonderful views; outdoor dining much of year

CREDIT CARDS: MasterCard, Visa, American Express

RATES: $$$-$$$$

HOW TO GET THERE: From Phoenix drive north on I-17; take Arizona 179 to Sedona. In town go west 3 miles on Arizona 89A to West Sedona; turn right on Tortilla Drive, and right on Hozoni Drive.

uilt new in 1992, Casa Sedona was designed by an architect schooled in the Frank Lloyd Wright style, with Southwestern emphasis. You can't help but appreciate the harmony it achieves with the natural environment of the region and the vast skies. From the porches and decks surrounded by thickly wooded property, you're treated to stunning views of the legendary red rocks.

Each of the guest rooms has a fireplace, spa tub, glass shower, and a little refrigerator. Among the tempting room choices are the Cowboy, an Old West theme with lodgepole bed and a patio; the Pueblo, with lodgepole bed, garden view from redwood deck, and a minikitchen; and the Juniper Shadows, with its shade trees and terrace.

Mornings begin with a full gourmet breakfast that includes muffins, breads, scones, and savory entrees. John and Nancy are adept at helping you figure out the day's plans, and they have maps and hiking books to loan. In the afternoon they serve appetizers, but you might just want to while away the dusk in the hot tub.

The Graham Inn and Adobe Village

150 Canyon Circle Drive
Sedona, AZ 86351
Phone: (520) 284-1425; (800) 228-1425
Fax: (520) 284-0767

E-MAIL: graham@sedona.net

INTERNET SITE: www.sedonasfinest.com

INNKEEPERS: Roger and Carol Redenbaugh

ROOMS: 10 rooms with private bath, TV, telephone, including a luxury suite

ON THE GROUNDS: Pool, hot tub, bicycles, TV/VCR, videos, CD player, CDs, library, Jacuzzi tubs, fireplaces, private balconies, bread makers, waterfall showers; orchard

CREDIT CARDS: MasterCard, Visa, American Express, Discover

RATES: $$$$

HOW TO GET THERE: From Phoenix take I-17 north to exit 298. Drive 8 miles to Village of Oak Creek. At second traffic light turn left on Bell Rock Boulevard, then right at second Canyon Circle Drive, on corner.

Graham Inn, built in 1985 by Bill and Marni Graham, was the first inn in Arizona built as a B&B. Within two years the accolades were pouring in. In 1992 the Redenbaughs arrived on vacation from Virginia and were immediately swept up by the red-rock beauty of Sedona and decided—never having stayed at a B&B—to buy the Graham Inn.

Carol and Roger were wise to keep the style, comfort, and hospitality for which the Contemporary Southwestern-style spread was known, and they added to it by putting in five fireplaces and Jacuzzi tubs, TV/VCRs and CD players, and the like. They added a luxury suite, too.

Next the couple bought the lot next door and erected Adobe Village, known as one of the most luxurious B&Bs in the nation. This addition of four luxurious, adobe-style casitas is what Carol describes as "a gentle escape for the soul." In each casita is an individually chosen painting and combination of fabrics and furniture.

Guests staying at Graham Inn and Adobe Village find special pleasures in a day of hiking, equipped with the hosts' backpacks, walking sticks, and trail maps; in mountain biking; or cooling off on the natural slides at Slide Rock State Park. The shopping stops in Sedona are legendary, of course, as are other sight-seeing options.

At the inn you'll be spoiled by breakfasts of fresh fruit, chilled peach soup, fresh vegetable frittatas, blue corn waffles with prickly pear syrup, and homemade breads. The afternoon snack will be either a layered Mexican dip or avocado-crab spread. When you're planning dinner, Carol and Roger can make recommendations.

The Inn on Oak Creek

556 Highway 179
Sedona, AZ 86336
Phone: (520) 282–7896;
(800) 499–7896

E-MAIL: theinn@sedona.net

INTERNET SITE: www.sedona-inn.com

INNKEEPERS: Rick Morris and Pam Harrison

ROOMS: 11 rooms with private bath, TV/VCR, telephone, fireplaces, whirlpool tubs; 1 with wheelchair accessibility

ON THE GROUNDS: Dining room, great rooms, decks, balconies, patio

CREDIT CARDS: MasterCard, Visa, American Express, Discover

RATES: $$$$

HOW TO GET THERE: Go 110 miles north of Phoenix via I–17 to Highway 179. Continue north on 179 until you reach inn.

Originally built as an art gallery in 1972, the multilevel building was converted to a B&B in 1995 and given an updated, highly sophisticated western decor treatment. The results are more than successful, as the inn has been given a four-diamond rating by AAA and has been named Sedona's best B&B by local publications.

The Angler's Retreat and Rose Arbor rooms are among the inn's most popular, thanks to private decks overhanging the creek and the incomparable views of Oak Creek Canyon. Details vary from room to room: In Apple Orchard, for instance, there is a vaulted ceiling and decor appropriate to Sedona's orchard industry; in Trading Post you'll find a collection of Native American crafts, such as baskets, pots, and jewelry; and Rested Rooster has a queen bed in one room and an adjoining Hen House with a trundle bed and a cedar deck. Throughout you'll find Pottery Barn furniture and Ralph Lauren and Laura Ashley fabrics.

Breakfast is absolute bliss. Expect to have such wonders as homemade granola with creamy maple yogurt, cherry spirals with lime butter, peppered bacon, and fresh apricot sauce with French toast. That's guaranteed to give you plenty of fuel for a day of hiking the red rocks.

The Lodge at Sedona

125 Kallof Place
Sedona, AZ 86336
Phone: (520) 204-1942; (800) 619-4467

E-MAIL: lodge@sedona.net

INTERNET SITE: www.lodgeatsedona.com

INNKEEPERS: Barb and Mark Dinunzio

ROOMS: 14 rooms, including suites, with private bath, some with fireplace, Jacuzzi

ON THE GROUNDS: Library, sunroom, garden, lily pond, labyrinth

CREDIT CARDS: MasterCard, Visa, American Express, Discover

RATES: $$$-$$$$

HOW TO GET THERE: Drive north from Phoenix on I-17 to Arizona 179; take 179 north to Arizona 89A. Go west 2 miles, then south on Kallof Place.

Originally a doctor's residence and then a treatment center, the Lodge became a B&B in 1993 with Barb and Mark's thorough remodeling effort. They added eight and a half bathrooms and hung some 250 sheets of drywall to soundproof rooms, then set about doing some serious decorating to provide the warmth that quickly earned the inn statewide awards from the *Arizona Republic*.

Known for its gracious atmosphere, lovely country pine antiques, soothing red-rock views, and utter privacy on two and a half acres of woodlands, the Lodge at Sedona offers sculptures; an open, airy kitchen; and a wonderful fireplace in its large common room. At breakfast time you'll be pampered by fresh fruit, homemade granola, juices, hot entrees, and baked goodies.

Guest room choices are impressive. There's the master suite, with a red-rock fireplace, outdoor Jacuzzi, two decks, and a queen bed; the Meadow Suite, with decor that includes Mission Arts and Crafts styling, a two-person Jacuzzi, fireplace, private deck, and king bed; and Nature, with a fireplace, Jacuzzi, and French doors that open onto a spacious deck.

A Sunset Chateau

665 South Sunset Drive
Sedona, AZ 86336
Phone: (520) 282–2644; (877) 655–BEDS

E-MAIL: stay@asunsetchateau.com
INTERNET SITE: www.asunsetchateau.com
INNKEEPER: Rosemary Corneto
ROOMS: 8 rooms in suites with private bath, Jacuzzi tubs, TV, phone
ON THE GROUNDS: Patio, porches
CREDIT CARDS: MasterCard, Visa, American Express
RATES: $$–$$$$
HOW TO GET THERE: Take I–17 to the Sedona exit. Take Highway 179 to 89A, turn left, go to the third light, and turn left on Sunset Drive. Proceed to the top of the hill and Chateau is on the right side.

A Sunset Chateau offers one of the best options in Sedona, in that you can pick between B&B suites or the more economical chalets. The B&B suites, bearing names like Magnolia, Katarina, Carmella, and Mesa, feature Jacuzzi tubs, separate stand-up showers, king-size beds, gas fireplaces, telephones, TVs, and computer hookups. You'll be instantly spoiled: From your private patio you'll have uninterrupted views of Sedona's magnificent red rocks.

A gourmet breakfast is served every morning in the inn's large dining room in the main lodge. You'll find a cozy fireplace in the lodge's gathering room—a wonderful place to hang out after a day of hiking, golfing, balloon riding, fly fishing, or Jeep touring in the desert.

The less-expensive chalet rooms are each 600 square feet and have full kitchens. Some have fireplaces and are furnished with queen, double, or twin beds.

What's Nearby Sedona

You'll be tempted to do nothing but gaze on the famed red rocks, with formations called Bell Rock, Courthouse Butte, Capitol Butte, and Bear Mountain. As a testament to the wholly spiritual feel of this glorious place, Sedona has an exquisite Chapel of the Holy Cross jutting out from one of the countless cliffs. An artists' colony since the 1960s, the town is filled with galleries for your perusal. Trails are there for hiking, and hot-air balloon rides will let you see the rocks from above. In September the town jams with the annual Jazz on the Rocks festival.

Cactus Cove Bed & Breakfast

10066 East Kleindale Road
Tucson, AZ 85749
Phone: (520) 760-7730; (800) 466-0083

E-MAIL: cactuscv@azstarnet.com

INTERNET SITE: www.azcactuscove.com

INNKEEPERS: Ivan and Sally Gunderman

ROOMS: 3 suites with Jacuzzi, TV/VCR, refrigerator, private entrances, private courtyards, telephone; 1 with wheelchair accessibility

ON THE GROUNDS: Large covered patio with fireplace, large pool with waterfall

CREDIT CARDS: MasterCard, Visa. American Express, Discover

RATES: $$$-$$$$

HOW TO GET THERE: Take I-10 to the Houghton Road exit. Turn north on Houghton Road and follow it to East Kleindale Road. Turn left onto East Kleindale Road and look for number 10066.

One of the original homes in this area of Tuscon, the inn occupies a 1963 adobe brick home in an irresistible Sonoran Desert setting. Completely remodeled, the inn offers suites that have been named for Saguaro, Agave, and Ocotillo cactus. Each suite has king or twin beds, roomy baths, two-person Jacuzzi tubs with showers, cable TV and VCR, microwave, refrigerator, terry cloth robes, private outdoor entrances, and private courtyards with sitting areas and outdoor showers.

At breakfast time your hosts will pamper you with a full breakfast of juice, coffee, tea, fruit, breads, pastries, and such main course options as eggs or pancakes. There's nothing nicer than lingering over breakfast on the patio next to the large pool—with its waterfall—while gazing at mountains on the horizon.

As though all that doesn't spoil you enough, Ivan and Sally will arrange on-site massage therapy and facials for you. And when you're ready to venture out, they'll point you in the right direction for hiking, horseback riding, and bird-watching—don't forget to bring your binoculars. Nearby places to explore include Saguaro National Park East, Sabino Canyon, and Agua Caliente Park.

Casa Tierra Adobe Bed & Breakfast Inn

11155 West Calle Pima
Tucson, AZ 85743
Phone: (520) 578-3058

E-MAIL: casatier@azstarnet.com

INNKEEPERS: Barb and Dave Malmquist

ROOMS: 4 rooms with private baths, queen bed, refrigerator, private entrance, phone

ON THE GROUNDS: Media room, fully equipped gym, hot tub, telescope, two courtyards with fountains, private patios

CREDIT CARDS: MasterCard, Visa, American Express

RATES: $$–$$$$

HOW TO GET THERE: From I-10 in Tucson take Speedway Boulevard west to Desert Museum. Go 2.6 miles past Desert Museum, turn left onto dirt road, and follow signs.

This charming adobe home will remind you of haciendas deep within Mexico, thanks to its fifty archways, courtyard with fountain, and entryways with vaulted brick ceilings. Each of the sun-baked adobe bricks was laid by hand in a design whose natural color and texture are easily appreciated. Throughout handmade ceramic light fixtures, viga-and-latilla ceilings, brick floors, and brightly patterned Talavera tiles lend an even greater Mexican authenticity.

Casa Tierra's four gorgeous bedrooms offer private baths, queen-size beds, refrigerators and microwaves, and private entrances with patios overlooking the desert landscape. Each of the rooms opens onto the common courtyard, where you can listen to the fountain and collect your thoughts. Guests also share a large common room with TV, movies, and games, as well as a library and a fully equipped gym. A separate hot tub area sits in desert surroundings, where you can see the sun set and the moon rise.

Barb and Dave serve a lavish, gourmet breakfast that happens to be vegetarian. Homebaked breads, fruit, and juices are included, and it's served in a formal setting. You'll eat the feast on the lovely portal, which overlooks the central courtyard with its birdbath and fountain, or in the formal dining room with a Sonoran Desert view.

Casa Tierra is closed from July 15 through August 15.

Catalina Park Inn

309 East First Street
Tuscon, AZ 85705
Phone: (520) 792-4541; (800)
792-4885
E-MAIL: cpinn@flashnet
INTERNET SITE: www.catalina
parkinn.com
INNKEEPERS: Mark Hall and
Paul Richard

ROOMS: 6 rooms with private bath, TV, telephone

ON THE GROUNDS: Large living room with fireplace for guests; nice gardens around the inn

CREDIT CARDS: MasterCard, Visa, American Express, Discover

RATES: $$-$$$ December through May; reduced rates rest of the year

HOW TO GET THERE: Take I-10 to the East Speedway Boulevard exit and go east on Speedway. Turn right on North Sixth Avenue, then left onto East First Street. Look for number 309.

Built as a residence in 1927 by a well-to-do Philadelphia family, this gorgeous home is noteworthy for beautiful Mexican mahogany doors and moldings, gleaming oak floors, neoclassic symmetry with several exterior columns, and an unusual green-glazed terra-cotta roof. The extraordinary craftsmanship and attention to detail that went into the construction of this home is evident throughout, and you'll be impressed also with the lovely garden areas that Mark and Paul have crafted.

Spend some time exploring the interiors: An impressive collection of blue-and-white china is displayed in built-in cases that flank the fireplace in the living room, and original paintings, weavings, and objets d'art add to the home's sophistication.

The East and West Rooms have private awning-covered porches, and the Bower Room has a romantic wrought iron bed and fireplace, as well as an extra large shower tiled in Mexican limestone. With eight windows on three walls, the Oak Room provides wonderful light and views of the Catalina Mountains. The Catalina Room is a very private basement room with high ceilings, a scored and polished concrete floor, beautiful mahogany woodwork, and a jetted tub in a cedar-lined bathroom. The Cottage Room has a cheerful botanical theme. Large cast iron urns with tiled tops, which Mark created, serve as bedside tables. A Saltillo tile floor and nice views of the garden give this room a warm and soothing feeling. Every guest room features luxurious touches: bathrobes, all-cotton sheets, irons and ironing boards, hair dryers, and bottled water.

Breakfast, served in the dining room on Port Meirion china, is usually something along the lines of papaya and lime scones, lemon-ricotta pancakes, poached pears, fresh-squeezed orange juice, and plenty of strong French roast coffee.

The Mesquite Tree Bed & Breakfast

860 West Ina Road
Tuscon, AZ 85704
Phone: (520) 297–9670; (800) 317–9670

E-MAIL: minker@mesquitetree.com

INTERNET SITE: www.mesquitetree.com

INNKEEPERS: Barbara and Jeffrey Minker

ROOMS: 2 rooms with private bath, TV, telephone

ON THE GROUNDS: Patio, pool, garden, fountains, mature trees on seven acres, bird feeders

CREDIT CARDS: None accepted

RATES: $$$$

HOW TO GET THERE: From the Tucson airport take I–10 west; from the Phoenix airport take I–10 east. Go to the Ina Road exit 248 approximately 10 miles north of Tucson. At Ina Road go east approximately 4 miles. You will pass through a traffic light at La Canada Boulevard. Continue on Ina Road approximately 0.7 mile to the next traffic light at Paseo del Norte. Make a U-turn, now going west on Ina Road to the first mailbox and driveway on your right.

At this spectacular mud adobe Mexican Colonial home is a separate guesthouse B&B that faces the pool and garden. Called the Mesquite Tree, this B&B is part of Quinta San Francisco, a gorgeous private residence that has been on the Arizona Opera League Home Tour and a featured property in the "Home" section of the *Arizona Daily Star*.

The B&B guesthouse has two distinctively decorated bedrooms and two bathrooms that are separated by a photo gallery entrance hall. The grand bedroom has a queen bed, fireplace, and a sitting area with a sofa-daybed. The second bedroom has a king-size bed. Both are furnished with Mexican antiques and artifacts that Barbara and Jeffrey have collected from around the world. From the Mesquite Tree you have unbelievable views of the pool and garden, as well as the Catalina Mountains. You can't beat this location in the northwest foothills of Tuscon, right across the street from the desert botanical park known as Tohono Chul.

To get the breakfast that's included with your stay, you'll take a short walk through the desert to a tearoom at Tohono Chul Park. After breakfast you can wander the self-guided nature trails to examine the desert flora and fauna, which include some feathered friends, hummingbirds, dove, gila woodpeckers, finches, cactus wrens, cardinals, quail, and roadrunners.

In the evening you'll want to unwind at the spa beneath the mesquite tree, privately situated on a walled patio next to the guesthouse. Can you think of a better way to enjoy a starry night in Tuscon?

The Mesquite Tree is open May through December.

What's Nearby Tucson

Surrounded by Mount Wrightson and the Santa Catalina, Santa Rita, and Tucson Mountains, this southern Arizona city unfurls itself across a ruggedly beautiful desert basin. Make time to explore the sensational Arizona-Sonora Desert Museum, Saguaro National Park, and the downtown historic districts, Barrio Historico and El Presidio. Good side trips include those to the mission church at San Xavier del Bac, the mission at San Jose de Tumacacori, Tombstone, and Nogales, Mexico.

Other Recommended B&Bs Nearby

Coyote Crossing Bed & Breakfast, a Southwestern hacienda with library, hot tub, heated swimming pool, fireplace, in-room refrigerators, and four guest rooms with private bath and TV; 6985 North Camino Verde, Tucson, AZ 85743; telephone: (520) 744–3285 or (877) 740–3200. *Ramsey Canyon Inn,* known for hummingbirds and the flora-and-fauna biodiversity of the world-famous Ramsey Canyon Preserve, about 90 miles southeast of Tuscon; managed by the Nature Conservancy, the inn has eight guest rooms with private bath, 2 with telephone, 1 with wheelchair accessibility, a library, verandah, garden, and front porch; 29 Ramsey Canyon Road, Hereford, AZ 85615; telephone: (520) 378–3010; e-mail: lodging@theriver.com.

Sheridan House Inn

460 East Sheridan Avenue
Williams, AZ 86046
Phone: (520) 635-9441; (888) 635-9345
Fax: (520) 635-1005

E-MAIL: sheridanhouse@thegrandcanyon.com

INNKEEPER: Steve Gardner

ROOMS: 8 rooms with private bath, TV/cable/VCR, CD player

ON THE GROUNDS: Decks, patio, hot tub; dining room, fitness room

CREDIT CARDS: MasterCard, Visa, American Express, Discover

RATES: $$-$$$$

HOW TO GET THERE: Take I-40 to the North Grand Canyon Boulevard exit. Turn south on North Grand Canyon and follow it across a set of railroad tracks. This road will become South Second Street. Stay on South Second, turning left onto East Sheridan Avenue. Look for number 460.

On two secluded acres in historic Williams, the inn offers you the best of mountains and the cool ponderosa forest. But you're not any great distance from civilization, either. Close enough for walking is the quaint town, which offers antiques shopping and gallery browsing. Golf and fishing are also just a few minutes away, and hiking begins outside the inn's door. After a long day of adventures, you won't be able to resist a long soak in the hot tub. If you're feeling sociable, join in the inn's happy hour with other guests and the occasional local dignitaries who stop by to welcome visitors to town.

Named for the flora that flourishes in northern Arizona, rooms include the Willow, a large bedroom with queen bed and views into the pines; the Aspen, a luxurious room with king bed; the Sycamore, with king bed, sitting area, and a sunset view through bay windows; and the Fernwood, a suite with a living room, minibar, queen bed, and sleeper sofa. Everyone has access to the inn's library, which includes books, videos, and CDs.

Steve, the owner-chef, will spoil you with his culinary repertoire. There are wonderful appetizers at happy hour, gourmet spreads at breakfast, and—for an additional charge—lavish lunches and dinners in the dining room. If you're so motivated, you can work off those sins in the inn's fitness room or head off to the nearby eighteen-hole golf course.

Terry Ranch Bed and Breakfast

701 Quarterhorse Drive
Williams, AZ 86046
Phone: (520) 635-4171; (800) 210-5908

E-MAIL: terryranchbnb@usa.net
INNKEEPERS: Glenn and Leisa Watkins, Del and Sheryl Terry
ROOMS: 6 rooms with private bath
ON THE GROUNDS: Pool, gazebo spa, patio with waterfalls, library
CREDIT CARDS: MasterCard, Visa, American Express, Discover
RATES: $$–$$$
HOW TO GET THERE: From Phoenix drive north on I-17 to I-40. Go west on
I-40 to exit 165. Turn south on Route 66 to Rodeo Road. Go left to the
corner of Rodeo and Quarterhorse.

Terry Ranch guests might be forever spoiled for B&B visits after this one. Besides a comfortable family room and other common areas with fireplaces, there's a wraparound verandah with rocking chairs, a rustic log gazebo, a barbecue area for guests to use, and a shady yard with a swing and hammock.

But that's assuming you'll ever want to leave your room. You won't if you're booked into the Eliza Jane, where you can relax in a two-person, clawfoot tub or curl up in front of the fireplace on a sofa to watch TV or a video. If you're in the Hannah Louisa, you'll have a hard time tearing yourself away from the porch glider and the sensational mountain views. Much can be said of the other rooms, as well.

After a restful night's sleep, you'll be lured out of the room by a big breakfast of breads, meats, egg dishes, waffles, or French toast, along with juice and coffee or tea. There you can mull over your sightseeing options, which might range from Grand Canyon expeditions to joining in the Mountain Village Holiday Festival in November and December or the Rendezvous Days on Memorial Weekend. In summer you can fish and hike, of course, or kick up your heels at the Cowpunchers' Reunion Rodeo in late July.

What's Nearby Williams

Spend some time exploring this Grand Canyon gateway, long ago a bawdy frontier town, where historic Route 66 serves today as the major artery. Along the brick streets of the historic district are saloons, bordellos, and shops that tell a colorful story and bring to mind images of cowboys and gunfighters. Visit the historic Fray Marcos Hotel and Williams Depot, now home to the hugely popular Grand Canyon Railway, where the steam whistle, clanging bell, and restored rolling stock help transport you to another era. Take time, too, to play the wonderful Elephant Rocks Golf Course.

Another Recommended B&B in Williams

Red Garter Bed & Bakery, occupying an 1897 bordello and saloon that later became a general store and rooming house, with four bedrooms and private baths, bakery, and Victorian decor, skylights, and historical photos and artifacts; 137 West Railroad Avenue, Williams, AZ 86046; telephone: (520) 635-1484 or (800) 328-1484.

Indexes

Alphabetical Index to B&Bs

Family-Friendly B&Bs

B&Bs with Farm/Ranch Setting

Pet Friendly B&Bs

B&Bs with Separate Cottage/Guest House

B&Bs That Serve Dinner

B&Bs with Hot Tubs

B&Bs with Wheelchair Access

B&Bs That Offer Outdoor Adventures

B&Bs with a Pool

B&Bs with a Pub or Happy Hour

B&Bs with a Waterside Setting

B&Bs with a Mountain Setting